The New Central Asia

The New Central Asia

The Creation of Nations

• • •

Olivier Roy

NEW YORK UNIVERSITY PRESS
Washington Square, New York

Published in the U.S.A. in 2000 by New York University Press
Washington Square
New York, NY 10003

Originally published as *La Nouvelle Asie centrale ou la fabrication des nations*,
copyright © Editions du Seuil, 1997

First United Kingdom publication in 2000 by I.B.Tauris & Co Ltd

Translation copyright © I.B.Tauris & Co Ltd, 2000

Published with the assistance of the French Ministry of Culture

CIP data available from the Library of Congress
ISBN 0-8147-7554-3 (cloth)
ISBN 0-8147-7555-1 (paper)

Typeset in Bembo by Dexter Haven, London
Printed and bound in Great Britain by MPG Books Ltd, Bodmin, Cornwall

Contents

Introduction

On 19 August 1991, a conservative coup d'état threatened Mikhail Gorbachev and jeopardised his reform of the Soviet Union. Most of the leaders of the Muslim Soviet republics promptly approved the putschists' actions. A few days later, these same people went on to declare the independence of their respective countries, which was then carried through during the next three months. Out came new flags and new slogans in celebration of independence, fatherland and nation. Competitions were organised for the writing of national anthems and the design of national emblems. The communist parties transformed into presidential parties. The national language became the language of official communication, even if a lot of people made a hash of it because they could only really speak Russian. Leaders who in 1991 had come directly from the Soviet nomenklatura, and who only a few months previously had still been servilely repeating Moscow slogans, now became the mouthpieces of a nationalism that was more hostile to Russia and open to the West. In 1996, we saw the seventy-year-old president of Azerbaijan, Haidar Aliyev, giving Moscow a hard time and upbraiding the only one of his ministers unable to express himself in Azeri. Was this not the same man who had been a former KGB officer, a member of the Soviet Politburo and the ruler of Soviet Azerbaijan for the best part of 18 years?

How do we explain these sudden changes of tack? Are the rulers of Central Asia unreconstructed communists, with their power undermined by the demise of the Soviet empire and intent on rebuilding little Soviet republics, as might seem to be suggested by the personality cult that surrounds the Turkmen president? Or did the collapse of the USSR simply uncover the continued existence in Central Asia of traditional society, with its new potentates, its clanism and ethnic quarrels that date back to the beginnings of time? Are we seeing something old here, or something new? for the Western observer, this poses something of a problem. However, what is happening here is neither a return to some pre-Soviet past, nor is it neo-Sovietism. The new nations have to be taken seriously in their own right.

Their achievement of independence was sudden, and not necessarily wanted. There was no historical memory of a nation lost, nor had there been nationalist movements preparing the ground, as there had been in Armenia, Georgia and the Baltic countries. The Muslim republics of the ex-USSR were the creation of decrees that were issued between 1924 and 1936, which determined not only their frontiers, but also their names, their re-invented pasts, the definition of the ethnic groups that they were reckoned to embody, and even their language. This artificiality led many observers to predict that the fall of the USSR would see the return of supra-national identities (for instance pan-Islamism, pan-Turkism or pan-Turanianism, and even a return to Sovietism reincarnated in the Commonwealth of Independent States). However, it is obvious that, with the exception of Tajikistan, the newly-independent nations had immediate prospects of growth, built on the state apparatus inherited from Sovietism. In the limited memories of their citizens, these new republics have a solid and tangible reality. These citizens have no names for their nation and language other than what they have inherited from the Soviet period, and they do not really question what their schools, newspapers, televisions and neighbours tell them about their national identities. The rootedness of this identity became reinforced after independence, despite the economic difficulties and a certain nostalgia for the Soviet system (interestingly, this system is no longer viewed as a gift from Bolshevik Russia, but as a common heritage which has been betrayed by the egotism of 'big brother' in Moscow). Uzbekistan is not Poland, but neither is it the GDR or Bosnia. A nation exists, and a state is firmly in place. But nobody has ever had to fight in order to bring it into existence. How can a nation arise without being brought into being by a nationalism?

Unbeknownst to itself, the Soviet Union was a formidable mechanism for the manufacture of nations in Central Asia. Soviet nationalities policy had been conceived first and foremost to break the existing nationalisms, particularly Russian, Ukrainian, Georgian, Tatar and Kazakh. To this end, a multitude of 'small' competing peoples was manufactured, and in theory they had the same rights as the 'big' peoples: thus nationalisms were brought into being where previously they had not existed. The aim was obviously not to turn these new peoples into viable nation-states, but rather to reduce them, along with all the others, to a purely administrative appearance, as a prelude to their fusion in the greater Soviet whole.

While the broader ideological project of the USSR was indeed that of the fusion of peoples into a *homo sovieticus* (who, incidentally, would be exclusively Russian-speaking), the strategic aim at the time of the founding of the new empire was to break up the large linguistic and cultural blocs founded on language (Turkic) and religion (Islam). In order to do this Stalin advanced the concept of 'nationality' (*natsionalnost*). Every national political entity had to have its corresponding titular nationality, defined as an ethnic community which had preserved an identity founded on language throughout the whole process of its history. Such peoples were presented as living natural facts which developed independently of any political contract or conscious choice among their members.

The Soviet paradox in relation to this ethnic conception of the 'people' is that it attributed this status of objective reality to regroupments of populations which were in fact largely artificial, because they had been carried out piecemeal among the Muslim population of the Russian empire. In that empire not only had no nation in the modern sense of the term ever been created, but the meaning of the word 'national' itself (*milli*) referred to a religious and cultural community which had no territory and no state of its own. Rather than first identifying the strength and vitality of a people which might then be empowered to be the basis of a modern nation-state, with its appropriate territory and institutions, the Soviet authorities worked in reverse. In 1924, they decreed the creation of Soviet republics to which titular peoples were then subsequently attributed. It was then left to the anthropologists, linguistics experts and historians to explain how this virtual people had been waiting for centuries for its political incarnation to be achieved. The aim of this great national division was, among other things, to provide a multi-ethnic empire with a system of government that would make it possible to fuse many different populations into a single Russian mould, a process defined as 'internationalism', while at the same time respecting multilingualism and the rights of peoples. These republics were not supposed to be viable as independent entities, although they all had the the formal trappings of statehood. No stone was left unturned in order to achieve this: peculiarly-aligned frontiers, enclaves, capitals where the titular nationality was always in a minority (Tashkent, Dushanbe, Alma Ata and Frunze), the enclosure of minorities within minorities (or rather their transformation from minorities into majorities and vice versa), economic dependence on the centre, the absence of direct communication between states etc.

However, the fact remains that the peoples selected in this manner and presumed to have arrived at the final stage of their development – that of the nation – were accorded the trappings of statehood: a political apparatus (the Communist Party of the republic concerned), a state structure (Council of Ministers and head of state), a national language, a university and an academy of sciences. Thus it was the Soviet system that implanted the model of the nation-state into a region where it had previously been unknown. The Soviet system forged the conceptual instruments (historical, ethnographic and linguistic) which provided the Muslim republics with the elements of their legitimacy and their self-definition. The proof of the existence of these peoples, given the lack of pre-existing nationalism, was the national form which they were suddenly accorded. Certainly the Soviet postulate, endlessly repeated, was that this was only a form, and that the content, whether in literature or politics, had to be Soviet. But this form ended up creating the life of its object.

A Soviet republic is an empty frame which produces an effect of reality. The existence of institutions and an administrative apparatus results in the generation of a political class, a bureaucracy and an intelligentsia which owe the fact of their social being to that framework. The fact of having a national territory, national symbols, a language and references in school to the existence of a national culture, however superficial it may be, result in the implantation of a vision of the world which is not so much nationalist as simply national. Nationalism here is not an ideology, it is a *habitus*, a way of being which is internalised and which accords well with the actual ideology of communism, inasmuch as this latter does not question the functioning of the national framework. It was when Andropov (1983) and Gorbachev (1985) set about attacking national cultures and local apparatuses in the name of 'socialism' and the struggle against corruption that local cadres and public opinion in the republics no longer recognised themselves in the compromise that had been put in place during the long period under Brezhnev: to each according to their needs – in other words, strategy, the military and ideology were the province of Moscow, while exercising local power, making money, and being rooted in a national framework was what mattered for the apparatchiks in the republics.

The major effect of the Soviet period was the territorialisation and systematic ethnicisation of populations, which led in turn to an exacerbation of regional and ethnic conflicts that had been unknown up until that point. This took place within a framework of collectivisation, the assignment of individuals to collectives (the *kolkhoz*), the structuring of the Communist Party on the basis of territorial administrative divisions (soviets at the level of village, district and province, and the republic's communist party). In a parallel development, identity became univocal: the ten-yearly censuses and 'line 5' in people's internal passport required that all people declare themselves as belonging to one, and only one, of the 'nationalities' (ethnic groups), to be chosen from an official list drawn up by the state. Generalised territorialisation went hand-in-hand with a systematic ethnicisation of identity: the foundations of the ethnic nation-state were thus imposed to the detriment of a strictly political identity, that of citizenship in relation to a Soviet state which foundered amid the vapours of petrol and alcohol at the end of August 1991.

Benedict Anderson's thesis, drawn from an analysis of colonial Latin America, is broadly relevant here in explaining how the model of the nation-state came to be implanted within the framework of the Soviet system in Central Asia.[1] Nationalism was created by the administrative, cultural and political *habitus* installed by the colonial power, within an entity that had no antecedents of nationhood.

But this thesis does not explain everything. The building of a nation-state structure from above does not necessarily explain the rooting of a national identity, and even less the setting up of a social fabric, of a 'civil society', which maintains an ambiguous relationship with this state structure, neither confronting it nor pushing for an alternative state structure. The role of the colonial power in setting up the state structure is important but not sufficient:[2] the shift from colonial administrative structures to modern nationalism supposes a process of re-appropriation of these structures by local élites and society. And this re-appropriation is done through the social patterns and historical memory of the given societies, not by using an abstract model of what is or should be a 'nation-state'.[3] This process of re-appropriation is the main issue that we address in this book.

How was it that traditional society in Soviet Central Asia proved so adept at appropriating this imported model? After all, on the one hand these societies had been subjected to a direct and violent attempt to destroy them, and on the other, the imported model of the nation-state was itself only an element of a radical and much broader project of social engineering which was supposed to render traditional society obsolete by integrating it into the Soviet mould.

Two elements here are slightly different from Anderson's 'imagined communities'. First, in Central Asia the colonial state apparatus has been sociologially re-inhabited by a traditional society, or at least, after the collapse of the former society, by traditional patterns of political life, which have largely voided the ideological content of the Soviet system, without challenging it. The 'community' here is not imagined, it has a sociological reality. The second point of difference is about the role of the intellectuals: in Central Asia, the intellectuals did not care to give a real content to the concept of national culture. Although managing in a professional way what was allowed by the centre in terms of national culture, they did not care to beef it up. This lazy intelligentsia never cared to provide an 'imaginary' for the 'imagined communities'. Creating nationalism does not neccessarily need intellectual effort.

Any analysis of the installation of the nation-state model needs to be accompanied by a study of the concomitant social processes which enabled a social space to restructure itself around elements that had been conceived in order to destroy it. In this book I would like to demonstrate how the society reconstructed itself around three axes: the shift into the kolkhozian communitarian system of pre-existing solidarity groups (kinship groups, clans, *mahallas* – in other words, grouped habitats of families having links with each other); the recomposition of the world of politics around regional factionalism; the internalisation of ethnic identity in line with criteria defined by Soviet anthropology and the Soviet administrative system (language and univocality of ethnic identity). These three levels generally run into each other: conflicts between local solidarity groups do not prevent the emergence of a regionalist solidarity, and regionalist factionalism is not an obstacle to sentiments of national belonging.

However, Tajikistan provides an instance of a patent failure of this hierarchy of identities: the violence of relations between regionalist factions rendered the emergence of any coherent national sentiment difficult. Curiously, the Tajik identity is the only one that was also the bearer of a universality prior to the Soviet recomposition: the Islamic-Persian culture which is the foundation for the civilisation of the whole of Central Asia. The failure of the Soviet model of 'republicanisation' is only visible in countries where it has not been able to conceal and bury the past. But this past functions in a register which no longer offers an identity-based model of political mobilisation, other than that of an Islamism which has basically been captured by a purely regionalist logic. Islamic identity has shared the same fate as the preceding 'socialist' ideology, and has ended up trapped by the logic of group loyalties.

I refer to a recomposition rather than an ongoing continued existence of traditional society. Although local solidarity groupings managed to preserve their existence at the time of sovietisation, it was a different matter for the élites. The traditional notables were eliminated (the war against the *basmachis*, the struggle against the *kulaks*, collectivisation, and the purges of 1937). However what one sees today is a continued existence of a category of rural notables (the chairmen of *kolkhoz*), who function as the interface between the state and the rural community and who draw their status (and income) from the systematisation of this function. In effect, the Soviet system fixed the basic local communities within the framework of the *kolkhoz*. It gave them a reality that was both economic and administrative (brigades, *kolkhoz* and village soviets). While campaigning against traditional society, it fostered the basic kernel of that society, the solidarity group, as a mediator of relations between the individual and the state. It thus immediately recreated similar forms of notables, who were no longer the old-time tribal chiefs, but representatives of a new tribe: the *kolkhoz*.

But the Soviet system also meant that the state – which held a monopoly in the distribution of energy and the marketing of goods produced – was their sole interlocutor. The articulation between the neo-traditional kolkhozian system and the state took place via the apparatus of the Communist Party, which of course had a monopoly in the area of politics and the control of administration. There was no autonomy of the state apparatus (and thus there was also no appearance of a class of professional managers). In the rural areas the party was entirely in the hands of kolkhozian notables and regional élites (because, unlike the situation in the European part of the USSR, in the south there was no real turnover of cadres). In a system of scarcity and of a monopoly of trade that works to the advantage of the state, the solidarity group necessarily has to pursue a strategy of entrism in relation to the political power system, which then recasts it in return. The solidarity group endeavours to connect to the state apparatus, in other words to the party. The principle of the state is not questioned; on the contrary, it is the framework within which conflicts between groups take place. This rooting of the state model, sometimes strong (Uzbekistan) and sometimes weak (Tajikistan), is an effect of sovietism, made possible not by the void created in civil society, but by the recomposition of civil society around an apparatus – the Communist Party – which it has subverted and turned to its own ends. This explains how the party was able to disappear so suddenly, hardly leaving a trace, while at the same time the state, or at least the quest for a state, remained.

Power struggles strengthened the cohesion of the base groups, while at the same time making possible the emergence of a new political élite, which necessarily has to pass through the mill of the apparatus, of its logic of power and its official ideology, which are geared to one single horizon: the state and the new nation. During the Soviet period, these élites followed a fairly uniform professional training (as engineers), they joined the party, they underwent a formal Russification, they accepted (or rather internalised) the rules of the game (respect for an ideological code). But the aim is not to become a player at the level of the USSR, which would anyway be barred to them (practically no Muslim cadre could expect to make a career outside his republic, except in a minor role in the army or as a diplomat). The low-level rural official thus automatically becomes the interface between solidarity groups and a state which is very distant, and which one needs to know how to approach in order to obtain subsidies and energy supplies. The Soviet notable re-embodies not only the function of the khans and the beys, but also their behaviours and their social *habitus* (conspicuous spending, maintaining a set of client relations etc). The Communist Party becomes the ladder to social promotion, but within a traditional structure of clientism.

What appears as a 'retraditionalisation' is in fact simply an adaptation to a demand for social organisation induced by the state: the solidarity group, whether translated or recomposed, is the individual's entry point into the system; it is the mediator of the relationship to the state and to the rest of society. It provides the only access to 'goods', to social welfare and to administrative existence (passport, holidays, personal mobility). In this system, the fact of the state is not challenged. On the contrary, it is the keystone, the referee and sometimes also the stakes in competition between solidarity groups. The national space is the arena in which competition takes place. But this competition also implies a sort of solidarity. For competition to function, a national space is actually needed.

The paradox of Sovietism is that it brought simultaneously a crystallisation of political factionalism on a regionalist basis (conflicts over land and access to power arising out of a territorial and administrative realignment which is the basis of all power) and a homogenisation of the national space (the assimilation of minorities which have no administrative status; the uniformisation of solidarity groups within the territorial and social framework of the *kolkhoz*; the bringing of the business of politics exclusively into the framework of the Communist Party; a standardisation in the training of cadres). Factionalism is more a consequence of Sovietisation than an inheritance from the past. Although the new order assigns everyone a new place and fixes them to a given territory, within a given social order and a given classification of ethnic groups, it is little concerned with the overall management of this totality. In fact, the Soviet system is more totalising (bringing everything within its order and its registers) than totalitarian (gathering the whole of society into the state): the physical presence of the administration in the countryside was slight; the myth of the omni-presence of the party has led people to think that there was no space for independent activity, but in the rural areas the party itself was entirely captured by traditional solidarity groups, as were the KGB and the militias.

Thus it was precisely because of the nature of the Soviet system that the new élites came to operate within a national framework – but without seeking to construct a nationalist culture, and even less a nationalist ideology. The gap between the national *habitus* and the national imaginary is striking: between the two there is a lack of the more or less necessary relationship that

Benedict Anderson highlights in his examples. In particular, one does not find a category of nationalist intellectual trying by its writings and research to awaken this national imaginary. On the contrary, the real intellectuals are universalists, such as the Kyrgyz Chingiz Aymatov, or the Tajik poets attempting to revive Persian classical culture.

In Central Asia, the establishment of a national *habitus* has been preceded by a previous deculturation. This *habitus* took root not as an ideology but as a code, operating at several levels (dress, cooking, ethics, personal relations, marriage etc). It is striking to note that this kind of national positioning was not preceded (and so far has not been followed either) by a serious and complex intellectual construction. I do not consider the legitimation discourse produced during the Soviet era by official academics (linguists, ethnologists and archaeologists) and writers (poets and novelists) as the creation of a national culture. These academics were technicians working on a body of knowledge the meaning of which had been given by others – by politicians and ideologues. The poverty of the existing body of literature in bringing these new identities to life is self-evident: there was no new creation, and not even the exhuming of past creations. The reason is simple: in the eyes of the Soviets, the construction of nations was only a temporary step towards the establishment of *homo sovieticus*, so it should not be given too much reality. Hence derives the explicit limitation of national creative arts to a code and a form, following the adage 'national in form, socialist in content'. Folklore (national ballet) takes priority over musicological research (such as Bela Bartok had pursued in Hungary); translation has priority over literary production in the national language; ethnography (the study of rural customs) has priority over sociology etc. The nationalist ideologues of the Europe of nations filled whole libraries with books in the national language, while the manufacturers of nationalities in the Soviet era were content with just a few showcases.

It is thus striking the extent to which the code, the form and the appearance have a reality effect equal to the far richer and more complex efforts of the nationalist ideologues of Europe in the nineteenth century and Turkey in the twentieth, as regards setting in place a national culture. In this book, we shall several times have occasion to note that Atatürk's reform not only preceded by a year or two, but was also more radical than most of the Soviet reforms (except, of course, in the socio-economic domain: but this latter was precisely the very locus of the recomposition, of the retraditionalisation of the Soviet system). Atatürk had a greater modernising effect than did Stalin: today the social structure of Central Asia is more traditional than that of Turkey (a low degree of urbanisation, high birth rates, and the weight of regional clanism).

The poverty of ideological production (both in the Soviet and in post-independence periods) is a constant: it shows that nationalism can perfectly well develop outside any sophisticated elaboration, as a *habitus* and not as ideology. This explains why the future nationalist leaders were able, right to the last moment, to be perfect apparatchiks, taking orders, hammering the slogans of the day and toeing the line coming from the centre. This does not imply schizophrenia, nor a vacuity of all ideological discourse, but is rather a sign that the Soviet order could not exist without an ongoing discourse on and about itself, whereas the national level of things derives more from a practice than a declaration. The statement of nationhood is made in relation to the external world: we are independent, look at our flag. It is interesting to note that the newly-independent republics have been less concerned than the Afghan state of the same era to mark their symbolic membership within the world order by a currency, by stamps, the opening of embassies etc, all of which were done with some delay in Central Asia. This delay was interpreted, wrongly, as the sign of an independence that had not been fully completed, a feeling reinforced by the maintenance of a Soviet symbolism and iconography (street names, layout of newspapers, slogans etc). But the truth is that the national *habitus* came about in the realm of the unspoken. The élites of the newly-independent states did not need grand rhetorics, at least in the first years. Moreover, in the republics of Central Asia one does not find the daily scenarios of nationalism found in other recently-emerging countries (saluting the flag and singing the national anthem in schools, the omnipresence of the national emblem etc).

Thus the Soviet heritage has little to do with doctrine. What was stamped on the South was neither communism nor socialism but Sovietism: Sovietism is a form, an apparatus, a technique of power and an organisation of the social which is permanently out of step with the ideology on which it is supposedly based, like a film out of synch with its sound-track. The ideological register, that of speeches, slogans, textbooks, symbols, billboards and newspapers is simultaneously saturated and empty. It is the only possible language, but it leaves the field free for effective practices which are either unstated or state themselves only in patois: people say in Russian what is politically correct, and use the local language for what is effective (and affective). As we shall see, while the national language became degraded under the effect of Russification and politically correct jargon, it was not 'regenerated' in the Kemalist manner, and thus it remained more traditional (a political 'fault' is called a *gunah*, or 'sin', in Uzbek and Tajik). The perverse effect of the ideology is to block and render impossible all intellectual research in universities; but this opens the way for a whole range of traditional practices among the new élites. These practices (eg *tuy*, or feasts involving ostentatious expenditure; clientism, endogamy) are the grammar of the really-existing social relations, and are out of step with the ideological stated position which, anyway, will only be expressed in Russian.

So this is the way in which civil society was rebuilt, not in parallel but within the very framework of the Soviet institutions. It borrowed from that framework not only the social grammar (communitarianism), but also the very logic of its installation as nation. The present ruling élites are pursuing to the utmost the Soviet logic of creating nations and differentiating them from their fellow republics.

The newly-independent states are in effect keeping Soviet methods in order to give themselves authenticity (language and alphabet reform and a rewriting of history). They are also moulding themselves within the strategic constraints which have presided over their birth: the rejection of all 'pan-...ist' blocs (pan-Islam, pan-Turkism etc). And they are adopting the model of the strong, personalised state tending towards a monolithism which is challenged not by democracy but by regionalist factionalism or ethnic diversity.

This plasticity of the model for manufacturing nations, which functions within very various ideological frames of reference, is all the more obvious when one realises that many Soviet pseudo-innovations were already in operation in the tsarist period: the policy of ethnicisation by the promotion of so-called 'national' languages; the bureaucratic integration of the Muslim clergy; a policy of integrating Muslims within the Russian administrative system by means of an ideological project (orthodoxy, Sovietism), which made integration possible without requiring assimilation, etc.

Underlying the apparent break-point of 1917 there is therefore a continuity in Russia's relationship with its Muslim subjects, breaking with the Western models which swing between crusade and assimilation. The drama of Russia is that the machine for manufacturing nation-states does not work for Russia itself, since it is condemned to remain an empire, endlessly shrinking, and dragging with it a perennial Chechen drama that is as much an identity crisis as political. However, in another space, despite tensions and conflicts, the new nations are taking root.

This book is an attempt to shed light on the process of the manufacture of these nations, the recomposition of traditional solidarity groups, and the emergence of new nationalist élites from within the Soviet framework. It is thus necessary to take an historical perspective. Here I owe much to the work done in French by Alexandre Bennigsen and Hélène Carrère d'Encausse. In English, coming out of Chicago, the 'Bennigsen school' has produced two generations of researchers who have published some remarkable monographs, to which the first part of this book is much indebted. The contemporary perspective is based on my fieldwork between 1990 and 1996, mainly focussed on Uzbekistan and Tajikistan, which are thus the strong points of the book, to the detriment of the other republics, which I visited less regularly. My point of view comes from the South: I study Tajikistan from the standpoint of an *afghantsy* (a veteran of the Afghan war, in Russian slang), rather than from the standpoint of a Sovietologist, which is not what I am.

It is impossible to reach a unified system of transcription for the geographical area which concerns us, since not only are the languages (not to mention dialects) different, but so too are the alphabets. Thus the classical Arabic word *khotba*, with the emphatic letter 'ta', meaning preaching in the mosque, a word which is common to the whole Muslim world, is pronounced (without the emphasis) as *khotbe* in Iran, *khotba* in Afghanistan, *hitabe* in Istanbul Turkish (which is also how it is spelt), *khutba* in Uzbek (which becomes *xutba* in the Latin alphabet) etc. Since it is the same word and the same concept, it would be ridiculous to change the transcription every time one crosses a border, particularly because the concept in question ignores borders. It would be pedantic and ethnocentric to adopt the transcription norm of classical Arabic, which anyway would not be applied to words of Turkish or Persian origin.

It is thus necessary to use a transcription that is not too scientific, because the more scientific a transcription is, the more it isolates and particularises, according to the Stalinist recipe applied to the nations, thus losing the important elements, in other words the notion of a cultural area which is simultaneously homogeneous and diversified. As long as concepts and proper names are recognised, it is sufficient.[4]

1

History and Identity

THE WEIGHT OF HISTORY
Space

Central Asia is a concept which has a variable geography, in the sense that it can be taken as referring only to Transoxiania, or can be expanded to take in everything from Istanbul to Sinkiang.

In administrative and political terms, the Soviet definition of Central Asia comprised the four republics of Turkmenistan, Uzbekistan, Kyrgyzstan and Tajikistan. This area corresponds broadly speaking to the Transoxiania of the ancient world, and to the Mawarannahr ('beyond the river' in Arabic) of the Muslims, in other words the basin of the two darya ('sea' or 'river' in Persian): the Amu Darya (the classical Oxus) and the Syr Darya. But given the interconnectedness of their political destinies, a further republic – Kazakhstan – ought really to be added to these four, as it was in the Soviet era, when the muftiyya (directorate of religious affairs) based at Tashkent was officially known as the Muftiyya of Central Asia and Kazakhstan. This is the region which is the principal object of study in this book. At the same time, it is hard to leave out the sixth ex-Soviet Muslim republic, Azerbaijan, particularly since the new geo-strategic space which has appeared since the collapse of the USSR gives economic primacy not to the steppes which stretch from the Aral Sea to the Chinese frontier but to the Caspian, with its oil and gas reserves which will sooner or later make the region one of the world's largest oil export areas. Finally, one cannot study relations between Russia and the Muslim republics without taking on board the history of the Muslims in Russia itself, from the Chechens to the Volga Tatars, who, between 1552 and 1990, regularly set themselves up as champions of a Russian (or at least Russian-style) Islam which respected the structures of empire.

However, if we analyse the area in terms of cultural space, then Central Asia in its broadest sense is the area of Turco-Persian civilisation which was

1

THE NEW CENTRAL ASIA

the crucible of languages and cultures from Istanbul to Delhi, from Esfahan to Bukhara, with its Turkish emirs, its Persian administration, and, up until the Iranian split in 1501, its Hanafi school of Sunni Islam. Gradual shifts from one dialect to another, from blue ceramics to azure, from one musical mode to a variant mode in a slower tempo, this was an area of transitions. There were hardly any rigidly defined frontiers until the nation-states of the twentieth century solidified minor differences into a principle of exclusion. If there are cultural frontiers today, they are more subtle: for example, the caste system, which begins at the Indus and takes you beyond the Pashtun world; the space where people celebrate Newruz, the Iranian New Year (from the Kurds to the Uzbeks and from the Baluchis to the Azeris); the places where people take *naswer* (a green, bitter powder), from Peshawar to Samarkand; the peoples who, whatever their language, use the same words for referring to nation, assembly, tribe, clan, genealogy, hope and bread.

This Central Asia, divided by the descending slopes of the large ranges of mountains that reach across from China (called Tien Shan, Pamir, Hissar or the Hindu Kush), is an area of plains and high plateaus traversed by lines of poplars and oases where the ranges of vegetation are not unfamiliar to the Western eye. Agriculture relies on irrigation, even in the upper valleys, and the necessity of organising around a system of channels to draw water from one of the three big rivers is what consolidates the existence of village communities, whatever their formal name (tribe or *kolkhoz*).

However, this area is also divided by a fracture line which is more cultural than ethnic or political. Transoxiania saw the development of an old urban and Muslim civilisation around the oases of Zarafshan (Samarkand and Bukhara) and the Syr Darya (Ferghana, Kokand and Andijan). This was the focal point of the Turco-Persian synthesis which spills over into present-day Kazakhstan and Kyrgyzstan. On the other hand, the steppes of Kazakhstan, extended by the Tien Shan mountains, were the domain of Turkic-speaking tribes who were not Islamicised until the eighteenth and nineteenth century, and were only settled from the end of the nineteenth century and the period of the first Five Year Plan (1928–32). Here the Persian influence is weak. The frontier between these two areas is not ethnic: the Kyrgyz of Osh and the Kazakhs of the town of Turkestan are close to this civilisation. While this split also corresponds to two visions of Islam – more mystical and influenced by shamanism in the steppes, and more doctrinal and orthodox in Transoxiania – the two worlds have gradually interpenetrated each other.

Languages and populations

Before the establishment of the present republics by Stalin in the 1920s, Central Asia had never known the principle of creating a state by associating a given territory with an ethnic or linguistic group. The successive political entities in Transoxiania were built on loyalty to dynasties and fidelity to

Islam. In the era preceding the great division of 1924, the three emirates of Transoxiania (Kokand, Bukhara and Khiva) were ruled by Uzbek dynasties presiding over a multi-ethnic population among whom it would have been hard to establish a clear distinction between what we would today call 'ethnic groups'. At that time, terms such as Uzbek, Tajik, Kyrgyz and Turkmen were certainly used, but they did not really take into account the complex interplay of identities: the notion of ethnic group is far more a political construction than an observable fact.[1]

This concept of ethnic group was largely invented *post facto* by Soviet theoreticians in order to justify an imposed territorial realignment, the eminently artificial, manipulatory and strategic nature of which has been well documented. More importantly, these identities were not matched by the existence of nationalisms, even embryonically (except perhaps among the Kazakh élite of the nineteenth century, with their concern for the codification of their language): the 'ethnic groups' were intermingled with each other, and were distributed more according to ecological and socio–economic criteria than by territory. They accepted the political framework of multi-ethnic and generally bilingual 'emirates' in which the competition for power had more to do with dynasties, clans and tribes than with 'ethnic group' as such. Even if the rulers were Uzbeks, the court language was Persian at Bukhara and Kokand, in other words the language of the Tajiks, which at the time was seen as the main cultured language. The idea of associating a territory with an ethnic group defined by language was alien to the political ideas of the Muslims of Central Asia. These populations were, and still are, widely intermingled, so that infra-ethnic identities (tribal, clan, locality, family, etc) were more important in determining loyalties than strictly ethnic origin.

The populations of Transoxiania shared one culture up until Sovietisation: the Persian and Muslim civilisation which was established during the course of the eighth and ninth centuries, following the Arab conquest which had touched on Iran less than a century previously. There was no massive Arab settlement in Central Asia (the groups which today call themselves 'Arab' were established much later). Modern Persian, with its very Arabised vocabulary, emerged from the encounter between Iran and Islam. The channels of Islamisation in Central Asia, Afghanistan and northern India were the Persian language and civilisation which developed in Greater Khorasan (from Mashhad in Iran to present-day Tajikistan); the founding fathers of Persian culture (Rudaki and Firdawsi in the tenth century) come from this region and not from the historic heart of Persia, Fars, which much later would see the emergence of great figures such as Hafez and Sa'adi. The towns of Transoxiania (Samarkand and Bukhara) became centres of Persian and Islamic culture, whereas the countryside long remained faithful to the old languages, and also to Zoroastrianism. Persian functions as both the court language and the language of the urban élite, and is also the language of Islam (in Afghanistan it is still known as Dari, in other words the language 'of the court'). After

Mahmud of Ghazni, the conqueror of northern India (d. 1030), the channels of Islamisation are no longer military: the mission of Islamisation is gradually taken up by the Sunni Sufi brotherhoods. Islamisation migrated from the urban centres and advanced peacefully eastwards and southwards down the trade routes.

The ancient populations of Transoxiania (also of Sinkiang and Afghanistan) generally spoke languages of the East Iranian group, such as Sogdian; they became Persianised during the course of Islamisation, even though pockets of East Iranian are still to be found today (the Yaghnobi and Pamiri dialects, whose area incidentally corresponds to a heterodox Islamisation in its Ismaili form). The Turkic peoples who were Islamised in turn were also 'Persianised' culturally. Persian was the language of civilisation *par excellence* from Delhi to Samarkand, passing via Lahore and Kabul, and this remained the case until the early twentieth century. The emirates of Kokand and Bukhara, ruled by Uzbek dynasties, had Persian as their official language right up to their dissolution (in 1876 and 1920 respectively), as did the Moghul empire of Northern India until its abolition in 1857. From New Delhi to Bukhara and Baku, poets and writers were happier using Persian (even if they were themselves 'Turks' – a term used to denote Turcophones, whatever the dialect spoken) such as Ali Shir Nava'i in the sixteenth century. In the nineteenth century, the British and Russian colonial administrations taught their agents Persian, which was also the language of correspondence between the Ottoman caliph and the court of China. Bombay was a major centre of Persian-language publication. The great poet of the Indian sub-continent, Iqbal (d. 1938), wrote more in Persian than in Urdu. The intelligentsia of Central Asia at the time of the Russian Revolution also expressed themselves mainly in Persian: Abdurrauf Fitrat, the Bukhara reformer and Bolshevik sympathiser, published his work Munazare ('The Debate', 1909) in Istanbul in Persian.[2] The great Russian Azeri author Mirza Fath Ali Akhundzada (1812–78) wrote equally happily in either Persian or Turki. When a 'Jadid' (reform) school was authorised by the Emir of Bukhara in 1908, the pupils were taught in the Persian language. Finally, the principality of Chitral, part of Pakistan, maintained Persian as its administrative language until as late as 1962.

However, linguistic dynamics were tending slowly to veer towards Turkic languages. After the Islamic conversion of the Mongols, a highly Iranicised vehicular Turki language (the Chaghatay of the fourteenth through nineteenth centuries, which was to be replaced by Uzbek) spread among the populations of the plains of Transoxiania. While Turkic slowly became the language of the masses in Transoxiania, Persian still remained the language of culture. The decline of Persian was further accelerated by the Bolshevik revolution: nowadays in Central Asia it is restricted to the centres of the major historical cities (Samarkand and Bukhara) and the foothills of the Pamir and the Tien Shan, while the plains speak Uzbek, and the higher mountain areas Pamiri or Kyrgyz. This split between town Tajiks and mountain Tajiks was to weigh heavily on the difficult process of emergence of a Tajik political identity.

Changes of language one way or the other do not necessarily imply military conquest or forced imposition: they derive from social dynamics and questions of cultural prestige, and bilingualism was often the norm. The recent setback suffered by Persian in Central Asia has been abrupt, and can be related to the disappearance of the great multi-ethnic empires of which it had been the *lingua franca*, and to the development of nation-states eager to promote their 'national' languages. This has resulted in Persian going into decline since the 1920s, in the face of Turkic languages (Uzbekistan), Urdu (Pakistan) and Pashtu (Afghanistan). Today we have the combined impact of ethnic nationalism, the appearance of nation states with national language policies, and the split between Shiite Iran and the Persian-speaking Sunnis of Central Asia. This has led (at least outside Iran) to the definitive decline of Persian. Nowadays it exists as an official language only in Iran and Tajikistan, while in Afghanistan it shares this status with Pashtu.

'Turkisation'

After an Islamisation in the Persian mode, linguistic and demographic Turkisation was the second major element which fashioned the present face of Central Asia. The political history of the region during the second millennium of our epoch has been one of tribal confederations, generally Turkic (Pashtun in Afghanistan), carving out empires in an area that had been peopled since the preceding millennium by settled populations of Iranian stock, some of whom would go on to adopt a Turkic language; at the same time, some Turkic peoples, as they settled, became Iranicised in turn – if not in language, at least in culture. The strong earlier differences between nomadic Turkic tribes and sedentary Indo-Europeans began to become less marked from the fourteenth century onwards. The Turks penetrated into Central Asia *en masse* from the eighth century onwards. This was not an invasion but a displacement of tribes which often resulted in short-lived tribal confederations building empires, such as the Karakhanid empire in the middle of the ninth century, which extended from Transoxiania to present-day Sinkiang. The Persian-speaking Muslim kingdoms of Afghanistan and Khorasan took on some of these Turks as soldiers; they adopted the Muslim faith and soon moved into positions of power, the best known of them being Mahmud of Ghazni. Among the Turkic tribes that moved to the frontiers of the Muslim world in this way, a clan belonging to the Oghuz language group, the Seljuks, conquered Iran and took Baghdad in 1055: from that point on, there was no longer a frontier between the Turkic and Persian worlds. The Turco-Persian culture which resulted from this fusion continued in existence for eight centuries: from Anatolia to Samarkand, taking in Iran, Herat and northern India, emirs and sultans were all Turks (with the exception of some Pashtuns in Afghanistan and northern India), while the administration was Persian in both its language and its personnel. This model was still to be found in the Afghan territories of General Dostum in the mid-1990s. The Turkic tribes are classified into three major language groupings: the Oghuz to the south and west of the Aral Sea, the Qipchaks to the north and east, and the Turki of the settled populations of Central Asia (Chaghatay, present-day Uzbek and Uighur).[3] The first of these groups shifted virtually wholesale in the direction of Iran and Anatolia, leaving Central Asia with today's Turkmens. The second group remained between the Volga and the Kazakh steppes, and this language group contains the Volga Tatars, the Kazakhs, the Kyrgyz, the Karakalpaks and the founders of the tribal confederation who were to take the name Uzbeks. The third group became ethnically 'Uzbekised', but its language is at the base of what is 'modern Uzbek'.

The shifting movements of the Turkic populations did not follow a logic of territorial continuity with the steppes. The mass of the Oghuz who crossed the Amu Darya towards the west left the Iranian plateaux, which remained Persian, and established themselves more to the west, in Anatolia. Here they divided into Ottomans, who were Sunni and settled, and Turkmens, who were nomads and in part Shiite (or, rather, Alevi). The latter were to keep the name 'Turkmen' for a long time: from the thirteenth century onwards they 'Turkised' the Iranian populations of Azerbaijan (who spoke west Iranian languages such as Tat, which is still found in residual forms), thus creating a new identity based on Shiism and the use of Turkish. These are the people today known as Azeris. The adoption of Shiism by these nomads and their conquest of Iran in 1501 established the long-term (and still current) frontier of Iran: it is a religious frontier (Shiites versus Sunnis) rather than ethnic or linguistic. In the desert areas of present-day Turkestan, Turkmen nomadic tribes were already present before the Arab invasion; they did not follow the Anatolian branch in the transition to Shiism. This is the only place where one can speak of a marked opposition between nomadic Turks and sedentary Persians, an opposition which rests more on religious incompatibility than ethnic antagonism. Finally, the Oghuz language group divided into three branches (Ottomans, Azeris and Turkmens) according to both religious criteria (Shiism-Sunnism) and political ones (with the Sunni Turkish dynasty of the Ottomans, the Shiite Turkic dynasty of the Safavid Iranians, and also Sunni Turkmen nomads rejecting supra-tribal structures).

The Mongol invasion in the thirteenth century tended to lead to an inter-mixing of populations. In particular, various Qipchak Turkic tribal segments were brought into the Mongol confederation. One paradoxical consequence of this was the rooting of Turkic languages in Central Asia; the Mongols effectively became simultaneously Islamicised and Turkised, from the reign of Chagatai onward (the son of Genghis Khan, who had been given Transoxiania as his vassaldom). All the dynasties which followed the Mongols in Central Asia (Timurids, Uzbeks and Moghuls) claimed descent from Genghis Khan. In the late fourteenth century Tamerlane (Timur Leng, 1336–1405), originally from the Mongol Barlas tribe, was to found a short-lived empire which stretched from Ankara to Delhi. This empire definitively consolidated the Turco-Persian cultural synthesis in Transoxiania: a literary form of Turkish (Chaghatay) sits alongside Persian as both cultural and official language; the orthodox religion is strictly Sunni; and Samarkand becomes the jewel of an Islamic art which owes everything to Persian artists. Timurid culture lived on after the death of its founder.

Meanwhile, in the steppes between Aral and Ural, Abul Khayr (1412–68), another descendant of Genghis Khan (via his grandson Shayban, who was to give his name to the Shaybanid dynasty), attempted to regroup the tribes which his grandfather had received as his prerogative. These tribes, which belonged to a Qipchak linguistic group, then divided: one part (the Qazak or 'fugitives', from which the Russians derived the word 'Cossack') refused to join the confederation and went off to live nomadic lives in the steppes which today bear their name – Kazakhstan, which ought to be written Qazakistan. The others took the name Uzbek and set off in conquest of Transoxiania. The grandson of Abul Khayyir, Mohamed Shaybani, took Samarkand in 1500. The power of the Uzbeks was born. But the Uzbek sovereigns were formed in the Timurid mould: they took their languages (Persian, and a highly Iranicised Chaghatay Turkish, which was thus very different from the Qipchak of their origins), their culture and their state apparatus. Once again the integratory power of the old Persian culture had its effect on the new arrivals. The frontier between Transoxiania and the steppes counterposed, on the one hand, a town–based culture that was statist and orthodox Sunni, and on the other tribes which had remained nomadic, had no state entity, and were barely Islamicised (sometimes as late as the eighteenth century, by the Tatars of Kazan), and which had never been subject to Persian cultural influence. The descent of the Turks towards the south and west thus involved a major differentiation in their culture and their way of life.

The last mass migration of Turkic tribes was that of the Kyrgyz, who moved into occupation of their present habitat in the sixteenth and seventeenth centuries, having been chased from the steppes by the Buddhist Oyrats.

Empires and Political Culture

The political formations which occupied the area were therefore not the direct expression of ethnic groups. They were built on dynasties whose tribal legitimacy transformed into dynastic legitimacy, which was then reinforced by a religious legitimacy, able to maintain sway over very varied populations thanks to a state apparatus that was inherited from the Persian tradition. We have a paradigm of this in the first Seljuk government in Iran: the emir was Turkic (Arslan, succeeded by Malik Shah), the 'vizier' (the great Nizam al-Mulk, 1018–92) was Persian; the latter organised the system of *madrasahs*, and created the corporation of *ulemas* (doctors of law) who were guardians of religious orthodoxy and of the *sharia* (Muslim law) and who, whatever their 'ethnic' origins, were educated in both Arabic and Persian. In the court administration, civil functions inherited from the Persian world sat side-by-side with military titles that were expressed in Turkish. An Islamisation of names (the adoption of names deriving from the Quran, for example 'Abd' followed by one of the names of God) means that it becomes no longer possible to identify people's 'ethnic' origins. At best, their geographic origin (al-Bukhari, al-Tirmizi etc) may offer a suggestion. But this does not enable us to identify the mother tongue of the person concerned. This paradigm functioned for the best part of eight centuries.

Nevertheless, the rise and fall of empires, and the regroupings and subsequent fragmentation into dozens of short-lived emirates, did not prevent the crystallisation of Central Asia, in the broad sense, around three poles which still make sense today. This crystallisation took place right at the start of the sixteenth century, at the time of three simultaneous founding events: the conquest of Iran by the Safavid dynasties (which ruled from 1501 to 1727), which made Shiism the foundation of the state and nation; the conquest of Transoxiania by the Uzbeks, who controlled all the political structures up until the arrival of the Russians; and finally the foundation of the Moghul empire (from northern India to Kabul) by Babur, who was chased from his ancestral lands of Ferghana by the Uzbek invasion, and who took Delhi in 1526. The Shiite legitimacy of Iran, eclipsed under the Pahlavis (1921–79), returned in strength with the Islamic revolution of 1979. The Moghul empire in northern India (1527–1857) was taken up by the British from 1857 to 1947 in the 'great game' with Russia which resumed the Uzbek tradition of pressure towards the south.[4] Meanwhile, Pakistan, under General Zia ul-Haq (1977–88), was able to take advantage of the war in Afghanistan, the fall of the USSR and the taking of Kabul by its Taliban allies (September 1996) to revive its great dream of becoming the Muslim and Sunni focus for a recomposition of Central Asia. At the time of independence, Uzbekistan laid claim to Tamerlane as its founding father and went on to claim the Timurid heritage, making itself a focal point in Transoxiania to the benefit of Uzbeks. At the intersection of these three focal points, Afghanistan hovers between a role as battlefield between the three neighbouring empires (from the sixteenth to the eighteenth centuries), whose heirs today support their respective clients (the Hazara Shiites in the case of Tehran, General Dostum in the case of Tashkent, and Hekmatyar, followed by the Taliban, in the case of Islamabad), and its status as a buffer-state designed from 1881 to 1907 by the Russians and the British.

Such a configuration, which first appeared between 1500 and 1526, is not necessarily the unavoidable fate of greater Central Asia, but it has nevertheless left a powerful mark on its present geo-strategy. The Shiitisation of Iran undoubtedly had the longest-term effects: it led to a radical split between the Sunni Persian-speaking world and Iran, which would never again succeed in getting a foothold in Central Asia, even in support of the newly independent republics and through the crisis in Afghanistan. Only the Afghan Shiites (Hazaras) have, belatedly, identified themselves with Iran.[5] The Sunnis of Transoxiania, Afghanistan and India have always seen the Shiites as heretics, to be either converted or reduced to slavery.[6] The Turkmen tribes, who incidentally are none too orthodox themselves, took steps during the nineteenth century to provide themselves with *fatwas* authorising them to enslave Iranians, on the basis that they were infidels (*kafir*). Iran, for its part, has never had any interest in anything that may have been written in Persian in the Sunni world. Iran, instead of being a bridgehead between Central Asia and the Middle East, became a barrier from the sixteenth century onwards: the pilgrim routes to Mecca were cut, forcing the emirates to negotiate rights of passage with Russia. Right up until the fall of the USSR, Russia would remain Central Asia's route out of its enclave, and towards contact with the West.

Deprived of a political centre, the Sunni Persian culture of Central Asia atrophied. Anglo-Russian rivalry in the nineteenth century cut the route to India. At the end of the nineteenth century, caught between Christian Russia and Shiite Iran, the élites of Central Asia sought a new path in pan-Turkism as a way of enabling them both to preserve their Islamic identity and to embark on social and political reform. But their attraction to Ottoman Turkey was too late in coming: in 1921, the newly-emerging Kemalist Turkey abandoned pretensions to being a focal point for the Muslim world, and entered the era of the nation-state. This dual isolation, from both Iran and Turkey, explains why neither the Iranian revolution nor secular Turkey have had a real impact in Central Asia. One should add that, contrary to claims that one regularly finds in the specialist literature, there are almost no Shiites in ex-Soviet Central Asia, and those that are found are never Tajiks (they are urban and even Uzbek-speaking in Samarkand). The confusion between Tajiks and Shiites derives from the fact that the Pamiris are often classified as 'Shiite Tajiks', even though they are neither one nor the other, but are Ismailis speaking East Iranian dialects.

This radical split between Shiites and Sunnis remains of far greater importance than any ethnic or linguistic proximity. But the opposition between the Sunni Moghul empire and the Uzbek emirates of the sixteenth century has also left its mark. For a long time the two sides shared the same court language and the same religious culture (Hanafi-school Sunnism). The opposition was not ideological but purely political: despite various attempts, the emperor Babur was never able to reconquer Transoxiania from his Kabul bases, and the various Uzbek rulers never succeeded in crossing the barrier of the Hindu Kush towards the plains of the Indus. The dynastic rivalry between Moghuls and Uzbeks in the sixteenth century gave way in the nineteenth century to rivalry between the major colonial powers, Russia and Britain, and then to rivalries between modern states. But the British never got a

9

foothold north of the Hindu Kush, and the Russians paid dearly for their 1979 intervention in Afghanistan. This ill-defined frontier between Central Asia and the Indian subcontinent is being reconstituted before our eyes, with the Uzbeks attempting to turn General Dostum's little kingdom into a new buffer zone, while the Pakistanis are set on restoring Moghul-style indirect sovereignty over the Pashtun tribal regions from Kandahar to Kabul, through the Taliban, and commander Massoud has failed to create an Afghan state that can act as a mid-point between the three poles, Iranian, Uzbek and 'Indo-Muslim'.

While these three poles established in the sixteenth century — Iranians, Uzbeks and Moghuls — are still meaningful, it is worth repeating that none of these empires was ethnic. They all had Persian as both their court language and the language of culture, and all the successive sovereigns in each of the three instances were of Turkish origin: the Safavids, followed by the Qajars in Iran; the Moghuls in India (Babur, the founder of the dynasty, wrote his Memoirs in Chaghatay Turkic); and the Uzbeks in the various emirates of Transoxiania (Bukhara, Khiva and Kokand). The Afghan ruling dynasty, which was Pashtun in origin, was the only indigenous one.

If I use the terms 'focal point' and 'pole', this is because these empires were not really territorial. They ruled over an area that was extended or reduced by military conquest. At the political level, the pre-1920 states were not built on a vertical integration of society. The palace directly controlled the town, and it left society and solidarity groups untouched (the latter were eventually rewarded or punished according to their loyalty or otherwise to the dynasty). Administration was largely indirect. In a sense, the state had an interest in ethnic and tribal diversity, and in competition between solidarity groups, because these enabled it to maintain its authority over a society which it ruled only indirectly, via the medium of local notables acting in the name of solidarity groupings (khan, malek, bey, katkhoda, aksaqal etc). The power of these 'representatives' thus rested largely on their function as inter-face between their respective solidarity groups, and by this means the state contributed to strengthening the role of notables, and to fixing/freezing the groups by putting them into competition with each other. This *schema*, paradoxically, was also to be found under the Soviet system. The act of sovereignty *par excellence* was the collecting of taxes, based on the state's claims to the eminent ownership of land (*amlak*), except where they were classified as being the property of a charitable foundation (*waqf*). In the emirates of Transoxiania, when revolts occurred they were first and foremost against taxation.

★   ★   ★

The major innovation in the course of the twentieth century has been the transition from a logic of empire (in which questions of language and ethnicity were secondary and where loyalty went to a dynasty, and more recently to an ideology, socialism in the USSR and Islam in Iran and Pakistan) to a nation-state logic (in which nationality tends to be defined as a function of one's linguistic and ethnic belonging, and there is a direct relationship between the citizen and the state, unmediated via solidarity groupings or religious affiliations). In the 1920s, in Iran (Reza Shah), Turkey (Atatürk) and Afghanistan (Amanullah and Nadir Khan), as well as in the USSR (Stalin), there was a shift from a legitimacy of empire to a legitimacy of the nation-state. The specificity of the Soviet Union was that it combined a logic of empire at the level of the central state (hence the problems of today's Russia, which has inherited its identity from a USSR which was never a nation state), and a logic of ethnic group-based states for the 14 'Soviet Socialist Republics', each of which was defined by an ethnic group and a territory. Even though the sovereignty of these republics was only symbolic, the symbolism was materially effective, because it necessarily translated into a political and administrative apparatus, and into the development of a pseudo-scientific rationality (in this case history and ethnography). Given that it was permanently caught in the interplay between ideological legitimacy and 'nationalities', the USSR made considerable efforts, in the name of socialism and through the medium of Russification, to combine the 14 non-Russian republics into an ideological supra-national entity: the collapse of the USSR has left a heritage which is asymetrical – a Russia in search of nationhood, and an Uzbekistan or a Turkmenistan that no longer have doubts about their identity. This development took place within the actual framework of the USSR: in the process of operating a logic of ideological empire (the adherence to socialism and respect for 'nationalities', while at the same time keeping them on the sidelines of political power) the Soviet system actually established the conditions for the emergence of nation-states.

Iran is the sole case in which a logic of empire transformed seamlessly into a logic of nation-state, but there was a reason for this, which the last Shah had forgotten: Shiism was the ideological foundation of politics. The return of Islam with the Islamic Revolution is only the affirmation of the identity link of a nation-state. The last remaining ideological state in the region today is Pakistan.[7]

Unlike empire, which willingly subcontracts the management of local solidarity groups to notables and satraps, the nation-state is integrative: it does not accept indirect administration of society and a preservation of the autonomy of solidarity groups. In the nation-state, nationalism is intrinsic: the citizen is defined by a direct relationship to the political community. He is above all a 'national'. His identity is not a question of ethnology but a matter of political strategy: all nation-states, even the 'liberal' ones, mobilise the human sciences – beginning with archaeology and history – as part of their founding process. Thus from the 1920s onwards, throughout the region of greater Central Asia (from Turkey through to Afghanistan), there has been a process of vertical integration, in other words the setting up of direct state administration. The reaction of solidarity groups would thus be to oppose that administration, or to circumvent it. We shall see how, under the Soviet system, solidarity groups were simultaneously able to subvert and bypass the system.

★   ★   ★

Present political developments in Central Asia suggest more than a return of the pre-existing ethnic groups – the emergence onto the political stage of 'macro-ethnic groups' in forms which may have been structured, modelled, even invented, by states, but which have acquired a reality, at least among the politicised élites. The reality of these macro-ethnic groups is today based on language plus religious difference (basically the Shiite-Sunni split). The question of the relationship of identity to ethnicity is thus a key element of political analysis.

ETHNIC GROUPS AND IDENTITIES

When people comment on the political problems of ex-Soviet Central Asia two notions are repeatedly advanced: that of 'ethnic group' and the vaguer notion of 'clan' (or faction, tribe, group etc). The elements differentiating the two notions are not to be found at the level of anthropological analysis: in a traditional society such as Afghanistan, where political intervention is less marked, it is much harder to establish a clear dividing line between 'ethnic group' and 'solidarity group'.[8] And while it is possible to distinguish between these two levels in the Muslim republics of the CIS, this is because they were shaped by the political order, and are part and parcel of it at two different levels. In the USSR, the concept of ethnic group was formalised and defined by a political and administrative approach which sometimes flew in the face of reality: a closed list of 'ethnic groups' or 'nationalities' was established each time there was a census, and this list corresponded to an administrative reality on the ground (ranging from simple recognition of a language to the establishment of an eponymous Soviet Socialist Republic).

Here I shall use the terms 'macro-ethnic group' or 'titular ethnic group' to define the groups which were granted a 'republic'. The notion of 'clan' on the other hand, in all senses, ranging from tribal subdivision to regional grouping, and including political faction, is seen only as a negative category, and is denounced by the political class as a leftover from the past. However, this very denunciation confirms it as a phenomenon that is politically relevant. There is no doubt that these 'clans' – all of which, for the purposes of this book, I shall define as 'solidarity groups', whatever their sociological base (tribal, regionalist, family etc) – have real meaning. They apply in everyday life (marriage preferences, proximity of residence, client networks, mafia etc) and also in political life (political faction, the social base of a chief or party etc). It takes only a few examples to show the relevance of the two notions of ethnic group and solidarity group; the problem then becomes how to analyse the ways in which they are constituted, and their usefulness in explaining the workings of the political system.

The newly emerging states have each laid claim to a defined ethnic and linguistic group: if Turkmenia renamed itself Turkmenistan in 1991, this was very much to affirm its existence as the country of Turkmens. In the same way, none of the new states (except Kazakhstan) has taken up the suggestion of various international diplomats and officials to make a distinction between, for example, 'Uzbeks' and 'Uzbekistanis' – in other words between ethnic origin and political citizenship. So what one has here is ethnic nationalism. As regards the regional importance of 'solidarity groupings', one might note that the two principal factions fighting in Tajikistan are regionalist 'clans' or factions: the 'Kulabis' and the 'Gharmis', both of which are of Tajik ethnic origin. One might also note that power in Uzbekistan is held mainly by the Jizak-Samarkand 'faction', in Turkmenistan by the Tekke tribe, and in Kazakhstan by the 'Great Horde'. Clan, tribal and regional factionalism is very much a key to the political life of the republics of Central Asia.

It is clear that these two notions, ethnic group and 'clan', do not refer to ongoing historical human groupings that have been produced over long periods of time. The notion of 'ethnic group' is a modern construction which state strategies have played a key role in creating, rather than a strictly anthropological or linguistic concept. And the 'clan' is not some unvarying entity deriving from traditional society which has maintained itself throughout the Soviet period and now suddenly re-emerges: clan and factional alignments are equally products of the recomposition of traditional society by the Soviet system.

My concern here is therefore not to categorise and write the history of these various groups, but to show how two different registers – ethnic group as a founding political construction of the nation state, and factionalism as one of the keys to political loyalties – structure the political field and are, in return, per-petuated by it. Identities which are not, or are no longer, relevant (tribalism in Uzbekistan, for instance) wither away, while the requirements of politics bring about the creation of more up-to-date networks, based on new social realities and no longer on the reworking and reformulation of 'traditional' iden-tities (for example, the promotions of such-and-such an institute). Obviously, it would be reductive to see the whole of politics simply as a matter of identities and networks. Plainly there are other issues at stake, particularly at the ideological level (Islam and democracy, for instance), but my thesis is that, at least for the moment, they are not the key to political mobilisation.

★   ★   ★

If we take as our starting point the terminology used in local languages to refer to one's identity in terms of community belonging, it is striking that the terms used correspond neither to the official *schema*s defining ethnic groups, nor to the distinction outlined above (the macro-ethnic group on the one hand and the solidarity group on the other). The semantic content of the terms used to define levels of community belonging (*awlad*, *qawm*, *qabila*, *tayfa* and *millat*), which are common to Persian, Uzbek and Turkmen (together with the Uzbek, *urugh* and Turkmen variant, *tire* or 'lineage segment')[9] is thus variable, and refers to different levels of solidarity which are not hierarchised, even though *millat* (or *mellat* in the Iranian pronunciation) is generally taken to mean nation, and *qabila* to mean tribe. One should not go looking behind this terminology hoping to find a rigorous system of social organisation. When one questions people about their identity using any of these terms at random, they may reply with one self-description or with different descriptions when you use a different term. For example, in the region of Kurgan-Teppe in Tajikistan, where two antagonistic Persian-speaking Sunni groups (the Gharmis and Kulabis) are in conflict, one person will describe himself as a Gharmi if you use the terms *qawm*, *qabila* or *millat* in the question, while his cousin will reply 'Tajik' when asked about his *millat*. The Turks of the province of Kulab will refer to themselves as members of the *qawm* of the Turks, but when questioned as to their *millat* they may reply either 'Kulabi' (a localist identity) or 'Tajik' (a reference to their citizenship or ethnic identity, since the term *millat* is here the translation of the Russian term *natsionalnost* used on identity documents).

This vagueness of terminology indicates clearly that there is no 'essentialist' view of people's identity groupings. People's replies vary according to circumstances.[10] But it also indicates the difficulty that interviewees have in conceiving their identities in the administrative or anthropological terms used by their interviewers. At the same time, when one moves into the field of politics it is the 'external' terminology which imposes itself. For example, in Tajikistan there is a neologism in current usage to define community belonging when it determines political loyalty: the term *mahalgera'y* (literally 'tropism of the place') translates the Russian word *mestnichestvo*, or 'localism', which appeared in the Tajik press in 1947 in what was obviously a pejorative sense.[11] This is sure proof that the identities which make sense today at the political level are a recomposition, and not the simple continued existence of ancestral conflicts.

The Soviets tried to impose a terminology of levels of identity which was supposedly rigorous and hierarchised (*plemya*, *narod*, *natsia* and *natsionalnost*: 'tribe', 'people' or 'ethnic group', 'nation' and 'nationality'), but a quick glance at Soviet bilingual dictionaries (between Russian and any of the languages of Central Asia) shows that this seeming good order soon disappears: for every specific Russian term the translation draws indiscriminately from the whole list of available terms in the local languages.[12] You find *millat* for both *narod* and *natsia*; *milliyat*, *qawmiyyat* and *khalqiyat* for *natsionalnost*; *khalq* for *narod*, *narodnost* and *liudi*. You also find neologisms which have not passed into current language (such as *khalqchilik*, to translate *narodnost*, 'the fact of constituting a people', in Uzbek). The only term which is given with a single meaning would be *millat* (and its associated adjective *melli* or *milli*), to refer to an ethnic group qualified to establish nationhood: but this term has experienced the same semantic development throughout the whole of the Turco–Persian region, independently of Soviet influence. Thus in Iran, *melli* takes on the sense of 'national state' as an adjective only at the start of the twentieth century, for instance in the expressions *bank-i melli* (National State Bank) and *mellikardan* (nationalise); previously *mellat* referred to society as against the state, in the sense of 'private individual' or civil society.[13]

Anyway, Soviet authors are not particularly concerned to take into account the terminology actually used by the populations in question. They prefer to apply, however artificially, their own ideological vision of ethnography (see my analysis of Soviet ethnography below). Thus we have two registers in juxtaposition: one is explicit, that of ethnicity as it was defined and imposed by the Soviets; the other, more implicit, is that of multiple forms of identity and solidarity which are either ignored or ruled out as leftovers of the past. Thus we are here working in two different registers: the reality effect of ethnic categories imposed by a political apparatus attempting to conceptualise a territorial realignment which is actually driven by opportunism; and the subversion of that apparatus by practices of networking and factionalism based on a recomposition of a political culture founded on the 'solidarity group'.

Ethnic Groups and Political Constructs

The history of the peopling of Central Asia is, as we have seen, extremely complex. One should be wary of simplifications such as identifying Turks with nomadism and mongoloid features, or Tajiks with sedentarism and 'Indo–European' features, the kind of thing that one all too often finds in travellers' descriptions. While one might note that Kyrgyz and Kazakhs have been at once nomads, tribalised, and superficially Islamised, while at the same time having clearly mongoloid features, such criteria become inoperative as soon as you enter the Ferghana Valley, or even Turkmenistan. An Uzbek is somebody who speaks Uzbek and who calls himself Uzbek, and not somebody who has 'Turkic' features. Nor is the linguistic criterion sufficient to determine group affiliation: the Jews of Bukhara, the 'Arabs' of Shartuz (south of Tajikistan) and the 'Joggi' (gypsies) of Ferghana are Tajik-speaking, but they do not call themselves Tajiks. The 'Irani' (Iranians) of Samarkand are Uzbek-speakers, but what distinguishes them is their religion (Shiism).

The major ethnic affiliations, corresponding to the 'nationalities' as they exist today, do not date back to the origins of time, as the protagonists would have us believe. The only major objective distinction in terms of the peopling of the region (Turkic-speaking populations having gradually taken over a previously Indo-Iranian space), no longer really explains anything. Modern identities are the products of history. The history of the macro-ethnic groups

(Uzbeks, Kyrgyz, Kazakhs, Turkmens and Tajiks) is marked by ruptures and transformations. The Uzbeks, like the Kazakhs and the Kyrgyz, were first tribal federations which appeared at a given moment and pulled together groupings of diverse peoples. These groupings then 'crystallised' into ethnic groups more by effect of political process than by some natural evolution. The Uzbeks become an 'ethnic group' only after the sixteenth century, in the sense that a population takes on the name independently of any tribal affiliation, rather as the term 'Frank' changes meaning between Clovis and Charlemagne.

However, things begin to change when a fifteenth-century tribal confederation under the leadership of the Shaybanid dynasty takes the name of Özbek and takes over Transoxiania in 1500. In the strict sense, an Uzbek is a member of this confederation, where Qipchak dialects were spoken; the settled Turcophone populations that had long been established in Transoxiania – such as Babur, driven out of his native Ferghana by the new arrivals – saw the Uzbeks as a foreign and conquering population. But a part of the conquered settled populations ended up calling themselves Uzbeks in turn, although still keeping their language, Chaghatay, which by the nineteenth century was known undifferentiatedly as either 'Turki' or 'Uzbek'. All it took was for Soviet linguists to call it 'Old Uzbek' at the end of the 1930s, and the matter was settled: the Uzbeks of today have always been Uzbeks, and have always spoken Uzbek.

However, present-day memory maintains an ethnic division between the Uzbek tribes and a settled population speaking Chaghatay. Questioned as to their 'group' (qawm), families from Kulab and Penjikent (Tajikistan) referred to themselves as 'Turk', while the former were Tajik-speakers and the latter Uzbek-speakers. Questioned as to their ethnic and tribal affiliation, people from Andijan (in the Ferghana Valley) referred to themselves as 'Uzbek' by ethnic group and 'Moghul' by tribe, in other words members of the tribe of Babur, the enemy of the Uzbeks.[14] R. Wicksman advances the hypothesis that today's Uzbeks comprise at least three groupings: the Sarts (settled non-tribal people, often of Iranian origin); the 'Turki' speaking Chaghatay and representing the Turkish-speaking populations that settled before the Timurid era (Karluk, Barlas, Karaltai etc); and finally the Qipchaks (Qipchak, Kungrat, Mangit, Kurama etc), in other words the component members of the Shaybanid tribal federation which invaded Transoxiania in the early sixteenth century.[15]

However, it is clear that this quest for ethnogenesis (defining a ethnic group by the history of its formation) so dear to Soviet ethnographers is not always the answer: for example, the Karluks of Kabadian (South Tajikistan) would call themselves Shaybanids, although in historical terms they correspond to a tribal population that settled much earlier, and even though the only true Shaybanids of the same kolkhoz are the Durman who settled in the valley at the time of the Uzbek conquest in the sixteenth century.[16] This confusion is not a 'mistake' on the part of those concerned; it is explained by the fact that

16

identities are in a state of permanent ongoing recomposition, partly for political reasons (for example the Turki group was reclassified as Uzbek in the census in the late 1930s)[17] but also, even without external pressure, for reasons of 'status', or the need to establish a common past with other groups with which one shares a common identity. In Kabadian, the Karluks in question are part of a *kolkhoz* (Yangi Yol, the 'new way') which in formal terms comprises five or six named tribes, but in which everyone insists on their Shaybanid identity. In other words they assert themselves as 'true' Uzbeks in a region where the rival *kolkhoz* are Tajik or Pamiri.

This recomposition of identity as a result of constraints imposed by the political environment happens frequently. For example, an Uzbek language group called the Khidyr-Ali redefined itself as Turkmen at the time of the territorial division in 1924, in order not to be cut off from its traditional economic space, which had suddenly gone over to Turkmenistan.[18]

What defines the group is not so much ethnicity and language as its place within society, and the ecological space it occupies. A good example is the term 'Sart'. Up till the start of Sovietisation, the term referred to sedentary non-tribalised peasants of Transoxiania, whatever language they spoke (Turki, Uzbek or Tajik).[19] The Sarts effectively shared the same culture and the same economic 'niche'. However, this term, which defined a social, economic and cultural category, was accorded an ethnic meaning by Russian anthropologists in the late nineteenth century, to such an extent that attempts were made (fruitlessly, of course) to define a 'Sart language' when the Soviets first embarked on their attempts at classification. Interestingly, the Russians lacked a clear vision of the ethnic groups of Central Asia even at the time when they were claiming to want to promote the rights of nationalities. Lenin's appeal to the 'Muslim workers of Russia and the East' (December 1917) was addressed to, among others, 'Kyrgyz and Sarts'. As it happened, neither of these words made sense for the people to whom the appeal was addressed: Lenin's 'Kyrgyz' referred to Kazakhs, and the 'Sarts' to the Uzbeks and Tajiks.

In the same way, as we have seen, the name Kazakh refers not to a ethnic group but to a political choice: the split with the Uzbek confederation and the maintenance of a nomadic way of life. As for the Turkmens, they were never a people or a nation. They were in fact members of the Oghuz language group who remained tribalised and nomadic, in contrast to those who had become sedentary. This is why today one finds 'Turkmens' in Turkey and Iraq, speaking the present-day Turkish language of Turkey. Their name derives from a very longstanding way of life (tribalism and nomadism) and not from any particular linguistic connection. As for the Tajiks, this is today a residual term, referring to those Sunni Muslims of Central Asia who still speak Persian. A former Tajik who has become solely Uzbek-speaking is no longer seen, and does not see himself, as a Tajik. We shall return to the specific case of the Tajiks later on and the impossibility of taking on the form of nation-state which the Soviet system had conferred on the other titular ethnic groups.

The concept of an Azeri identity barely appears at all before 1920. Up until that point Azerbaijan had been purely a geographic area. Before 1924, the Russians called the Azeri Tatars 'Turks' or 'Muslims'. Prior to 1914, the reformist leaders of Azerbaijan stressed their Turkish and Muslim identity. The great Azerbaijani author Mirza Fath Ali Akhundzada (1812–78), who wrote in the vernacular and campaigned for a simplified and adapted Arabic script, chose to refer to himself as Persian.[20] He referred to the language which he used as 'Turki' rather than Azeri. It was the brief period of Azerbaijan independence in 1919, following the collapse of the Trans-Caucasian Federation, which led political leaders such as Rassulzade to advance the concept of an 'Azerbaijani nation' – but not that of an 'Azeri ethnic group', which was to be a construct of the Soviet era.

It is thus logical that the titular ethnic groups, elevated by the granting of a state, were far from exhausting the range of possible identities. This substantiation of ethnic group by means of politics had, as we shall see, a reality effect. But a direct inquiry as to people's identities ('what would you call yourself?') elicits answers that produce multiple denominations and registers, referring to realities that are often very heterogeneous.

Infra-ethnic Identities: Solidarity Groupings

When questioned as to his identity, an individual will often give multiple identity references: ethno-linguistic (Uzbek or Turkmen), tribal (Barlas or Kungrat), regional (Kulabi or Gharmi), religious (Jewish), socio-religious (*sayyad* or descendant of the Prophet; *khwaja* or *ashraf*, kinds of caste which were until recently endogamous and combined a religious origin with a superior socio-economic status); or sometimes simply by a name without any religious or linguistic specificity (such as the Ghazi Malek of Shartuz in Tajikistan, who speak Tajik and are Sunni; or the 'Arabs' of Kabadian, who don't speak a word of Arabic). These are groups that one might call pseudo-ethnic.[21] There can also be combinations of multiple determinants: the Pamiris have a specificity which is religious (Ismailism), linguistic (languages of the East Iranian group) and regionalist (from the Pamir mountains); the *khwaja* of Ferghana claim religious origins (the first to convert voluntarily to Islam), but they also invoke a social category (as former landowners) which transcends language divisions (one finds both Uzbek-speaking and Tajik-speaking *khwajas*). This same dissociation can be found in the names of tribes: one finds Qipchaks and Karluks in different language groupings (Kazakh and Uzbek). Finally, in rural areas people may relate to an extended family (*awlad*) which groups the descendants of a single ancestor over several generations.

The word most generally used to designate these infra-ethnic solidarity groups is *qawm*, but one also finds the term *awlad*. For groups that are united by closer kinship relations, people tend to use the term *khish-o tabar* (the relations, in other words the extended family) and *oila* (family in the strict sense).

The usual definition of a *qawm* relates to a shared genealogy. But one finds that only a limited number of tribal lineages and families claiming Sufi descent are able to go back further than four generations (these are the *haft-pusht* in Tajik, the 'seven generations'). If genealogy is thus downgraded in importance, it is not so much a result of the upheavals of the Soviet era as because the real foundation of the *qawm* is the fact of living together, a degree of endogamy, and a relationship of differentiation-opposition in relation to others.

In the villages, the various solidarity groups coalesce within the *mahalla* (or *gozar*), in other words neighbourhood, which is identified by a mosque which is built and often served by members of the group. The number of mosques has less to do with the number of believers than it has to do with the number of local solidarity groups. The sudden wave of mosque-building in 1990–1 proved very useful to the researcher: one could count the number of *mahallas* and solidarity groups even before beginning to make one's enquiries. It should be noted that in towns people also coalesce readily into *mahallas*, generally bringing together people originating from one region, and these tend to constitute solidarity groups in themselves. But the urban *mahalla* only plays a direct political role if it also reproduces a division at a higher level: the fact that there are streets of Samarkandis and Ferghanites in the town of Kulab does not have political implications; on the other hand, the *mahallas* of Pamiris and Karateginis in Dushanbe at the time of the 1992 civil war each mobilised in support of their respective regional factions.

What is at work here is not so much the origins and alleged legitimacy of any of these groups, but rather the fact that clearly definable solidarity groups exist. From one village to another the terminology used to name the *qawm* and the source of its legitimacy may change,[22] but the principle of association between a *qawm* and a *mahalla* is so general as to have been perennialised, as we shall see, in the setting up of *kolkhoz* and their subdivision into *uchatska* and brigades.

Here I would give some examples, collected in both Tajikistan and the Ferghana, to illustrate the complexity of the names given to qawms.[23] In the Ferghana Valley there is a fundamental division between the *khwaja* and the *fukara*. The exact nature of these two groupings is difficult to determine. The *khwaja* say that they are descendants of often indigenous peoples who converted spontaneously to Islam, or even of companions of the Prophet, whereas the *fukara*, the 'common ones', are supposed to be descendants of those who were converted by force. This thereby justifies the dominant social position of the *khwaja* prior to Sovietisation – in their eyes, naturally.[24] A *khwaja* from Isfara (Tajikistan) defined the *fukaras* for us as *bi-nasili* ('without genealogy'), but he himself could barely go back beyond his great-grandfather, which suggested that genealogy was not actually the issue.[25] The *ishan* – religious leaders of Sufi origin – are generally *khwaja*.

Today, in Chadak (a Tajik valley in northern Ferghana, in Uzbekistan) the split between these two groups still remains tangible, at least among older people: there one finds a *mahalla* of manifestly well-off *khwaja*, while all the members of the executive committee of the district's soviet are *fukara*. The *fukara* liken the *khwaja* to the former beys, landowners from the period before the Bolshevik revolution who were expropriated in the collectivisation supported by the *fukara*. In private conversation, some *fukara* denounce the refusal of the *khwaja* to give their daughters in marriage to a group that they judged inferior. The Tajik Soviet encyclopaedia juxtaposes these two (social and religious) dimensions in its definition of *khwaja*: 'A feudal social class – someone who follows the *sayyad* [a religious category of person] in supporting the ruling class'. This Marxist reading leaves the question of the historic past untouched. The *khwaja* would have acted as a political group, or even as a caste, at the time of the Bukhara emirate, whereas the term *fukara* seems to refer much more vaguely to anybody who is not *khwaja*, in other words, the 'common ones', as can be seen by the modern usage of the term *fukara* in Uzbek to denote a citizen or somebody belonging to a country.[26]

But it would be mistaken to conclude that the *khwaja* represent the old aristocracy as opposed to the new communist élites: a few hundred kilometres to the south, at Khojent in Tajikistan, the Communist Party élites are *ashraf* (the 'very honourable ones'), who also claim descent from old religious élites. They are often likened to *khwaja* and distinguish themselves from the *fukara*, but here they are the ones who benefited from Sovietisation, or have been able to turn it to their own advantage. That explains how it was that in Khojent we had a bourgeoisie of businessmen, originating within the former aristocracy, who had control of the Communist Party in the republic. The principle of political domination and control of resources by a single largely endogamous group in the name of ideological legitimacy translated perfectly from the epoch of the emirates to that of the USSR, and then on to independence.

At Isfara (also in northern Tajikistan) we find that the village of Chehel Ghazi is divided into into several *awlad* (a term here equivalent to *qawm*): *khwaja*, *ghazi*, *mohammadi*, *aliha* and *fukara*. One should note that the first four terms refer to 'noble' religious origins. In Mazar-i Sharif (Penjikent), the village is divided into three *qawms*: *sayyad*, *sheykh* and *fani* – two religious references and one geographical (the people of the valley of the Fan). But the *sheykhs* contest the claims by the *sayyad* to the title of 'descendants of the Prophet'. There are, needless to say, three *mahallas* and three mosques in the village. Incidentally, the present notable of the *sayyads* and the builder of the new mosque in the *mahalla*, is the son of the former bey who was deported as a *kulak* in 1932. Here too the aristocracies have survived the travails of Sovietism, although the history of how and why still remains to be written: how is it that the son of a deportee has succeeded in reconstituting the traditional social position of his family?

There is thus no symmetry in the order of the *qawm*: each person has his own reading of the past which explains the historical precedence of his group, a reading which is denied by others who employ different registers of legitimation, including those of Sovietisation (being a member of the family of the founder of a *kolkhoz*, for example). The terms classifying solidarity groups are thus drawn from heterogeneous and often reconstructed registers: they are religious, social and tribal, and may even be professional (in north Tajikistan one finds a village of *ustayyan*, 'artisans', representing an endo-gamous professional grouping). The historical reality of the group has little importance. Some of these groups undoubtedly have a real history, an ethno-genesis, a peregrination or a permanent settlement, but this really hardly counts in the way in which they function today. The groups themselves are a product of an ongoing process of intermixing[27] which is often consolidated by a reconstruction of their origins, in which pseudo-historical stories occupy a far more important position than legend.

★   ★   ★

How do these different levels of identity combine together? They are not organised in concentric circles, in which, for example, one might be first Tajik (ethnolinguistic group), then *khojenti* (region), and finally *ashraf* (local sub-group). A native of Andijan (or his descendant) will be an *andizhani* before being a Tajik or Uzbek; an inhabitant of Samarkand will be a *samarkandi* whatever his language. In the region of Kurgan-Teppe in Tajikistan, an Uzbek belonging to the Lakay tribe will define himself first as Lakay, because this ancient tribe has preserved an identity of its own and has its own *sovkhozes* and *kolkhoz*. But in a district further south, other Uzbeks will only give their tribal identity (Kungrat, Barlas etc) if the questioner insists, because for them it has less meaning than their ethnic identity: here tribalism is a thing of memory and has no social meaning. Networks here are constructed, rather than preserved from the past.

There exists no system of 'solidarity groups', but the important thing is to belong to a group, to the extent that one's relationship to the state or to resources (water, *kolkhoz* etc) necessarily passes through the network to which one belongs. Before the Soviet period, when the state was external and dealt through 'intermediaries', the solidarity group had a very real existence: it was collectively responsible for taxes and corvées, and enjoyed certain rights (over land and water) and certain duties (collective responsibility). As we shall see, Soviet collectivisation only brought up to date and 'modernised' this necessary communitarian belonging, which is not some remnant of a communitarianism or traditional tribalism, but an adaptation to a demand for social organisation occasioned by the state.

The nature of the solidarity group thus tends to alter in line with its function, in other words depending on how successful it is in responding to political or social demands. We lack data for analysing the evolution of the answers to questions relating to identity. My experience is that the Soviet system has, indirectly, reinforced certain tendencies, while others are no more than residual. The identities which still function are those that are embodied in one of the administrative or political categories which are explicitly or implicitly active: the *kolkhoz*, the brigade, the *mahalla*, the district, or indeed the political faction. But other identities are now merely a matter of memory: for example, in the Uzbek-speaking areas, apart from among the Lakays, only people over the age of fifty are really interested in tribal belonging in the 1990s, whereas this is a major area of concern in Turkmenistan and Kyrgyzstan.

Some identities which remain in popular memory are deliberately brought up in conversation in order to explain particular events, but they are not functional, whether sociologically or politically. For example, the non-Uzbek sedentary Turcophone people known as 'Turks' generally merge into the dominant group, but in the event of a marriage or a dispute, you will often hear the proverb (which I collected in Persian from an Uzbek of Penjikent, where the Turks are Uzbek-speaking): *'Turk o Tajik yek kas ast/Turk wa Uzbek dushman ast'* ('the Turks and the Tajiks are as one, the Turks and the Uzbeks are enemies'). It says a lot about the inadequacy of using only linguistic criteria to account for differences.

However, to the extent that these affinities favour matrimonial alliances, they are also meaningful within the political order. For instance, in Ferghana, during this same period, the distinction between *khwaja* and *fukara* was only mentioned by young people in relation to marriage problems. But since the new solidarity networks rest largely on marriage alliances, or on relationships established on the occasion of reciprocal invitations to *tuy* (feasts given on the occasion of a circumcision or a marriage), this question of matrimonial exchanges cannot be neutral. It traces a virtual dividing-line between two groups, which could be re-actualised within the framework of a competition for local power, so the important thing is to equip oneself with solidarity networks and not with a community of ideological viewpoints. Thus the use of the term *ashraf* to refer to the communist (and economic) aristocracy of the town of Khojent is meaningful in contemporary Tajikistan: this group provided the three prime ministers of the period 1992–6.

A group like that of the Ghazi Malek, between Kabadyan and Jilikul in southern Tajikistan, was only able to emerge onto the political scene thanks to its ability to raise a local militia which, having allied itself first with the Gharmis and then with the Kulabis, made the difference locally at the time of the civil war in 1992. This group subsequently made the most of its role by establishing a quasi-monopoly over local power and taking control of the National Football League within the framework of distribution of perks between victors. It was subsequently laid low, in November 1995, by the arrest of its chief, Khwaja Karimov. The specificity of this group is neither ethnic nor religious: it is Tajik and Sunni, but it cultivates a difference, which is simply that of being a *qawm* unto itself and of pursuing the interests of its own group above all others in relation to the state which is the basic source of power and potential incomes.

The Specific Case of Tribalism

Tribalism is simply a particular instance of 'group solidarity'; it offers a more rigorous genealogical 'grammar', but is preserved only to the extent that it has a real existence within the framework of Soviet organisations, particularly in connection with the *kolkhoz*. Tribalism in the strict sense (lineage groups defined by a genealogy which organises them into a system, into circles or branches, with the possibility, of course, of the whole being deliberately recomposed subsequently) makes sense among the Kazakhs, Kyrgyz and Turkmens: tribal belonging is generally recognised and plays an important role in the functioning of the society and of political life, at least in rural areas.[28] Among the Tajiks there have never been tribes. To talk of tribalism there is to use metaphor. Among certain Uzbek groups, as we have seen, there is a memory of tribalism, but it is rarely relevant to explain political affiliations and is often discarded disdainfully by younger generations, who affect ignorance of it. But the memory of a tribal belonging remains alive in certain rural sectors and may even re-emerge by a process of symmetry with other groups, as during the Tajik civil war.[29] Among the Turkmens and the Kazakhs, the system is rigorous. The Kazakhs are exogamous, which is the exception in Central Asia. Two groups (the 'white bones') dominate a gathering of tribes, clans and sub-clans. They are divided between an aristocracy (claiming descent from Genghis Khan) and the *khwaja*, supposedly of Arab origin but Kazakh-speaking, who supply mullahs and *pirs*. The mass of ordinary people (the 'black bones') are organised into tribes and clans, the basic unit being the *awl*, a group of 'tents', which pursues nomadic life together. The awls and the clans are headed by begs or beys, who are both richer property-owners than the others, and notables who are recognised as representing the group. But none of these powers is acquired automatically: aristocrats and beys have to get themselves admitted by the groups that they head. The division into three hordes or *juz* (small, medium and large), which took place in the eighteenth century, expressed a reorganisation which was both political (each is ruled by a branch of the 'white bones' with a khan at its head, originating from the 'genghiskhanid' aristocracy) and economic (each horde organises itself around a given area of transhumance). The khanates were abolished by the Russians between 1822 and 1845, but the Kazakh aristocracy continues to exist as such.

Tribalism may be either an innovation or a *post facto* reconstruction. Tribal identity is a shifting thing: clans and tribes reshape, merge and even invent origins for themselves.[30] After 1801, a Kazakh khan of the Small Horde split and founded a new horde (Bokei juz) under Russian protectorateship. The recomposition here took place under the pressure of political events. We have already seen how one same tribal name might be found among different 'ethnic groups' (the Qipchak) and how 'Moghuls' might call themselves Uzbeks. While the nomenclature of the Uzbek tribes hardly changes over a period of a century,[31] what varies is the meaning that is given to these names.

The Uzbek Lakays of the south of Tajikistan use the term 'clan' to refer to groups which elsewhere are seen as self-standing tribes: these Lakays (between Vakhsh and Kafirnehan) were divided in 1920 into the Ishan-Khwaja (a dominant tribe, of which Ibrahim Beg was a member), the Badra-Oglu (which went over to the Bolsheviks), and the Karluks, Durman and Kungrat.[32] By 1992, these internal distinctions seem far less relevant. The Karluks, Durman and Kungrat of Kabadian district distinguish themselves explicitly from the Lakays: for them, as we have seen, what now dominates is their Uzbek ethnic identity. The recomposition of these identities as a result of intermixing populations, territorialisation and localism has meant that only regionalist and ethnic identities are really relevant in the Uzbek-Tajik area, whereas among the Turkmens, Kazakhs and Kyrgyz, tribal organisation has much greater meaning, inasmuch as it has been moulded within the Soviet territorial context. Sovietisation is very much the key to the recomposition of infra-ethnic identities.

2

The Russian Conquest

GENERAL OUTLINES OF THE RUSSIAN CONQUEST

The Russian conquest of Central Asia between 1865 and 1920 was the outcome of a centuries-long process of expansion of the Russian empire, to the detriment of the region's Muslim populations. This colonialism had two characteristics which distinguished it from other European models: it was pursued continuously through time, and in territorial continuity with the Russian land-mass; and it also juxtaposed different systems of colonial administration in time and space, accentuating differences within the Muslim world that it conquered. Europe, on the other hand, saw a break in time and space between the period of the Crusades, concluding with the Spanish *reconquista* in 1492, and the colonialism of the nineteenth century, inaugurated by Napoleon's expedition to Egypt in 1798. The protagonists ('Franks' and Spaniards, and later the French and English), the manner of fighting (between armies that were more or less symmetrical up until the sixteenth century, and then in forms of warfare totally modified by the technical and institutional superiority of the West), and the attitude towards the conquered populations (expulsion, followed later by direct or indirect administration) clearly differentiate the two separate epochs. For Russia, things were different, because from the taking of Kazan in 1552 to the taking of Bukhara in 1920 there was a continuity in the confrontation with Muslims, both in time (with just one pause in the seventeenth century) and in space. The two spaces, Russian and Muslim, have always been territorially continuous, and on occasion even interpenetrated each other. For example, on the present frontier between the Russian Federation and the republic of Kazakhstan, in the region of Kustana, there is an instance of 'ethnic inversion': on the Russian side you are only a few dozen kilometres from the autonomous republic of Bashkortostan, with a strong Muslim population, while over on the Kazakh side you find yourself in a region that is almost exclusively Russian.

The only comparison that one could make with another European power would be with the Habsburgs' descent into the Balkans between the seventeenth and nineteenth centuries. Here too territorial continuity put Muslim and Christian populations right next to each other. However the Austro-Hungarian advance was a form of *reconquista*: the lands conquered from the Ottomans were formerly Christian, and the Turkish-speaking Muslims withdraw *en masse* to Turkey, leaving behind more or less only indigenous Islamised populations (Bosnians and Albanians). The situation with the Russian empire was different, inasmuch as it was established under Ivan the Terrible by the conquest of a Tatar population that had settled in ancient times and had become Muslim at more or less the same time as the ancestors of the Russians were becoming Christian. Another difference, with effects that can still be felt today, is that Russia was built precisely on this imperial expansion: Russia has never been anything other than an empire, a centre with permanently shifting frontiers.[1] The third characteristic is that this empire, despite its Orthodox and Slav heritage, always chose to incorporate its Muslim populations rather than expelling them as the Spanish did. However – and this is the final characteristic – this incorporation took place in variety of ways, depending both on the strategic context and the 'culture' of the era: conquest and forced conversion in the sixteenth century; political treaties in the eighteenth century, and granting Islam a status; settler colonisation, indirect administration and protectorate status at the end of the nineteenth century; and then division into 'nationalities' during the Soviet period. The aim has always been integration, either by assimilation or by cooptation.

⋆   ⋆   ⋆

Ivan the Terrible took over the territories formerly under the Golden Horde (Kazan in 1552 and Astrakhan in 1556), and this brought him to the Caspian, to the banks of the Terek, which is today the 'military' frontier with Chechnya. At the time, this was a crusade: the conquered Muslims were forced to convert to Christianity, or were reduced to second-class status (confiscation of *waqf* property, demotion of the Muslim nobility, a ban on owning property in towns etc). The seventeenth century saw a pause in the process of conquest. In the eighteenth century, the advance resumed along two fronts: against the Ottoman empire on both sides of the Black Sea (towards the Balkans and towards the Caucasus), and towards the Kazakh steppes. But the Russian advance was accompanied by a series of accords and treaties. The Muslims conquered to the west were subjects of the Ottoman empire with whom the Russians negotiated under a form of international law. The status of the Muslims of the Crimea was governed by peace treaties (Kuchuk Kaynarji in 1774); Islam was recognised, *waqf* property was respected, and the Tatar nobility of the Crimea kept its status. At the other end of the empire, the first contacts were also contractual: already in 1715 the Kazakhs were appealing for Russian protection against Oyrat invaders arriving from Jungari; in October 1731, the chief of the Little Horde, Abul Khair, swore allegiance to the Tsar, and he was followed by the Middle Horde, and then, by part of the Great Horde (1742). To the extent that their tribal chiefs swore oaths of allegiance, the members of the tribe or horde in question became 'alien subjects' of the tsar (*inorodtsy*), but not citizens. The Kazakhs were controlled from the town of Orenburg and the line of forts which extended from it, which today mark, broadly speaking, the frontier between Russia and Kazakhstan. This was a useful mechanism, on the one hand making it possible to prevent incursions by Kazakh nomads, and on the other serving as a base for future conquest. By the opposite token, the Kazakh and Turkmen nomads functioned as a protective shield for the three sedentary emirates of Samarkand, Khiva and Kokand, which were not to have direct contact with the Russians until the following century.

The Caucasus was a major concern in the first half of the nineteenth century, partly within the ongoing perspective of countering the Ottoman empire, but also as a way of ensuring direct liaison with the Christian kingdoms of Transcaucasia which had come into Russia's sphere of influence (1801 in the case of Georgia, and 1828 in that of Armenia, under the Treaty of Turkmanchai with Iran). The war against the *montagnard* tribal confederations was to be long and bloody, and it was followed by a massive voluntary exodus of many of the North Caucasians into the Ottoman empire.

The final stage was the settling of Kazakhstan and the conquest of Transoxiania along strategic lines that were familiar from the actions of other Western powers: settler colonisation in Kazakhstan, with a defeat of the indigenous nomadic populations (the American model of colonisation of the Far West, and the French model in Algeria); indirect and especially military administration of part of Transoxiania, involving the development of industrial agriculture, but non–intervention in traditional society (the British model in Egypt and North India); and finally protectorates established with conservative Muslim dynasties (Bukhara and Khiva).

Each of the stages of this conquest took place within a different strategic context. The Tatars of Kazan had no protectors: as outposts of the Islamic world in the north they were isolated and benefited from no movement of solidarity in the rest of the Muslim *umma*. The pincer advance around the Black Sea was directed essentially at the Ottoman empire, which was one of the elements of the international order of the time: none of the European great powers wanted to see Russia getting hold of Constantinople; they made this clear at the time of the Franco-British intervention into the Crimea in 1854, and in their efforts to prevent the taking of Constantinople (the Congress of Berlin in 1878). This concern to preserve the status quo was to reappear in Central Asia, when the British did everything in their power to slow Russia's descent towards India from 1839 onward (the first occupation of Kabul by the British). In Central Asia, the emirate of Bukhara, the symbol of Muslim independence, was not a great power, and had little inclination to take the lead in a 'holy war' against the Russian invader: the emirs of Bukhara were even to profit from Russia's attacks on their neighbours, using them to extend their influence. Their southern neighbours, the Afghan emirs, were eager to make the most of their status as a buffer state and opted for caution in their relations with Russia: the only real crisis occurred in 1885, when the Russians occupied the Afghan oasis of Panjdeh on the Murghab. The fact that the Afghan dynasty was Pashtun also explains why it looked more towards the Indian subcontinent than towards the north, in line with the old regional truism that there has never been an invasion of Central Asia from India, whereas there have been dozens in the other direction, from the arrival of the Indo-Europeans to the Soviet intervention of 1979. As for Persia, after a final flurry between 1813 and 1828, it renounced all attacks on its big Russian neighbour, upon whom its ruling dynasty occasionally depended for its survival. The Shah's regime was twice saved by the intervention of the Russian army, in 1909 and 1912. Despite an additional series of Russian interventions which were not agreed with the central state (1920, 1941 and 1945), Iran was to maintain great caution in relation to its northern neighbour, a caution which extended to the period of the Afghan war (1979–89) and the emergence of the newly independent ex-Soviet republics.

Thus it was Ottoman Turkey and not Iran which appeared to the Muslims of the Russian empire in the period 1878–1924 as the focal point of resistance to Russian imperialism, and as the bastion of Islam, an image reinforced by the fact of a shared language and religion (Hanafi-school Sunnism).

RUSSIA AND ISLAM

Islam has always been part of the Russian horizon. The Russians became Orthodox and the Tatars Muslim around the year 980. The Mongol invasion in 1237 gave rise to the Golden Horde, a fusion of Muslim Tatars and pagan or Christian Mongols which developed in favour of the former in terms of language and religion. The Golden Horde was established around Kazan on the Volga, in the heart of present-day Russia. Between that period and 1480, nine of the ten Russian principalities were vassals of the Golden Horde. This power balance was only reversed at the end of the fifteenth century. The taking of Kazan in 1552 marked the start of a Russian supremacy which lasted right through until the independences of 1991, when minority Russian populations handled down power in states with a Muslim majority.

Although Russian policy differed greatly at various stages of the conquest, there were a number of constants. From Ivan the Terrible through to Stalin, Muslims were never perceived as automatically hostile, external and unassimilable. Russia never had the kind of racial vision which created the situation in sixteenth-century Catholic Spain, where any converted Muslim or Jew was viewed with suspicion: the Spanish law on 'blood purity' which required an absence of Muslim or Jewish ancestors before one could be allowed to hold certain jobs was a good example of the confusion between 'race' and religion. In 1609, the Moriscos (Muslims who had converted to Catholicism) were expelled from Spain; in precisely that period, the Tatars who had been converted (probably equally superficially) to Orthodoxy (the *starokreshchennye*, or *kryashen* in Tatar) were being accorded favourable treatment, and were able to reach high positions in the state (a number of the great Russian princely families, such as the Yussupovs, are of Tatar origin). Russia has always had an optimistic view of its capacity for assimilation. Conversion, even forced, is the opposite of ethnic cleansing, particularly when the converts are allowed to keep their language. In the Russian and Soviet empires, the dominant view was that the Muslims could be loyal subjects, on condition that they chose to abide by the state ideology (Orthodoxy or Sovietism).

Needless to say, in the early Tsarist period adherence to the state's ideology presupposed conversion to Orthodox Christianity, although the tsars had no hesitation in making use of Muslim Tatars.[2] But this was not a policy of assimilation: in return for their conversion, the Muslims were recognised as a 'national' or ethnic group, in other words they preserved their customs and continued to speak their own language. The Bible was translated, and a Tatar catechism was published by the authorities in 1803 (it is hard to imagine the kings of Spain setting about converting the Moriscos via the publication of works in Arabic).

However, one also finds another tradition of handling relations with Muslim subjects, which is less widespread but more tolerant than integrating them by means of conversion: the instrumentalisation of the Muslim community. This presupposed a kind of pact between two separate communities that shared a common political legitimacy – the Muslims were seen as constituting a community subject to their own rules, but collaborating with the Russians in a common state project. This was the position of Catherine the Great, which one later finds emerging briefly among 'national-communists' of the Bolshevik era such as Sultan Galiev. Catherine II (who reigned from 1762 to 1796) embarked on a policy of collaboration with Islam which, leaving aside the tsarina's 'modernist' views, was based on two considerations: on the one hand the need for state control in the business of religion (in line with the tradition of 'Josephinism' in Austro-Hungary and of 'Gallicanism' in France), and on the other a new strategic approach to relations with the Muslim world. What mattered was to prevent the Ottoman sultan from being able to mobilise Muslim populations which would have everything to lose from a Russian victory. Muslim confidence was to be maintained. It was more sensible, politically, to guarantee them a decent status under Russian sovereignty, in order to avoid both war and the possibility of a massive exodus which would have impoverished the new possessions. Finally, at the time when Russia was penetrating the Kazakhs steppes, the empress considered it advisable to move towards 'civilising' the nomads through the mediation of merchants and Tatar mullahs, who were already well Russified and enjoyed the benefits of networks and establishments along the trade routes to China. In short, Catherine II offered the Muslims a historic compromise: status in exchange for loyalty.

In concrete terms, this policy found expression in the Holy Synod Act (1773), which decreed tolerance towards other religions and the setting up of a religious directorate for Muslims in Russia, the muftiyya, which was installed initially at Orenburg and then later at Ufa (an office to be held by a Volga Tatar). It was also embodied in transit rights for Sunni Muslims from Central Asia wanting to avoid a hostile Shiite Iran on their way to Mecca; by the encouragement given to Tatar mullahs in islamicising the Kazakhs; and by the reopening of *madrasas* and Koran schools. The empress was also to finance a *madrasa* in Bukhara.[3] In 1789, institutes of higher education were created in order to give a Russian education to children of the Kazakh aristocracy, thereby inaugurating the tradition of linguistic and cultural Russification of this aristocracy, without, however, threatening its Kazakh character, because it involved neither conversion nor an attack on the language.

This liberal policy of Catherine II was addressed to all Muslims, and not merely those protected by treaty. As a consequence, the Tatars, subjects of the tsar and very much integrated within the empire, came to replace the Bukhara *ulemas* as the source of Islamic thought and propaganda within the territory of the empire, and even beyond (as far as Bukhara itself). The Islam that they were to propagate would be reformist and more Westernised, but at the same time it was pan-Islamist, and as a result there was an anti-Tatar reaction at the end of the nineteenth century on the part of both the tsarist authorities and the emir of Bukhara.

The tsarina's benevolent attitude towards Islam was later re-evaluated. More 'orthodox' *schema*s were adopted under Catherine's successors, in particular Nicholas I (1825–55), but a number of the basic principles such as the muftiyya were preserved. A Muslim state publishing house was established in Kazan in 1802. The first mosque in Moscow was built in 1816 by a decree of Tsar Alexander I, in memory of the Muslim, Tatar and Bashkir soldiers who had died in the Napoleonic wars. Tatar was authorised, together with Russian, as the administrative language of the governorate of the Steppes. Conversion to Christianity was no longer required for employment in administrative posts. In 1846, for example, Nicholas I granted the Muslim aristocracy of Azerbaijan a status comparable to that of the Russian nobility (a concession which had the paradoxical consequence of reducing the local peasants to serfdom).[4]

The Russian military academies in the nineteenth century were open to Muslims (Tatars, North Caucasians, Azeris and Kazakhs, but hardly any from Transoxiania). Thus there were not only Muslim regiments – such as the Karabakh Battalion, who were all volunteers, since with the exception of Tatars and Bashkirs most Muslims were exempt from conscription – but also Muslim officers serving in ordinary regiments, which was very different to the French and British system, where native regiments had metropolitan officers. The Russian army had a number of Muslim generals: for example, during the 1914 war, the Azeris Sikhlinski and Hussein Khan Nakhishevanski, and the Lithuanian Tatar Suleyman Sulkiewicz. At the end of the nineteenth century, a mosque was built in the park of the royal palace at Tsarskoye Selo (Saint Petersburg) for the children of Muslim dignitaries educated in the Russian manner at the tsarist court, who included Alim Khan, the future emir of Bukhara.

This dual approach (an ideological assimilation which respects ethnic specificity, or a collaboration between two communities in a common state project) prefigures a debate which exercised the minds of Muslim reformers at the end of the nineteenth century, and of the Bolsheviks: should one adopt a communitarian and religious approach, whereby all Muslims are treated as members of a community which is then accorded juridical, and even political, status; or should one emphasise the ethnic and national specificity of each of the Muslim groupings, and ignore their common denominator in Islam? The drawing up of Stalin's nationalities policy was the eventual and definitive response to attempts by people such as Sultan Galiev to secularise (and 'proletarianise') the concept of *umma*.

THE RUSSIANS IN CENTRAL ASIA

The Russian advance in Transoxiania began after their defeat in the Crimea in 1854. The Russians started from positions that they had achieved in what is today Kazakhstan, after they had prevailed on the Great Horde to transfer to them the allegiance which they had previously given to the emir of Kokand (1847). The three emirates which held Central Asia (from west to east, Khiva, Bukhara and Kokand) were in the throes of permanent conflict. The Russians attacked first at Kokand, and occupied Pichpek in 1860 (present-day Bishkek, and previously Frunze), Chimkent in 1864 and Tashkent in 1865. The emir of Bukhara felt directly threatened, and he intervened, but he was defeated in 1868. The Russians under General Kaufman, having made peace with the emir of Kokand, in January 1868 occupied Samarkand, which was in the possession of Bukhara. A treaty with the emir gave the Russians the whole of eastern Bukharia (from Samarkand to Pamir). In 1869, Russian troops arriving from the Caucasus disembarked on the shores of present-day Turkmenistan, in the territory of Khiva, and established the port of Krasnovodsk. They took over the Turkmen coastline, reached the Iranian border, and thereby put an end to Turkmen raiding into Iran. The Russians thus defeated the three emirates. They annexed Kokand in 1876, but kept Khiva (minus the Caspian coast) and Bukhara (minus Samarkand and the valley of Zarafshan), under the authority of their ruling dynasties. Then they bypassed these two centres and headed directly for the frontiers of Iran, Afghanistan and India. They attacked the Turkmen Tekke tribes in 1879 (the tribes won early victories, but were defeated in 1881 at Gök-Teppe), took the Afghan oases of Panjdeh in 1885, and finally occupied the upper Pamir. At that point, however, reaction from Britain forced them to recognise the Iranian and Afghan frontiers (1887 and 1895). Afghanistan was established as a buffer state between the two great powers, a status marked by the return to the emir of Kabul (who had not asked for it) of the Wakhan corridor, a valley peopled by Ismailis and Kyrgyz, lying between Russia's possessions, the Indian empire and China.

In order to govern these areas, Russia established a province of Turkestan (1865), which was then promoted to a governorate under General von Kaufman (1867). This governorate was the the subject of various administrative reforms. It expanded from three provinces in 1886 (Syr-Darya, Ferghana and Samarkand) to five in 1898, with the addition of Semirechie from present-day Kazakhstan and the Transcaspian province (created in 1881) on the Turkmen side. On the Kazakh side, the governorate of the steppes had become administratively independent of Orenburg and Siberia and now contained only the provinces (*oblast*) of Akmolinsk and Semi-Palatinsk. The coming and going of different administrative entities inaugurated a practice of voluntarism and arbitrariness which was to reach its peak in the Soviet period. At the end of the century, Central Asia under Russian control was divided into four entities: the governorate of the Steppes (the north-east of present-day Kazakhstan), the governorate of Turkestan (Tashkent, Samarkand and the north and east of present-day Tajikistan), to which was added the Transcaspian province (the heart of what was to become Turkmenistan), and finally the protectorates of Khiva and Bukhara.

★   ★   ★

The occupation of Central Asia was carried out along lines similar to those of the British and French colonisations of the time: settler colonies in the Kazakh zones, an administrative and military occupation of Turkestan which eliminated the traditional political authorities but left the local élites intact – landowners or begs (beys) and mullahs – and finally the establishment of protectorates. Except in the Kazakh steppes, there was no attempt at religious proselytisation. The Orthodox churches and priests which were established were for the use of the small Russian settlements, generally living in a modern town to one side of the traditional Muslim town, where the garrison and the railway station were also to be found (this was the British 'cantonment' model in India). In the governorate of the steppes, the Russians proceeded to a settlement policy which was detrimental to the Kazakh nomads: the European population rose from 20 percent in 1887 to 40 percent in 1911 and 47 percent in 1939, a percentage which was to remain more or less stable until 1989. The Russian authorities made efforts to break the traditional tribal system and to administer the Kazakh populations as directly as possible. During this period, they tried to oppose Islam by limiting the building of mosques, hindering the activities of Tatar preachers, who up until then had been encouraged, and even attempting (unsuccessfully) to convert some of them to Orthodoxy. Reaction to this policy led to a more rapid penetration by Islam, and to revolts which combined defences of land, nomadism and autonomy (the most important of these took place in 1916).[5]

In Turkestan, on the other hand, right through to the Bolshevik period the life of the native population continued to be organised under *sharia* courts and customary law, and they were spared forced Russification. Expropriations were carried out solely in order to facilitate the setting up of a cotton monoculture, one of the justifications of settlement. As a corollary of this indirect administration, the Muslims of Central Asia, including the Kazakhs, had no status as citizens, and were classified as 'foreign subjects' (*inorodtsy*).

The tsarist authorities did not attempt to coopt the local élites, as they had done both with the Tatars of the Volga and Crimea and with the Azeris. In fact, the authorities were caught in a dilemma common to all colonisers. Colonisation was a major factor of social upheaval (the confiscation of Kazakh lands and the development of industrial-scale cotton production in Transoxiania from 1884 onwards), and it resulted in the pauperisation of part of the peasantry, but also the development of new élites, particularly those educated in the Russian schools. At that point, the colonial power could either push for modernisation, in co-operation with the new élites (albeit with the attendant risk that they might demand participation in power and reforms); or they could do the opposite and ally with the former élites who were under threat from the new order (with the risk of encouraging an Islamic fundamentalism which would reject all innovation). There was, in fact, political opposition from both sides: at Andijan in 1898 there was a fundamentalist revolt led by a Naqshbandi Sheikh (Mohamed Ali) against all forms of Russian influence, while the Jadids (Muslim reformers) campaigned against tsarist absolutism, but not the modernisation which the Russian presence brought with it. After having given thought to notions of modernisation, for example by supporting the Tatar reformers and their schools, the tsarist authorities backtracked in the mid-nineteenth century and turned to supporting the conservatives. They shared with the traditional notables and the emirs of Bukhara a suspicion of the reformers. The Muslim reformist movement that had been set in motion in the Russian empire by Tatars only really caught on in Central Asia among a small fringe of urban intellectuals who were in an anomalous position between two conservative forces: traditional Muslim society and the tsarist system.

On the other hand, the government no longer needed the Tatars as intermediaries in Central Asia: the setting up of a Russian administration and Russian schools, and the arrival of Russian merchants, meant that the Tatars were now competitors, and no longer the vanguard of Russification. Since the days of Catherine the Great, the Tatars had played a twin role, both as Russia's vanguard and as awakeners of Muslim awareness. They now found themselves in a delicate position. This explains why at this point their élites turned to two opposing models: on the one hand, pressuring the tsarist (and subsequently the Bolshevik) state to recognise a Russian Muslim entity which would take in all races; on the other, falling back on a Tatar national identity.

3

Reform Movements Among the Muslims of the Empire

RELIGIOUS REFORM AND AFFIRMATION OF IDENTITY

The reform movement among the Muslims of the Russian empire was part of the great reform wave (*salafiyya*) which stirred the Muslim world at the end of the nineteenth century, the most famous early advocate of which was Jamal ad-Din Afghani.[1] This activist current combined three characteristics: pan-Islamism, anti-colonialism and religious reformism. The view was that the confrontation with the West could only be won if reforms were enacted. What stood in the way of social and political reform was religious conservatism, a consequence of the monopoly exercised by the *ulema* over teaching. It was therefore necessary to reopen the door of interpretation (*ijtihad*), a door which had been closed in the Muslim world since the tenth century. This would make it possible to study sciences and modern languages, and to generate educational techniques with a view to spreading a new system of education among Muslim youth (hence the term 'jadid', which means 'new, modern'). Russia's Muslim reformers drew on the work of two Tatar theologians, Abul Nasr Kursawi (1783–1814) and Shehabuddin Marjani (1818–89). The religious reform movement had two aspects which today are often mutually contradictory but which in those days were difficult to separate and distinguish, since both derived from *ijtihad*: an Islamic fundamentalism which sought a strict return to the principles of Islam (for instance the Siberian Tatar Abdurrashid Ibragimov, or Ibrahimov, who died in 1944) and an attempt at updating and adapting the culture and everyday life of Muslims to the modern world by limiting the role of religion. This, perhaps slightly paradoxically, led to the creation of a secular pan-Islamism, as represented in the figure of the Crimean Tatar Ismail Gasprinski. If the opposition between these two tendencies was hardly noticed at the time, this was because they had the same enemies – Muslim traditionalism and Russian fundamentalist chauvi-nism – and the same ally, Ottoman Turkey (in its 'caliph' version for

35

the fundamentalists and the Young Turk version for secularists). Both tendencies campaigned in favour of pan-Islamism, the recognition and promotion of the Muslim entity within the Russian empire, the provision of new schools, a common language for the Turks, and support for Turkey, although both had a very different view of the place of religion in society. This inbuilt ambiguity of Jadidism was to explode after 1918, between those who opted (sometimes very temporarily) for alliance with the Bolsheviks (reform versus religion) and those who ended up joining the *basmachis* (religion versus reform).

★   ★   ★

The Tatars of Kazan and the Crimea were the driving force behind the Jadid movement. It was first and foremost a cultural movement, aiming to educate the whole community of Russia's Muslims, and to make them aware of their identity and their strength. This would then make it possible for them to negotiate a status for themselves within the Russian empire. The vector for the campaign was the press and the schools. The movement's figurehead was the Crimean Tatar Ismail Bay Gasprinski (1851–1914), whose weekly newspaper Tercüman, founded in 1883, reached all parts of the empire. It was written in a slightly artificial Turkish, as a way of getting round language divisions, and it used the Arab alphabet. Gasprinski set up a network of reformed schools, which were to spread particularly among the Tatars, with some limited penetration among the Kazakhs and in Transoxiania.[2] In 1916, there were 5,000 Jadid schools in the empire as a whole, while the 1897 census indicated a literacy of 20.4 percent among Tatars, as compared with a mere 18.3 percent among Russians, which shows how successful the movement had been.[3]

Attempts to translate this current of Muslim reformism into political movement were less fruitful. With the liberal opening of 1905, which opened the way for elections to the first Duma (parliament), the Muslim élites attempted to set up a joint political representation. In August 1905, a first pan-Russian Muslim congress at Nizhni Novgorod set up the Ittifaq ('union') Movement, which was dominated by Tatars and was politically close to the Russian Constitutional Democrats (KD). But in none of the four successive Dumas did Muslims succeed in forming a 'Muslim party', a shortcoming which was to be repeated within the Bolshevik Party between 1918 and 1923, and in the USSR under *perestroika* between 1990 and 1991.

PAN-ISLAMISM AND PAN-TURKISM

We need to take a closer look at the nature of this movement. What did pan-Islamism mean at that time? Historians often use the term 'national movement' of Muslims in Russia. However, it was not a nationalist movement in the modern sense of the term, because it defined a 'nation of Muslims' on religious and cultural criteria without reference to a state or a given territory. In a sense, it was a sub-grouping of the great *umma* of all Muslims worldwide. The word used to describe this community was variously *millat*, *mellat* or *millet* in the Iranian or Turkish pronunciations, from which derives the adjective *melli* (*milli*). Today this word means 'national' throughout the Turkic-Persian area, but before 1914 it referred essentially to a community defined in religious terms, as in the Ottoman *millet*.[4] This broader community sense also comes close to what many Islamic leaders are seeking to construct in the late twentieth century among Muslims living in the West. As we have seen in examining the meaning of the word in the Iran of the Qajars, the term *melli* does not refer to a state, but rather to the definition of a civil social space. Working within this conception of 'national', Muslim reformists of the Russian empire were not seeking independence in the modern sense (with a territory and a state). Gasprinski himself always said that the place for Russia's Muslims was within a reformed empire.[5] The same impulse emerged at the pan-Russian Muslim Congress held in Moscow in May 1917, which set up a *melli shura* or 'national council', in the broader community sense of the term. Such a demand for recognition of a deterritorialised entity was completely compatible with the structures of empire. But it emanated principally from the Tatars, who had no intention at that time of seeking territorial separation from Russia, any more than they have today. Azeris and Central Asians preferred the notion of federalism, but this too was not within a perspective of the formation of independent nation states. The majority of Azerbaijani intellectuals before 1914 defined themselves effectively as 'Turks' and not as Azeris, and many used Ottoman Turkish rather than the vernacular Turkish that had been promoted by the writer Akhundzade: this was the case with Husseinzadeh (1864–1941, who in about 1905 launched the slogan 'Turkify, Islamicise, Europeanise').[6] The Azerbaijani Mussavat Party, founded in 1912, pressed for a unification of all Muslims, and up until 1918 it studiously avoided calls for independence and even talk of an Azerbaijani nation. The short-lived Muslim government of Kokand in Transoxiania (November 1917–February 1918), under Jadid influence, called for an autonomous rather than independent Turkestan, and gave itself a Kazakh as president (Chokayev), which suggests that they were far from thinking in ethnic-nationalist terms.

★   ★   ★

Needless to say, the issue of language was not overlooked by the reformers: since the great majority of Muslims in Russia were 'turcophone', the language of pan-Islam within the Russian empire was bound to be a common Turkic language, but the question remained open as to precisely which language, after the decline of Chaghatay and hesitations about adopting Tatar. Writers such as Gasprinski made considerable efforts to establish a common Turkic language, written in the Arabic alphabet and usable as easily by Uzbeks as by Crimean Tatars. The advantage of the Arabic alphabet is that it does not register short vowels, the pronunciation of which may differ from one language to another (*millat, millet, mellat* etc), and also that it can represent the large numbers of words coming directly from the Arabic with their original spelling, thereby making possible a 'global', almost ideographic, reading whatever the local pronunciation. The problem is that it is by definition a learned language. Rassulzade, the leader of the Mussavat Azeri party from 1913 onwards, was opposed to the movement of the 'Azerijilar', who were seeking to create a literary language out of the Turkic dialect of Azerbaijan, and he argued for the use of a reformed Turkish on the model advanced by the Young Turks in the Ottoman empire.[7] But this was still within the context of a quest for a *koine* or common language.

As an expression of pan-Islamism, this linguistic pan-Turkism went hand-in-hand with a movement in support of the Ottoman caliphate which extended far beyond the Turcophone areas. At the start of the twentieth century, the great mass of Muslims in Russia (but also in India and China) were mobilising in favour of the Ottoman caliph as the commander of the faithful. But the twin concepts of pan-Turkism and pan-Islamism, which were held jointly among Russian Muslims, began to diverge within Turkey itself following the Young Turk revolution in 1908, when Turkish nationalists gave pan-Turkism a connotation that was purely ethnic, indeed racist, leaving the religious dimension largely out of the picture. One key proponent of this strictly ethnic and linguistic Pan-Turkism was the Turk Zya Gökalp. 'Turkism' and Islam thus became increasingly separate currents in the Near East at the time of the 1914–18 war, under the combined effect of an emerging Arab nationalism (encouraged by the British) and the transition from Ottomanism to Turkish nationalism among the heirs of the Young Turks, which would then lead to the secular and nationalist policies of Atatürk (who abolished the caliphate in 1924).[8] This secular form of pan-Turkism, emanating from Istanbul, did not take root among Russian Muslims, except among Azeri refugee intellectuals in Istanbul, people such as Aghayev, who had already been articulating anti-clericalism and pan-Turkism prior to 1914. In Azerbaijan, which was more subject to direct influence from Istanbul, a fundamentalist movement was created by way of reaction against this secular 'Turkism'. Significantly this organisation, created in 1917, was called Rusyada Musulmanlik (Muslim Community in Russia). Its programme argued for the organisation of Muslims within the Russian framework, and under *sharia* law.[9] This was to be exactly the programme of the Islamic Renaissance Party (IRP) in 1990.

It is therefore possible to argue that among Russian Muslims up until 1924 pan-Turkism was merely a variant of pan-Islamism. But pan-Islamists in Asia were dreaming of a restoration of the caliphate, a proposition which, after the Kemalist revolution, was no longer on the agenda in Istanbul.

This out-of-phaseness between a principally religious reading of pan–Turkism in Central Asia and an ethnic reading in Turkey partly explains why pan–Turkism appeared to be a dead issue in 1991: the only 'universalists' on the scene were the Islamists, and they did not recognise themselves in a Turkey that was secular.

*   *   *

Finally, pan-Islamism and pan-Turkism combined with a third dimension in the period prior to 1924: anti-colonialism or anti-imperialism. Japan's victory against Russia in 1905 had major repercussions among Muslims in Russia and India, subjects of the two major imperialist powers of the time. Among fundamentalists such as Abdurrashid Ibragimov (who was to move to Japan in the hope of coverting that country to Islam), but also among modernists such as Gasprinski and the Afghan Mahmud Tarzi (editor of the journal *Siraj-ul Akhbar*, published from 1911 to 1918 and also distributed in Central Asia), there developed the notion of a solidarity of the peoples of the East against the connivences of the Western imperialist countries.[10] This recurrent theme was to be taken up by the Bolsheviks, and explains why numbers of Jadids were to become Communist Party fellow travellers, even at a time when their political positions were close to the KD.[11] The Baku Congress in September 1920 was organised by the Bolsheviks precisely in order to mobilise Muslim anti-imperialist sentiment in support of the October Revolution, whatever the price in political gymnastics.[12] But the finest – and most short-lived – synthesis was that of the communist Sultan Galiev,[13] who actually invented the notion of the Third World before the term existed – in other words the idea of oppressed peoples where class divisions take second place in the face of the global exploitation that imperialism tries to impose on them. Here pan-Islamism prefigures a kind of anti-imperialist internationalism.

BETWEEN PAN-ISLAMISM AND ETHNICISATION

The tsarist authorities initially had some sympathy for the Tatars, seeing them as a people that might 'Westernise' the Muslims. But in the last quarter of the nineteenth century they recognised the dangers of such a policy: it paved the way for political liberalism, and played into the hands of the Ottoman empire, which had been Russia's principal enemy from 1877 to 1914 in its expansion southwards. They then turned to the most conservative elements in Islam, the 'Qadimists' (from *qadim*, 'old') as a way of combatting the influence of the Tatar thinkers among the other Muslims in the empire. The Russian authorities appointed as mufti at Ufa the 'Qadimist' Bajazitov, who remained in this post until 1917. On the occasion of the trial of a Jadid school in Kazan in 1911, the main accuser was a Qadimist mullah, whereas the Russian intelligentsia took the side of the Jadids.[14] The Russian authorities also collaborated with the emir of Bukhara in order to limit Jadid influence.

The direction taken by the emirs of Bukhara was also clear: they resisted all moves towards religious reform and counted on a body of *ulemas* who had been unaffected by the development of thinking in the rest of the Muslim world. At the start of the nineteenth century, Emir Haydar had the Tatar reformist theologian Kursawi sentenced to death, which meant that he had to flee Bukhara, where he had previously settled. The Jadids of Bukhara and Khiva would thus be forced to remain undergound until they succeeded in taking power in 1920.

But the Qadimists were not the only card played by the Russian authorities. They also discreetly encouraged another tendency, which had a far less marked presence among the Muslim intelligentsia: the 'nationalists' in the modern sense of the word, in other words those who took language and territory as the founding elements of identity. It may appear strange to have a tsarist government supporting ethnic nationalism. The aim was not, of course, to encourage independence movements, but to defuse what Russia viewed as the most important threat, that of a synthesis between pan-Turkism and pan-Islamism, because it hung on an external threat, that of the Ottoman empire, whereas the development of an ethnic identity could only take place within the framework of the empire. This would be precisely the analysis arrived at by Stalin.

The policy of ethnicisation thus found favour among a minority of Muslim intellectuals, particularly among the Tatars and Kazakhs. Here Muslim reformism and pan-Turkism were no longer in play. Instead, we had an attempt to affirm national identity built around a particular ethnic group. Ethnic authenticity (*tatarlik* for the Tatars) was counterposed to 'Turkicity' (*türklük*). Efforts were made at the creation of a modern written language, based on popular spoken forms and with no particular concern for convergence with other Turkic languages. In choosing this path the reformers benefited both from the work of Russian scientists who (obviously for different reasons) had emphasised the 'ethnicisation' of the various Muslim groups, and from official encouragement and even promotion within the government's educational system. The Tatar Abdul Qayyum Nassiri (1825–1902) campaigned for the teaching of a vernacular Tatar based on the language spoken in Kazan. The Russian authorities appointed him Professor of Tatar at the (Orthodox Christian) theological seminary in Kazan. He became a member of the town's (Russian) archaeological society, and published the journal *Zaman Kalendari*[15] in new Tatar. However, his school was then closed and he fell into disgrace. Among the Kazakhs, Ibrahim Altynsarin (1841–89) published the first Kazakh grammar and the first Russian-Kazakh dictionary. He was encouraged by a Russian academic from Kazan, Ilminsky, who had him appointed inspector of Kazakh schools in 1879. In the 1860s, the use of literary Kazakh became more widespread (although Altynsarin published his own works, rather unwillingly, in the Cyrillic alphabet, most works in Kazakh, including retranscribed works by Altynsarin himself, were printed at Kazan, in the Arabic alphabet).

In Azerbaijan, from around 1905, a minority of the intelligentsia began calling for the use of the vernacular language in place of Ottoman Turkish. These *azerijilar* (not Azeris, but 'those who speak Azeri') were criticised as allegedly playing the Russian game. Feridun Kocharli, who founded the journal *Sharq-i Rus* in 1905 (with the agreement of the Russian governor), spoke in terms of a 'nation' (*millet*) defined by its language.[16] This is the modern meaning of the term. Rassulzade was to make the distinction between the *umma*, a definition on strictly religious criteria, and the *millet*, defined by language; but up until 1918, for him this language was Turkish, and he would not hazard to say whether the Azeris were a nation unto themselves or a part of the Turkish nation. The term 'Azeri' was not used by any politician at the time. People spoke of 'Turks', 'Muslims' and (only among Russians) of 'Tatars'.

Nassiri, Altynsarin and Kocharli were in an ambiguous position: they were perceived as being pro-Russian by many of their co-religionists, and they were promoted and instrumentalised by the Russian authorities. But they were not Russifiers. They were searching, first, for an authenticity that had been betrayed or ignored by the traditionalists, and second, for a compromise with the Russian model of modernisation. Russian support was tactical and liable to be withdrawn, as happened to Nassiri in 1876. A similar balancing act was to reappear during the Soviet epoch (when an advocate of national rights might find himself being accused of nationalism after first having been used as a means of attacking Islam, and where the denouncer of a deviation to the left could as easily find himself under attack as a deviationist of the right).

★   ★   ★

Among Muslims, the reticence in relation to pan-Islamism often appears less as the expression of an already constituted ethnic nationalism and more as a reaction to Tatar hegemony. The quasi-monopoly which Tatars had over pan-Islamism in all its forms (from Gasprinski to Sultan Galiev), the role played by Tatar teachers and merchants in Central Asia, the fact that the Tatars, behind their pretentions to be a model, were perceived as the most Russified of Muslims, and the tsarist authorities' use of the Tatar language in administering the Kazakhs up until 1870 all engendered a certain resentment among the populations of Central Asia, particularly since the Tatar reformists made no secret of their disdain for the region's backwardness (for example Gasprinski approved of the forced sedentarisation of Kazakh nomads).[17]

Thus pan-Islam remained a majority tendency among the Tatars prior to 1918, a situation in which Gasprinski's *Tercüman* had a larger readership than Nassiri's *Zaman Kalendari*;[18] Tatars made up the core of the Soviet

Islamic Renaissance Party in 1990, just as they had controlled the Ittifaq in 1905. Pan-Islamism made some headway among Kazakhs who had become Islamicised from the late eighteenth century onwards, even though there were signs of growing divergences between the different Muslim groups.

*   *   *

The choice of options between a communitarian model conceived within the framework of a unitarian Russia and a national model within a Russia that should be federal was clearly posed at the pan-Russian Muslim Congress in Moscow in May 1917, following the fall of tsarism. A split occurred which ranged on the one side the pan-Islamists and socialists, who favoured a Muslim community within a united Russia, and the federalists, who argued for autonomy based on regional and ethnic considerations. The former comprised the Tatars and North Caucasians, the latter belonged to groups that had a more compact demographic presence in the territory concerned: Turkestanis, Azeris and Kazakhs, but also including Crimean Tatars. The latter point of view, which was promulgated by the Azeri Rassulzade (although he was still talking about Turks rather than Azeris) carried the day, and the Congress passed a motion calling for Russia to be transformed into a 'democratic republic based on national–territorial–federal principles'.[19] The same debates and similar protagonists would be found over 70 years later in 1990, at the founding congress of the IRP, which mobilised principally Volga Tatars and North Caucasians (this time with the support of the Tajiks). But the outcome was more or less a foregone conclusion: the IRP would split into national branches. Pan-Islamism died in the Russian empire in 1924, as a result of the abolition of the Ottoman caliphate, the marginalising of Sultan Galiev's nationalist communists, and the administrative realignment of the empire into 'nationalities'.

The Jadid heritage was not to be a reference point at the time of independence in 1991. The deeper reason for this was presumably that the Jadids were not nationalists in the modern sense. The real heirs of the Jadids are probably more to be found in the ranks of the IRP, but the party could hardly identify openly with such an ambiguous heritage, on account of the pan-Turkism of the Jadids, their hostility to the traditional clergy and their secularising tendencies.

MUSLIM POLITICAL PARTIES IN RUSSIA

At the time of the first revolution in February 1917 Muslim political parties, some of which had been created clandestinely post-1905, came out into the open. These were: the Hümmet (socialist) and Mussavat (pan-Turkist) parties in the case of Azerbaijan; Alash Orda among the Kazakhs; Melli Firqa among the Crimean Tatars; Ittifaq among the Kazan Tatars. In Transoxiania, two movements – both still underground – appeared in the emirates: the Young Bukharians and the Young Khivians. None of these parties was 'nationalist' in the strict sense (except perhaps Alash Orda), let alone independentist; most of them were campaigning for emancipation for all Muslims empire-wide, and they preached a pan-Turkist solidarity. On the Russian political scene they were all very close to the KD, except the Azeri Hümmet, which was split between Mensheviks and Bolsheviks. The specificity of the Kazakh situation became manifest on the occasion of the foundation in 1905 of the Alash Orda party by enlightened aristocrats and nationalists (Bokeykhanov and Baytursun). After an initial eclipse, the party was to be reborn in March 1917. Its principal aim was an end to Russian colonisation and a return of land to the Kazakhs. It was the only nationalist Muslim party in the modern sense to have appeared in Russia pre-1914. Moving in the opposite direction, the Baku Muslim Congress of April 1917 decided to avoid the term 'Azerbaijan' in the final motion in order to keep relations open with all Muslims in Russia.

Even though nationalism was not on the agenda of the Muslim parties, none of them was truly pan-Russian in make-up, and they each had a precise ethno-linguistic base, which was to lead them into defending nationalist positions in the modern sense of the term, against both Bolsheviks and the White revolution. There were various reasons for this. First, a growing dis-affection in relation to the Russian reformers, who were applauding the Russian offensive against the Ottoman empire (the taking of Erzurum in February 1916), at a time when the Muslim reformers were more or less in favour of the Ottoman empire and were making approaches to the revo-lutionary socialists and Mensheviks (but not the Bolsheviks). Finally, their various situations and strategic interests differed considerably. The Azeris, who had experienced the 1914–18 war very much at first hand, polarised in favour of the Ottomans against the Russians and Armenians; the Kazakhs' main concern was to keep out of the war, and there was a revolt against the conscription launched in 1916; the Young Bukharians and the Young Khivians, on the other hand, were counting on Russia's revolutionaries to help them to drive the emirs from the throne.

The first true declaration of independence of a Russian Muslim territory took place in Azerbaijan. The dissolution of the Transcaucasian Federation (May 1918) – as a result of internal dissension between Georgians, Armenians and Azeris, and the setbacks suffered by the Ottoman army – led the Azerbaijani National Council (under the control of Mussavat) to declare the independence of 'Azerbaijan' on 28 May 1918, with Ganja as its capital (since Baku was in the hands of the Bolsheviks and the Armenian Dashnaks). This was not only the first independent Muslim republic, but it was also the first time that the name 'Azerbaijan' had been used to refer to a nation. The arrival of Ottoman troops under Nuri Pasha paradoxically served to accentuate the Azeris' feeling of difference in relation to their new Turkish big brother, who behaved condescendingly and was wary of formally recognising Azerbaijani independence. On 7 December 1918, after the departure of the Ottomans and occupation by Britain, Rassulzade declared in parliament that Azerbaijan was henceforth a nation unto itself.

★   ★   ★

All the Muslim parties in Russia, to which we should add the fundamentalist movements in the mountains of the North Caucasus, were principally interested in using the troubles and the Russian civil war as a means of advancing their own interests. Where they were able, they set up their own local governments. They began by supporting the revolutionary cause, but from early 1918 they were being attacked on all fronts by the Bolsheviks, who were hostile to movements which they perceived as bourgeois and nationalist. In January 1918, sailors from the Black Sea occupied Simferopol, where Melli Firqa had established a Tatar government of the Crimea. The Tatars of Kazan created the Military Congress of Russian Muslims (*harbi shura*) in February 1917, and envisaged the creation of a republic of Idel-Ural. But the Bolsheviks crushed what they referred to derisively as the republic of Trans-Bulak (from the name of a local neighbourhood in Kazan) in March 1918, after the dissolution of the *harbi shura*. In Turkestan, the Council of Muslim Peoples created a government at Kokand at the end of 1917, but this was savagely crushed in February 1918 by the Tashkent soviet, composed exclusively of Europeans. In that same month, the Bashkir government of Zeki Velidi Togan was broken up. On 3 March 1918, the Bolsheviks took Alma Ata from the Kazakhs of Alash Orda. In March 1918, the Commune of Baku set up an administration that was basically in the hands of Europeans (Russians, Armenians and Jews), forcing the Mussavat party to take refuge in Ganja, under Ottoman protection.

Muslims of all tendencies then rallied to the White Russians, who launched their counter-offensive in March 1918. But rather ineptly, the Whites applied a far more rigid (and 'ethnic') Russian and Orthodox chauvinism than had the tsars. Meanwhile, the Bolshevik leadership readjusted their sights and began addressing the Muslims in more conciliatory tones. So at the end of 1918, most Muslims re-transferred their allegiance to the Bolsheviks. The latter used them as fellow travellers for as long as necessary in order to consolidate their power. Then, in 1919–20, the 'nationalist' movements would again be crushed, once the civil war had been won by the Bolsheviks, and their 'fellow travellers' would almost all disappear during the purges of 1937. The only ones to survive would be those who had managed to reach Turkey in time, and an isolated few who had remained in Soviet service.

THE NATIONAL-COMMUNISM OF SULTAN GALIEV

Sultan Galiev, a Volga Tatar (1880–1941?) only joined the Communist Party in 1917.[20] For him, the October Revolution was not so much an ideological revolution as a means of mobilising and organising the Muslim community in the empire against Western imperialism (within which he included the Russian variety). In June 1918, he joined the Commissariat for Muslim Affairs, which had been set up in January. He campaigned actively for the creation of an autonomous Muslim Communist Party, a Muslim army and a Muslim territory. In his view, such entities would constitute a revolutionary bridgehead in relation to India, Afghanistan, Iran and, of course, Turkey.

Sultan Galiev spoke all the time of 'the Muslim people', by which he meant the totality of Turcophone Muslims. He took up the notion of Muslim community as it had been defined by the pan-Islamists of the tsarist epoch, but played down the religious aspect. That left language and culture. In his view, this community required its own communist party (as a sign of its existence as a nation in Stalinist terms). This was effectively a secular pan-Islamism. It enjoyed some small initial success, before then being stifled by Stalin. In 1918 the Muslim section of the Russian Communist Party was transformed briefly into a 'Turkic' Communist Party, with the 'nationalist communists' vainly trying to oppose the partition of Turkestan into ethnic republics and calling for the creation of a 'Turan' or Greater Turkestan, with a communist party of its own.[21]

Galiev's theories were taken up in a lower key way by the Kazakh Turar Ryskulov (1894–1938), head of the short-lived Office of Muslim Organisations in Turkestan which had been set up within the Communist Party. Like Sultan Galiev and the other Bolshevik Muslims, Ryskulov only joined the Communist Party in 1917. Having become president of the Executive Committee of the Soviet of People's Commissars of the new Autonomous Republic of Turkestan, in January 1920 he persuaded the Congress of the Turkestan Communist Party (a short-lived concession on Lenin's part) and the Bureau of Muslim Organisations, to approve the creation of a 'Turkic' (Turki) Communist Party, and of a 'Turkic Republic'. He also won approval for a Muslim army, and agrarian reform to favour the indigenous population rather than the Russian settlers. However, such notions were soon to be shattered by the Turkestan Commission that was sent by Moscow in early 1920.

The centre's counter-offensive took place in various stages: first the re-absorption of the Turkestan Communist Party and the Bureau of Muslim Organisations into the Russian Communist Party (summer of 1920); then the elimination of all references to 'Muslims', to be replaced by the term 'peoples of the Orient' (Baku Congress, September 1920); and finally a restatement of the priority to be accorded to proletarian revolution in Europe, with the oppressed peoples of the Third World playing only a supporting role. As a consequence, there would be tactical support for anti-imperialist nationalists in other countries (Atatürk, Reza Khan and King Amanullah in Afghanistan), but such tendencies were to be eliminated from the domestic scene. Moscow abandoned the Turkic Communist Party, evacuated the Iranian province of Gilan occupied some months ago, and did not support the Kurdish and Turkmen rebellions of 1925 against the Turks and Iranians. But Moscow also repressed the 'progressive nationalists' within its own empire, whose survivors fled and sought refuge in Turkey. Thus one had the paradoxical situation of the king of Afghanistan being supported by Moscow against the British, but playing host to the last emir of Bukhara, and of Atatürk signing a treaty with Russia but offering asylum to Jadids and pan-Turkists such as Zeki Velidi Togan and Shokayev. Bolshevik Third Worldism was for external consumption only.

Ryskulov lost his position. Sultan Galiev was expelled from the Communist Party in 1923 and imprisoned in 1928. He then disappeared. His name later came to be used as a label for nationalist and pan-Turkist 'deviationism', and opposition to the division of Muslim peoples into separate national entities (*sultangalievshina*).

THE *BASMACHI* MOVEMENT (1918–31)

The revolt of the *basmachis* (the 'bandits') was a conservative rural movement drawing support from all ethnic groups (Tajiks, Uzbeks, Turkmens and Kyrgyz), first against the Soviets' attacks and requisitions (1918, after the sacking of Kokand), and then against the reforms imposed by the Bolsheviks. The armed groups followed traditional chiefs, the *kurbashi*. Their leaders might be religious figures, mullahs and *ishan* (eg Khâl Khodja in the Ferghana), or bandits with popular support (Irgash in the Ferghana); they might be heads of 'solidarity groupings', khans, begs, or tribal chiefs (eg Jomud Junayd Khan and Lokay Ibrahim Beg), or simply minor local notables (such as Madamin Beg in the Ferghana). More rarely, they might be former Jadids, such as Zeki Velidi Togan, or even Turkish officers, such as Enver Pasha. Leaving aside the last two categories, who were not local, the *basmachis*' prime loyalty was to a conservative and fundamentalist Islam, and they had no 'national' project such as the creation of an independent Muslim state. Guerrilla warfare was pursued on the basis of traditional solidarity groupings, lacking in coordination and central command. There was never any such thing as an 'Islamic army', and the small groups in the movement had no hesitation about switching camps in line with changing conditions and local rivalries. This was a reactive war, completely lacking in broader perspective. For all their stance of defending the Muslim community, they were never able to transcend the 'clan' (not ethnic) divisions that were expressed in rivalries between individual chiefs. Without abandoning their stance as conservative Muslims, when a given group found itself about to be dominated by another, it would have no hesitation in allying with the

Bolsheviks. The Bolsheviks were able to win by pouring troops into the war and using counter-insurgency tactics comparable with those being pursued in that period by the British on the North-West Frontier and by Petain in the Rif (the use of tanks and aircraft), but also by putting into the front line Muslim troops (including the Kazan regiment, half of which consisted of Tatars and Bashkirs) and highly mobile cavalry regiments. They also used more peaceful means of persuasion: Islamic courts were readmitted in 1921, and solidarity groupings were brought into line by playing on their perennial rivalries.

Here my concern is not to trace the history of the *basmachis*[22] but to examine the *basmachi* heritage in present-day Central Asia. The movement had three main strongholds: Upper Ferghana, the Turkmen tribes (particularly the Jomud) and the south of present-day Tajikistan. In these three zones, the Jadids had no influence. There was never a Turkmen Jadid. The revolt of the Turkmen tribes were motivated more by the need to defend the tribal system and by opposition to the Young Khivians, who were all Uzbeks, than by attachment to Islam. Today, the *basmachi* heritage is nowhere to be found in Turkmenistan. There is nothing to indicate that the Jomud tribe is more 'Islamic' than the others. On the other hand, Upper Ferghana is still a bastion of Islamic identity, as is the south of Tajikistan. Is it reasonable to regard this as a heritage of the *basmachis*?

In the south of Tajikistan, memories remain very strong. Older peasants, for example, will often date their present settlement to 'after the war' (*pas az jang*). They are referring not to the Second World War but to the *basmachi* war. The war effectively lasted until 1929, having been relaunched by the collectivisation which began in 1927. The battlefields were the same as those which appear in today's communiques announcing operations carried out by the Tajik Islamic Opposition movement. In 1929, Fuzayl Maqsum, the last beg of Karategin (in the Upper Gharm valley) led the last major *basmachi* military operation, coming out of Afghanistan and retaking control of the districts of Kala-i Khum, Tahvil Dara, Khait and Gharm, which are precisely the strongholds of the Islamic movement today (Tahvil Dara was held by the Islamists from May to August 1996). The Afghan bases used by the armed forces and the points where they crossed the Amu Darya to make their incursions into Tajikistan were the same in 1994 as they were in 1924. Furthermore, some of the communiques ('Frontier guards have intercepted a band of armed elements coming from Afghanistan and crossing the river at Panj and Dawraz') could have been issued in identical terms 70 years previously.

However, closer inspection produces puzzling results. The Kulab Valley was a *basmachi* stronghold, and was not reconquered until 1926. Enver Pasha, the former Young Turk leader who joined the Bolsheviks after having been thrown out by Atatürk, and who then went over to the *basmachis*, was killed there in 1922. By 1992, Kulab became the stronghold of neo-communists against the Islamists, who themselves recruit more logically among the people of Karategin (today known as 'Gharmis'), another *basmachi* stronghold. The tomb of Enver Pasha was rediscovered in 1996 in the upper Baljwan Valley (Kulab), which is the home territory of members of the hardline Kulabi faction currently in power – Rahmanov (president of the republic in 1994), Obeydulayev (vice-president in charge of security) and Salimov (minister of the interior during the same period) are all Baljwanis.

In the same way, a little further west, the Lakay tribe of Kurgan-Teppe province joined the neo-communist coalition in 1992 even though, with Ibrahim Beg, it had been in the vanguard of *basmachi* fighting. The same goes for the neighbouring Ghazi Malek group. Abdul Majid Dustiyev, the strong man of the conservative regime that governed between 1992 and 1995, is a Kulabi on his mother's side and Lakay on his father's side.

How is one to explain these developments? First, one should avoid the conclusion that in 1992 the 'neo-communists' were recruiting among de-Islamised sections of the population. Although their leaders were communist apparatchiks not particularly noted for their attendance at mosque, the population of Kulab, during the Soviet period, was often negatively mentioned by the communist press for its religious conservatism. With one or two exceptions, the Kulab mullahs (such as Haydar Sharipov) 'blessed' the uprising against the Islamic-democratic coalition in May 1992. In short, as in 1924, everyone was Muslim. The civil war of 1992 counterposed not Islamists and communists, but regionalist groupings whose antagonistic identity had been, if not created, at least reinforced by the Soviet system. The pre-1927 hostilities arose in relation to the *qawms* (solidarity groups formed in networks and not communities defined by the territory in which they live), and this is also the case today.

Any explanation of the present political alignments would have, in my opinion, to derive from the history of defections and alliances, vengeance and reprisal, during the *basmachi* period. In short, more than ever, the true political stakes were not those of ethnicity or ideology; here the conflict was between solidarity groups which had been fixed to a territorial space (district or province) by collectivisation and administrative realignments under the Soviets.

If we take the case of the Lakays, Marie Broxup notes that in 1924 one clan, the Badra-oglu, joined the Bolsheviks against the dominant clan of the Ishân-Khwâja, that of Ibrahim Beg (their name indicates that this was a 'religious' clan, and probably endogamous), which withdrew to Afghanistan. It is possible that today's Lakays in Tajikistan are the grand-children of the clans who allied with the Bolsheviks. In order to explain present-day hostility between Gharmis and Kulabis, as well as the mutual vying over land and power which followed collectivisation, one also needs to take on board the way in which the hatreds of that period have been passed down. We need to look at how they have slipped from conflicts between kinship groupings or clans into conflicts between regionalist communities, as a result of kinship groups and clans having been transformed into regional groupings.

A typical example illustrates this thesis. Sangak Safarov was the political-military head of the so-called 'neo-communist' faction during the civil war in 1992. He was born in 1928 in Khawaling (village of Sharq-i Shârdi, district of Shughnaw, Yakhsu Valley in the province of Kulab) into a family that had originated in the Khingao Valley (and thus from Karategin); his father, Pir Nazarof, came from a religious family, and Sangak Safarov was a *sayyad* on his mother's side. He was the grandson of Ishan Sultan, head of the brotherhood that had been influential in Karategin, Darwaz and Vakhsh at the start of the century, and whose son – Sangak's uncle, Mullah Abdulhaq – was the khalifa. Ishan Sultan naturally became a *basmachi*, and took part in the taking of Dushanbe under the command of Enver Pasha in January 1922, together with another *basmachi* chief, Fuzayl Maqsum, former khan of Karategin and originally from Khayt in the Gharm Valley. In the spring, Ishan Sultan went over to the Reds and fought against Enver Pasha in Baljwan; he became head of the revolutionary committee of that district, where his family then settled, and thereby became 'Kulabi'. After the death of Enver in June 1922, Ishan Sultan attacked Fuzayl Maqsum, who was forced to flee to Afghanistan. But in 1929, this same Maqsum led the last major *basmachi* raid coming out of Afghanistan, and temporarily occupied the region in 1929. Ishan Sultan was taken prisoner and hanged. Sangak Safarov has not forgotten.[23] This suggests that Kulab identity is recent, and that it has crystallised around political events, including the conflicts between *basmachis*. The father of Sangak Safarov was arrested in 1935. He himself, after having spent ten years in prison and having led the Kulabi counter-offensive in the summer of 1992, was killed on 30 March 1993 by one of his allies, Fayzullah Saidov, who accused him of being too soft on the conquered Gharmis. Here a new level appears – that of ethnicity. Sangak favoured a return by Gharmi refugees, for fear of seeing the ethnic balance shift in favour of the Uzbeks; Saidov, who had an Uzbek mother, rejected any such return of refugees. But it is clear that both the groups, that of Ishan Sultan and that of Fuzayl Maqsum, were originally from the same region. So the fact of their 'region-alism' is not historically long-standing: it comes about when the two groups find themselves separated administratively into Kulabis and Gharmis. It is at this point that they become regionalist groups struggling over land.

The *basmachi* heritage today functions through the prism of the struggles of regionalist factions such as they were structured by Sovietism. This explains why, as in the case of Jadidism, the *basmachi* movement is not seen as a precursor of the present nationalist movements, nor even as a model for the militant Islamists of today.

4

The Sovietisation of Central Asia

The October Revolution marked the fulfilment of a colonial enterprise, but within an ideological logic which opened the way for local élites and new political entities to emerge.

Russia's Muslims did not take sides in the October Revolution. At the local level, they were subjected to the setting up of the soviets either as onlookers or as victims, at the end of 1917 and the start of 1918. At that time, the soviets of Kazan and Tashkent contained no Muslims. In Baku, the Bolsheviks allied with Armenian militias from the Dashnak party against the Muslim Mussavat party, and the ensuing conflict was to result in thousands of deaths in the course of March 1918. In Tashkent, Russian settlers, Menshevik and ex-tsarist alike, joined the soviet, which was perceived as the expression of the power of the metropolis, and they then set about forced expropriations from the Muslim peasantry. Elsewhere in Russia the dynamic was one of class antagonism (in fact the urban proletariat versus the peasantry), but in the Muslim provinces the dynamic was more one of inter-ethnic conflict, with the peasantry being Muslim and the workers and functionaries European. The Bolsheviks came to be viewed as a power that was Russian and colonial. Only some Tatars in Kazan, plus members of the Hümmet party in Azerbaijan and the Jadids of Bukhara and Khiva played the Bolshevik card. The few Muslim members of the Bolshevik party (mainly Tatars) mostly joined only in October 1917 (Sultan Galiev and the Kazakh Ryskulov). This made them suspect in the eyes of the party leadership, which tended to see Muslims as culturally backward, not really suitable to be communists and needing to be kept under a kind of tutelage.[1]

Lenin was very aware of the risk that Muslim indifference might transform into hostility. On 24 November 1917, he issued an appeal to 'all Muslim workers of Russia and the East'. On 19 January 1918, a 'Central Commissariat for Muslim Affairs' was established, and Sultan Galiev joined it in the following August. A short-lived socialist-communist Muslim party, distinct from the Bolshevik Communist Party, was created in 1918, and Azeri communists were authorised to form their own national communist party. The repression of the national Muslim movements in the first quarter of 1918, and the resulting alliance between Muslims and the Whites; the revolt of the *basmachis*; the risk of Bolshevik power coming to be seen as colonialism; and finally the hope of being able to use Muslim go-betweens as a way of promoting political agitation in British India, Persia and Turkey – all these were instrumental factors in persuading Lenin to put a brake on outright Bolshevisation. Instructions were given not to attack Islamic institutions such as the veil and *sharia* courts directly. The priority was to indigenise the structures of the revolution, but there was a problem here, in the lack of Muslim 'revolutionaries', particularly in Central Asia. Fellow travellers' from the ranks of the Jadids played a major role as transmission cogs (often symbolic) of a Bolshevik power that was intent on masking the essentially colonial nature of its enterprise. In Azerbaijan and the emirates of Bukhara and Khiva, the entry of the Red Army in 1920 was preceded by an uprising of the Azeri Communist Party and the Jadids.

★   ★   ★

But at the same time there was no question of the Bolsheviks allowing the setting up of a political or territorial entity, even a communist one, bringing together the entirety of Russia's Muslims: the Muslim Socialist Communist Party was dissolved in November 1918 at the same time as the Commissariat for Muslim Affairs. The Bureau of Muslim Communist Organisations, created in 1919 to provide a specifically Muslim organisational framework, was no more than a department of the Bolshevik Communist Party, and was anyway dissolved in 1922. So what was on offer for the Muslims? In the ways that were developed to integrate Muslims, we find the same twin policies that were used under Tsarism: playing the religious communitarian card (albeit in a secularised version), and ethnicisation. This was the path chosen by the communists, at the prompting of Stalin.

CONSTANTS IN RUSSIAN AND SOVIET POLICY

The continuity between Soviet policy and tsarist policy has been amply documented in the broader strategic field (for example Peter the Great's mythical objective of finding outlets to warm seas). However, I would suggest that it was equally present in the elaboration of ideological and conceptual instruments to make possible the perpetuation of a multi-ethnic empire dominated by Russians. There is considerable convergence in terms of the methods used (dividing the Muslim community by playing up ethnicity and administrative realignment of borders), the aims (a long-term Russification, playing on ideology and the natural superiority of the Russian model) and even the vocabulary: a report of the Ministry of Public Education in 1870 stresses the role of the Russian language in bringing people together (*sblizhenie*), a stage then to be followed by fusion (*sliianie*) and a greater degree of Russification.[2] Identical terms were used in Soviet policy, particularly during the Brezhnev period. There was also an important constraint which remained a policy constant from the time of the tsars, through Stalin and down to Gorbachev. Russia was not a nation state but an empire, an ideo-logical state. Any definition as a nation-state would probably have excluded at least the non-Slavs, and certainly the Muslims. Another continuing factor was the fear of a pan-Islamism which might unite Russia's Muslims with their co-religionists abroad, citizens of countries that represented something of a threat to Russia (eg Turkey) – all the more so because a Muslim reform movement might be the bearer of values which would run counter to the official ideology of the moment.

In order to counter these threats the Russian authorities more or less systematically played the ethnic card against pan-Islamism, and religious conservatism against Muslim reform. The ethnic concept of nation was privileged against the millet, but with a risk of this later backfiring with the emergence of ethnically-based Muslim nationalisms (from Kazakhstan to Chechnya). The multi-ethnic character of the empire has thus always been accepted (except by the Whites between 1918 and 1921, which accounts for their rejection by the Muslims) but it remained an open question as to what institutional form should be given to this ethnic multiplicity. The Chechen crisis shows that the problem has still not been resolved. The demand for independence is in effect a logical consequence of ethnicisation.

In three fundamental areas of policy there is a clear continuity between tsarism and Sovietism: namely Islam, ethnic grouping and the re-alignment of administrative borders.

The Approach to Islam

An identical three-fold approach to Islam was pursued under both the tsars and the Soviets: repression, the attempt to instrumentalise 'progressive' mullahs, and finally a 'middle road' which organised the world of Islam by means of a clergy that was conservative and functionarised. Ivan the Terrible had wanted to abolish Islam, as had Stalin between 1927 and 1939; Catherine I envisioned a role for the 'modern' Tatars, in the same way that the Bolsheviks very briefly attempted to promote red mullahs between 1921 and 1927 (for example by appointing a Jadid as mufti, the Tatar Rizaeddin Fakhreddin, between 1922 and 1936). But both systems eventually settled on the establishment of a muftiyya in the charge of conservative court mullahs, preaching a relatively harmless Islam with no pretensions to theological research. In around 1813, the mufti of Orenburg appointed by the Russians issued a condemnation of the work of the first Tatar reformer, Abul Nasr

Kursawi, who had already been obliged to flee the emirate of Bukhara. The Soviets required official mullahs to support and legitimate the policy of the USSR and to make themselves available for international conferences, but there were never efforts (any more than there were among the Orthodox Christians) to develop a progressive theology. The Soviet authorities ensured that their mullahs were always perfectly orthodox, and their tactic was to play off conformism and sclerosis against a theological revivalism that otherwise they might not have been able to control. They had similar problems with Christian liberation theology in the 1950s, where they evinced the same preference for conservative fellow travellers.

Another constant was the functionarisation of the clergy. Catherine II had established the principle of the muftiyya (at Orenburg, and later at Ufa). The idea of one single mufti for the empire as a whole went too much in the direction of 'communitarianism'. The tsars, beginning with Nicholas I, preferred a policy of playing ethnicity against communitarianism. It was thus logical that the number of muftiyyas would multiply as a function of the division of the Muslim community into separate administrative entities. In Azerbaijan, when the province became a vice-royalty annexed to the empire two religious administrations were created, one Sunni (with a mufti) and the other Shiite (with a sheikh–ul islam), both of whom were based at Tiflis (Tbilisi). Religious personnel came under the authority of the minister of the interior and the viceroy; they had the status of functionaries and were independent of the muftiyya based in Ufa.

By the fact of having created, in 1941, four spiritual leaderships for the totality of Soviet Muslims, Stalin was thus simply continuing tsarist policy. The Sunni and Shiite leaderships were established in Azerbaijan: the sheikh–ul islam, now based in Baku, was Shiite, and his deputy Sunni. The muftiyya of Ufa was given authority over the European part and Siberia. There was to be a mufti for the North Caucasus (at Makhachkala in Daghestan) and another for Central Asia and Kazakhstan, established in Tashkent, who was to become the *primus inter pares* of the muftis, the only one authorised to represent Soviet Islam in the rest of the Muslim world – a further way of limiting the role of the Tatars.

Both the tsars and Stalin discouraged relations between the leading clergy of the empire and the rest of the Muslim world, out of a fear of pan-Islamism. One of the successes of this policy was the long-term cutting-off of relations between the Azeri Shiite clergy and its Iranian mentors, the effects of which are still felt today; the Caucasus Shiites who left for Najaf and Kerbala during the Russian period generally did not come back,[3] and the present sheikh–ul islam, Shukur Pashazadeh, is the only mufti from the latter end of the Soviet period not to have studied abroad.

This territorial division does not really tally with 'national' borders, except in the case of Azerbaijan. All the muftis have a constituency which is supra-national: the five countries of Central Asia were covered by Tashkent; Russia, Byelorussia, the Ukraine and the Baltic countries (with their population of Tatars) by Ufa, and the six entities of the North Caucasus by Makhachkala. The mufti of Ufa is still a Tatar, but Ufa is in Bashkiria. The mufti of Tashkent is still an Uzbek. The demand of the Kazakhs, formulated in 1917, for a muftiyya of their own was rejected.[4] The reason was presumably the fear of a synergy being created between Islam and nationalism. The establishment of one mufti per republic would have to wait until the various countries gained their independence in 1991.

The Invention of Ethnicity

Debate about the true nature of 'the people' (*narod*) was a major continuing theme throughout the nineteenth and twentieth centuries. It derived largely from German Romanticism (the idea of the Volk), and assumed a Marxist tinge post-1917. The idea was that 'the people' was a natural ethnic entity, in the process of becoming and defined principally by its language. This ethnic approach first appeared in Russia in the nineteenth century, under the Tsars. The first step was the recognition of a Tatar language and culture for Tatars who had converted to Orthodoxy; the Russians created a Cyrillic Tatar alphabet for their use (whereas the Muslim Tatars used an Arabic alphabet). A Tatar 'nation' was thus recognised.

The key figure here was Nicolas Ilminsky, professor of Turkic languages at the University of Kazan from 1861. As well as being a specialist in Turkic linguistics, he was a great supporter of integration by means of conversion to Orthodoxy, but maintaining national languages and cultures (substitute socialism for Orthodoxy and you have Stalin). In 1870, under Ilminsky's influence, the tsarist authorities introduced a network of Tatar schools for Christian Tatars. Although the Russian language played a major role, teaching was in Tatar. That same year, the ministry decided on the creation of Russo-Kazakh schools, a policy which would be implemented by the Kazakh Ibrahim Altynsarin. These schools were open to all Kazakhs, given that there were virtually no Christian Kazakhs.[5]

The invention of languages and writings was not an innovation of the Soviets. Ilminsky used Cyrillic to transcribe Tatar, and having experimented with the Arabic alphabet invented a Cyrillic transcription for a Kazakh language which he himself set about codifying (since Kazakh literary writers used both Tatar and Russian, and the illiterate, by definition, did not write). The idea was to use language as an effective way of achieving ideological Russification, or rather as an improved means of converting to Orthodoxy, since Russification was merely a consequence of such a conversion. But as in the case of Sovietism, the system succeeded only in promoting the emergence of ethnic identities without at the same time achieving the ideological fusion which was its ultimate aim.

Muslim intellectuals who worked in this direction were looked on with favour, for example the Tatar Abdul Qayyum Nassiri and the Kazakh

Altynsarin, even though of course with neither of these men was there any question of Russification or conversion to Christianity. Nassiri was to be honoured in the Soviet vulgate as an authentic precursor of Tatar identity and an opponent of pan-Islamism and pan-Turkism (which latter were espoused by Gasprinski, the *bête noire* of the Soviets) – even though Nassiri wrote religious works, and had never attacked Islam. The Muslim reformers did not really recognise themselves in the use that was being made of them. Altynsarin, while supporting a project of valorising vernacular languages against vehicular languages, protested against the anti-Islamic stance of the Russo-Kazakh schools, and pressed for the maintenance of the Arabic alphabet.[6]

At the same time that Ilminsky was pushing for the use of vernacular languages, codifying them and authorising them as languages for teaching, he made a policy of destroying the vehicular literary languages in use at the time, and successfully encouraged the tsarist administration of the governorate of the Steppes to abandon the use of Tatar, in favour of Kazakh. Thus we have a paradox: Tatar was being promoted as a 'national' language and destroyed as a vehicular language; it was forbidden in Kazakhstan at the same time as it was being institutionalised in Tatarstan. Stalin was to do the same in Daghestan: Azeri Turkish was promoted in Azerbaijan, but as the vehicular language of the Muslim Caucasus it was replaced by Daghestani languages in teaching, and more particularly by Russian as the language of official communication. These efforts were a key part of the struggle against pan-Turkism (which aimed at a common Turkic language) and pan-Islamism.

This struggle was conducted by means of an affirmation, albeit temporary, of the 'nationhood' and culture of an ethnic group, on condition that this was not in contradiction with loyalty to the state. In 1870, the minister for education, D.A. Tolstoy, formerly prosecutor for the Holy Synod, published his 'Instructions for the Education of Native Peoples', in which one's mother language was recognised as the language of primary school education, on the understanding that Russian would be the language for tertiary, and even secondary, education.[7] This was to be exactly the founding principle of Stalinist nationality policy. Progressive 'multi-culturalism' (the right to speak, write and learn in one's own mother language) concealed an integrationalist and ideological imperial project, the main aim of which was to break down religious and cultural solidarities.

The second stage after the recognition of ethnicity was to encourage the division of Muslims into national groups, in other words to strengthen their respective identities, obviously with a view to fostering antagonisms. This is the opposite of French-style integration: it was a 'multi-culturalist' policy *ante litteram*, the consequence of which, as with all multi-culturalist policies, was to lock people into ethnic definitions that were basically dictated by the state, since only the state was authorised to lay down the list of 'legal' ethnic groups (in the same way that racial and ethnic groups have occasionally been defined by law in the United States). The ethnic censuses carried out every ten years in the USSR were a tsarist invention, in which the ethnic group was usually defined by language. One finds the same anomalies in the tsarist census of 1897 as in subsequent Soviet censuses: since ethnic groups are defined by their language, the Sarts of Central Asia ended up speaking 'Sart' (a language which has never existed, since the Sarts speak either Turki or Tajik).[8]

In 1905, permission was given for religious teaching to take place in the Kazakh language.[9] In 1906, a Kazakh muftiyya was created (and subsequently abolished). These two measures were directed against the influence of the Tatars and Jadids. In 1911, the governor-general of Turkestan decreed that teachers were to be of the same ethnic group as their pupils.[10] This measure was directed at reformed (or modernist) schools which were run by Tatars. At the same time, the emir of Bukhara required Tatar schools to be moved out of the Muslim neighbourhoods to the Russian part of towns. A similar paradox afflicted the Tatars living in Central Asia in 1991: despite their history of pan-Islamism, they found themselves assimilated with the Russians by the local population.

In Azerbaijan for a brief period (the governorate of Vorontsov in the 1850s, and that of Goltsyn from 1896 to 1905), the Russians encouraged the development of an Azeri identity in order to weaken links with Iran and Turkey. This took place in particular through the use of a less Persianised Turkish, and by the authorisation given for publication of *Sharq-i rus* in 1904, which promoted an Azeri rather than Ottoman Turkish (*azerichi*).[11] This special position of the Azeris was also recognised by the Bolsheviks. The Hümmet party was both the only Muslim socialist party and the only party to be recognised as a national communist party by Lenin (the founding of the [Bolshevik] Azeri Communist Party in February 1920). Lenin, as we know, was very hostile to the recognition of national communist parties such as the Jewish Bund and the Communist Party of Turkestan. The exception in this case derived from the same strategic considerations which led the final tsarist administration to greater flexibility towards the Azeri Muslims: it was thought advisable to develop an Azeri identity in order to detach the Azeris from their marked pro-Turkism, a result of their linguistic and territorial proximity to Turkey.

The instruments of this 'nationalities' policy under both the tsars and the Soviets were ethnography and linguistics. Soviet ethnography in its empirical version was a direct inheritance from the Russian ethnography of the nineteenth century, as was Soviet linguistics. The University of Saint Petersburg came through the revolution of 1917 without too much trauma, maintaining its dogmas and its body of teachers intact, since both adapted relatively easily to the Leninist vulgate.

The Creation of New Administrative Entities

The two forms of administrative restructuring – by means of dividing up existing entities, and by the artificial creation of new national entities – were first initiated under the tsarist administration. In Central Asia, the tsarist authorities made much use of administrative division: for instance the governorate of Turkestan combined the former possessions of the three emirates (Bukhara, Khiva and Kokand), with the two protectorates (Bukhara and Khiva) being greatly reduced; in the same way, the vast territories of the Kazakhs were divided, and the governorate of Turkestan was given Semirechie, a territory populated with Kazakhs. In Azerbaijan, rather the opposite course was pursued, with the tsarist authorities attempting to give a political identity to what was not much more than a group of small khanates recently removed from Iranian tutelage: the abolition of khanates, the setting up of a provincial administration, and also the exiling of pro-Ottoman Sunnis following the wars of 1877, made it possible to give Azerbaijan an administrative unity and a new political personality.[12] The final tsarist administration, on the eve of the 1914–18 war, encouraged the emergence of an Azeri identity as against a Turco-Muslim one.

★   ★   ★

A final element of continuity, which was not a matter of choice but a legacy of the past, was the ambiguous role played by the Tatars of Kazan. They were simultaneously the agents of re-Islamisation (or simply Islamisation, in the case of the Kazakhs of the north), of Muslim reformism, and of the awakening of a national consciousness (in a pan-Islamist sense), but were also the agents of Russification and Sovietisation. Catherine the Great used them in this way at the end of the seventeenth century; a century later they came to be seen as suspect in the eyes of the tsarist administration, which limited their activities in Turkestan and the governorate of the Steppes. The Tatars were to be the first victims of Stalinist repression (the arrest of Sultan Galiev in 1923 and the establishment of Bashkiria as the first autonomous republic in order to counter a Tatarisation that was already well under way); however, they were to be found emerging again as agents of Sovietisation in Central Asia. Already in the 1920s, anti-Tatar sentiment was beginning to appear among the intelligentsia of Central Asia.[13] Numbers of Tatars were employed in the administration and in the KGB, because of their Muslim names and their more 'oriental' appearance.[14] The Tatars' problem is that they are seen as Muslims by the Russians, and as Russians by the Central Asian Muslims (today in the newly independent republics they live in Russian neighbourhoods and send their children to Russian schools). They have always seen themselves as the vanguard of the Muslim community, but for that reason they have negotiated with the Russians a position as privileged intermediaries, and this has often led them to act as agents of the central government.

SOVIETISATION AND REALIGNMENTS OF TERRITORY
The Completion of Conquest (1917–24)

The Sovietisation of Central Asia took place initially under the authority of institutions dominated by Russians, and within a territorial framework inherited from the Russian empire (the governorate of the Steppes, the governorate of Turkestan, the Transcaspian province, which was re-established as a governorate, and the two emirates of Bukhara and Khiva). The continuation of the revolt of the *basmachis* through 1924 required the Bolsheviks to act both speedily and cautiously. One of their major problems was the absence of indigenous *cadres* and of any social base for revolution. However, the population's discontent with the emirs was evident (tax revolts, protests against cruelty and injustice, even when one allows for Soviet exaggeration and the 'orientalism' of Western travellers such as Vambéry, always ready to portray the native populations as savage). However this discontent benefited neither the Russians nor the Bolsheviks, as the latter found to their detriment on the occasion of a failed expedition against Bukhara in 1918, where the population mobilised against the small Bolshevik expeditionary corps. The mass of Muslims proved unwilling to rally round either the Bolsheviks or the Jadids, preferring to back their *ulemas*, their local chiefs, and the *ishan* who ran the Sufi brotherhoods.

In November 1917, the Turksovnarkom (Council of Commissars of the People of Turkestan) was created in Tashkent, with *cadres* that were exclusively European. In response, the Central Council of Muslims called a conference in Kokand (Ferghana) in November 1917, where a declaration was made of the autonomy of Central Asia. This was not a 'nationalist' movement: one third of the members of this government were Russian, and President Choghai-oghlu (Chokayev) was Kazakh. Kokand was taken on 18 February 1918 by troops from the Tashkent soviet. Thus, in the eyes of Muslims, the revolution came to be viewed as merely a reincarnation of Russian colonialism.

Lenin decided that it was a matter of urgency to indigenise the soviet and to adopt a more conciliatory policy in relation to the Muslims. The Kazakh Turar Ryskulov was appointed vice-president of the Executive Committee of Turksovnarkom in March 1918. In April 1918, Moscow proclaimed the formation of the autonomous Soviet Republic of Turkestan, in place of the governorate of the same name. This republic was attached to the Russian Federal Socialist Republic. In July, the Soviet proclaimed Uzbek and Kyrgyz (presumably meaning Kazakh, since at that time the Russians used the term Kyrgyz for Kazakhs) the official languages of the autonomous republic.

In March 1919, Moscow created a Bureau of Muslim Organisations in Turkestan, which was an offshoot of the Russian Communist Party and was also to be headed by Ryskulov. Its aim was to rally Muslims around structures that they would see as their own rather than as variants of Russian colonialism.

The Jadids joined up *en masse*, but tension still remained between the Europeans and Muslims, who criticised the colonial attitude of the local Bolsheviks. On the other hand, the Jadids were viewed with suspicion by the Bolsheviks. They had influence in the government of Kokand, and were unhappy about the incorporation of the emirates into the new Russian empire. The majority of them refused to join the small Khiva and Bukhara communist parties created in Tashkent in 1918. However, they were the sole indigenous channel by which it would be possible to gain control of Bukhara and Khiva. Ryskulov was promoted from vice-president to president of the Soviet of Commissars of the People of Turkestan at the end of 1919. The pendulum seemed to be swinging back in favour of the Muslims, but this was not to last.

In order to correct past errors, but also to assert control by the central government, Lenin appointed a Turkestan Commission (Turk Kommission), which set off for Central Asia in early 1920. It was headed by Frunze and Kuybishev, who would be joined in June by Kaganovich and George Safarov, and it contained no Muslims. The purpose of the Commission was the pursuit of the military campaign against the *basmachis*, the reduction of the two emirates of Bukhara and Khiva, a co-optation of native cadres ('indigenisation'), and finally the consolidation of Bolshevik power in Central Asia with a view to stamping out separatism and ending special treatment for the Muslims. In particular, the intention was to integrate the various different communist parties (of Turkestan, Bukhara and Khiva) into the Russian Communist Party. The idea, in short, was to make space for the Muslims within the Soviet system, rather than adjacent to it. One of the Commission's first moves was to purge the Tashkent Soviet of tsarist and settler elements, in order to bring in Muslim élites. But it was later to turn against the Jadids. Between June and July 1920, Ryskulov lost his position, the Muslim Bureau was dissolved, and the autonomous communist organisations were integrated within the Russian Communist Party. The Turkestan Commission then promoted young Muslims who had no relation with the Jadids, and who came from the countryside and were often illiterate.

In August 1920, the other governorate, that of the Steppes, was transformed into the Kyrgyz Autonomous Socialist Republic (in other words Kazakh, in the Russian terminology of the time), which continued as a dependency of the Russian Federal Socialist Republic (the Kara-Kyrgyz, in other words the true Kyrgyz, were excluded from this republic, along with Alma Ata and the area surrounding the town of Turkestan, and were attached instead to the Turkestan Autonomous Socialist Republic). The republic's soviet was controlled by former members of Alash Orda. Kazakh was admitted as an offical language in 1923. Finally, in 1920, the Transcaspian province, which had been detached from the governorate of Turkestan, became the Autonomous Soviet Republic of Turkmenistan (1920–August 1924). This too was attached to the Russian Federal Socialist Republic, together with the Autonomous Region of the Karakalpaks.

Thus these two governates and the Transcaspian province, an inheritance from tsarism, were transformed into autonomous socialist republics attached to Russia.

It now remained to conquer the two independent emirates. Since 1917, the emirate of Khiva had been headed by the Turkmen war chief Junayd Khan, of the Jomud tribe, who had thrown out the Uzbek ruling dynasty and was now fighting against the Jadids of Khiva, who were all Uzbeks. On 1 February 1920, Frunze took Khiva and declared the People's Republic of Khwarezm. Junayd Khan took the leadership of the *basmachi* movement among the Turkmens, and was to pursue his campaign up until 1928. In March 1921, the Jadids of the Young Khiva movement who ran the new government were thrown out by Frunze, and joined up with Junayd Khan. The local communists, following an internal purge, then took power. In 1923, the people's republic became a soviet republic, as a first step towards integration.

As for Bukhara, its fate was decided on 2 September 1920: the town was taken by Frunze, and a People's Republic of Bukharia was declared. The Jadids – in other words the Young Bukharians, who included F. Khojayev and A. Fitrat – refused to join the recently created Communist Party of Bukharia, which had been set up in Tashkent by other Young Bukharians in 1918. They were supposed to have organised the town's uprising, but they simply went through the motions. Nevertheless, they attempted to mark their difference, playing on Moscow's need to foster the development of indigenous cadres. Osman Khojayev was the first president of the new republic, but he rallied the *basmachis* and set off for Istanbul to found a Committee for the Liberation of Bukhara (1921). Fayzullah Khojayev took his place, with the support of Kuybishev, who represented the Comintern and the Soviet government in Bukhara after 1920.

The ruling Jadids attempted to mark their difference from both the emirs and the Bolsheviks, to preserve a degree of independence. The new government declared that laws could not be enacted which were contrary to Islam. Fitrat made Uzbek the national language in place of Persian (even though he himself wrote mainly in Persian). However, this pseudo-independence was not to last: in February 1922 the Bukhara Communist Party merged with the Russian Communist Party. The 1923 Treaty with the Russian Soviet Federative Socialist Republic (RSFSR) placed frontier guards under Russian command.[15] In the course of a purge in 1923, Fitrat lost his position at the Ministry of Foreign Affairs. F. Khojayev remained, and on 19 September 1924 the fifth *kurultay* ('assembly', in the Mongol tradition) of Bukhara accepted, on 19 September 1924, the People's Republic's transition to a Soviet Republic, the last stage before the process of nation creation.

The Creation of Nations (1924–36)

The 1924 division into nations was the founding act of the countries of Central Asia which have today found their independence. There have of course been other examples of colonial administrative division bringing into being states which had not existed before – for instance in the countries of Spanish-speaking South America, or French-speaking Africa. But this was the first time that the colonial power forged not only countries, but also languages and national histories, not to mention folklores and literatures. It is this concern for totalisation which is so fascinating about the Soviet system.

1924 saw the dissolution of all the preceding administrative entities and a complete rewriting of the map of Central Asia, on the basis of 'one ethnic group, one territory'. The Soviet Union's constitution consolidated these divisions by transforming the empire into a union between the Soviet Socialist Federation of Russia and the Soviet Socialist Republics, within which could be included autonomous republics, autonomous regions and national territories. It took until 1936 for the choices to become definitive.

Over a short span of time new countries were created: on the one hand the Soviet Socialist Republic of Turkmenia and that of Uzbekistan (the latter took in the Autonomous Republic of Tajikistan and the Autonomous Region of Gorno-Badakhshan); on the other, the Autonomous Republic of Kyrgyzia (in fact Kazakhstan) and that of Kara-Kyrgyzia (present-day Kyrgyzia), both of which were attached to Russia; and finally an Autonomous Region of Karakalpakia, directly attached to the RSFSR.[16]

In 1929, Tajikistan was separated from Uzbekistan and turned into a Soviet Republic in its own right. It was also given Leninabad, until that point a simple *oblast* of Uzbekistan, as a way of making it economically more viable. On the other hand, Samarkand, which was actually a Tajik city, remained in Uzbekistan. At the same time (1930), Tashkent replaced Samarkand as the capital of Uzbekistan, which further contributed to the erosion of the common Uzbek-Tajik heritage, since Tashkent had always been a 'Turkic' city. This division was to leave bitterness on both sides: Tajiks cultivated a nostalgia for Samarkand, while the Uzbeks always saw the independence of Tajikistan as something that had been imposed on them. In 1929, Kyrgyzia was renamed Kazakhstan, and Kara-Kyrgyzia to Kyrgyzia, without change in their status.

In 1932, Karakalpia was proclaimed an autonomous republic, still within Russia, but in 1936 the republic was transferred to Uzbekistan. Also in 1936, Kazakhstan and Kyrgyzia were given the status of soviet republics. At the same time, in the Caucasus, the Soviet Republic of Transcaucasia was divided into three soviet republics: Georgia, Armenia and Azerbaijan. So now all the Muslim republics had achieved a defined status. In 1936, the territorial framework of the Muslim republics was definitively fixed. It was within this territorial framework that they would subsequently go on to achieve their independence.

I now turn to examining the meaning and impact of this territorial division.

NATIONALITIES POLICY

The nationalities policy of the USSR had three basic elements. The first was a body of theory elaborated by Stalin on the basis of a notion of 'people' inherited from nineteenth-century anthropology and the Marxist vulgate, and systematised into what one can call the Soviet school of ethnography. The second was a system of administrative and political classification based on territorialisation and language status. The third was a real practice of dividing up populations and territories on the basis of a political and strategic logic which had little to do with the above two principles, but which had to be expressed in their terminology.

The patent absurdity of some of the territorial realignments derives from this juxtaposition of three different logics. However, it is important to note that the first two are neither simple pretexts nor *post facto* constructions: the desire to ensure that peoples did actually correspond to the ideological criteria had an effect of creating a reality which largely laid the basis for the nationalisms of today. While there had always been an Armenian or a Georgian sense of nation, one cannot say the same for the Tajiks and the Uzbeks. Thus languages were invented as the occasion demanded: since it had been decided that there was a Tajik ethnic group, there would have to be an accompanying language – Tajik – since an ethnic group was defined by the fact of its having a language. In another example, Chaghatay was defined as Old Uzbek even though there were no Uzbeks among the populations that spoke Chaghatay before the sixteenth century.

Let us now look at the methods and motivations of this national division.

Soviet Ethnography

Soviet ethnography is built on the juxtaposition of two very different traditions: on the one hand, the idea of 'the people' as it was forged by German Romanticism and then erected into a system in the second half of the nineteenth century by German and Russian theoreticians; on the other hand, a simplified Marxist reading of the developmental stages of modes of production.[17] The founding text of this ethnography was Stalin's *Marxism and the National Question*, published in 1913. A people (*narod*) is defined by a 'historically formed stable community of language, territory, economic life and psychological formation, manifested through a common culture'. Although there will have been, at a given moment, an origin of this people (through the fusion of different groupings) it then evolves in a natural manner without the intervention of political process. A people is not defined by political contract (the nineteenth-century French concept), but by an accretion of objective and 'natural' characteristics. This is the German heritage (in which the *narod* translates the *Volk* and in which *narodnost* translates *Volkstum*, in other words the quality that makes a people exist as such). Its transposition into a Marxist matrix requires that the 'people' in question passes through different stages of political organisation related to the development of the means of production: from the tribe (*plemya*), the stage of primitive community, to the capitalist stage, that of nation (*natsya*), which is defined by a market, and thus a territory. There is an unvarying element which maintains itself through history. Evolutionism combines with essentialism. But what is it that finally indicates the permanence of a people? For Stalin, studying the final censuses of the tsarist period, it was to be language, a position which he outlined in his 1947 polemic with the linguist Marr, for whom, on the contrary, language was to be seen as a superstructure.[18]

This theory was rationalised *post facto* by Yulian Bromley, director of the Ethnography Institute of the Academy of Sciences from 1966 onwards: he used the term *ethnos* to refer to the unchanging element which is maintained through history. But since each *ethnos* is originally the product of a fusion, one can reasonably prepare for the ultimate fusion of nationalities within a Soviet ethnic formation (*sliianie*, or 'fusion'). Evolutionism and essentialism are thus reconciled in a kind of theory of stages. What we have here is a juxtaposition of history and immanence, rupture and permanence, the evolution and fixity of ethnic groups, Darwin and Linnaeus. The Soviet ethnographer, with his eyes fixed on some future voluntarist and purely ideological fusion, which of course he will mention in the introductions to his scientific writings, with the obligatory reference to the writings of the ruling secretary-general, devotes himself to the classification, or rather the 'thingification', of ethnic groups viewed as natural objects. Because of the hierarchical nature and centralisation of the Soviet university system, Bromley's paradigm goes on to become the accepted approach for the whole of Soviet ethnography, and was often taken entirely at face value by contemporary young Russian ethnologists. For instance, the manual of the Academy of Sciences, written in 1977, takes up wholesale Stalin's definition of nationality, but does not cite its source.[19]

In order to establish a firm foundation for the idea of 'ethnic groups', Soviet theoreticians adopted two approaches: ethnogenesis and linguistics. Ethnogenesis involves creating a genealogy of the ethnic group: thus it was shown that the 'Uzbek ethnic group' was formed in ancient times and had then followed the various stages of development expected by the Marxist vulgate, but that it had always been found on the territory which today made up its eponymous republic. This reconstruction is teleological: one moves from present-day ethnic administrative realignments and then explains them by recourse to history.[20] As for linguistics, this has less to do with looking into real language usages and more to do with codifying, formalising and classifying languages according to ideological or simply administrative criteria (spoken language, written language and literary language).

A constant problem for Soviet social 'scientists', which could cost them their lives under Stalin, was that the *a posteriori* justifications which they gave for any given political choice could become 'false' from one moment to the next, following a change of line. Tsarist colonialism was viewed as negative before 1934, but after that date it became positive, through a decision of a plenary session of the Communist Party – much to the chagrin of any historian who had written anything on the subject previously. Anything to do with Chaghatay (both the language and the literature) was viewed as counter-revolutionary up until 1936, when it was rehabilitated under the name of 'Old Uzbek'. Scientists therefore got into the habit of framing their scientific research with an introduction and a conclusion that matched the political line of the moment, guarding their rears with delicately phrased disclaimers. A model of the genre is to be found in a book by the linguist Oranski, whose erudition is universally recognised. When he wrote a handbook presenting an overview of ancient and present-day Iranian languages, he had to use three different terms to define one language (Persian) – Fârsi, or the Persian of Iran, Tâjik, and Dari, or Afghan Persian. Ruling policy made it impossible for him to describe Tajik as a Persian language, but the situation was more embarrassing in the case of Dari, because any Afghan speaker would refer to it as 'Fârsi'. So he resorted to the following circumlocution: 'The difference between the Tajik spoken languages of Central Asia and the spoken languages of this group [Dari] is to be found not so much in their structural linguistic characteristics as in historical, social and cultural factors... As regards the dialects that are found in the territory of Afghanistan, in the present state of academic research the problem of their classification and whether they belong to Tajik or Persian is not easy to answer in terms of linguistic factors.'[21] There could be no more elegant way of admitting that the definition of the status of a language, and by the same token of a ethnic group, is first and foremost political.

The nature of the process thus becomes clear: the ethnic group in question is not first defined by scientific analysis and then given administrative status. On the contrary, first it gets its status, and then it is up to the experts to find it a *post facto* scientific foundation.

The Administrative System: Territory and Status

In theory, any people defined by a language constituted a 'nationality' (*natsionalnost*), which was granted an administrative status in keeping with its level of development. Peoples that had reached the level of nation (*natsya*), because they have a capitalist mode of production and a market, were granted the status of soviet socialist republic (SSR). Less developed peoples were given, in descending order, the status of autonomous soviet socialist republic (ASSR), autonomous region (AR, or *oblast*) and national territory (NT, or *okrug*). Each of these levels had a matching administrative status. The SSRs had all the external signs of statehood: a head of state (the president of the soviet), a minister of foreign affairs (after 1944), a flag, a national communist party, a national language, an academy of sciences, a national anthem etc. The ASSRs had a soviet, whose president was not a head of state, a cabinet that dealt with technical matters, but no minister for foreign affairs; they had a national language, which was used in primary and secondary schooling, but no university in that language, and their academy of sciences was only a sub-section of the academy of the soviet republic which includes them, in the same way that their local communist party is a branch of the 'national' party. At the bottom of the ladder, regions and national territories had their soviets but no ministers. Finally, certain nationalities existed by the fact of having recognised languages but had no territory or institutions of government. The classification of languages here became the criterion of distinction between these groups. Languages had three possible statuses: unwritten language, written language and literary language. A 'nationality' which had no written language would not be able to have territory, but since the decision to 'write' a language comes from the administration, this meant that the status of the language is basically political. If there was a desire to give a territorial entity to a group that has no written language (for example Bashkirs or Karakalpaks), then a written language had to be invented. This could even be accorded the status of a literary language if a few authors could be persuaded to write poems or social realist novels in it.

A separate consideration was that of 'nationalities' which had written lan-guages but no territory: this involved expatriate minority ethnic groups, sometimes tiny, who were found living in the USSR. They were provided with schools, newspapers, even radio stations, in the event that they might prove useful later (here we are talking about Kurds, Lazes, Indians, Germans, etc). And then there were anomalies, such as the Koreans deported to Central Asia, who were Russian-speaking but recognised as a nationality even though they have no institutions of representation.

The final result was a list of nationalities which served for censuses and included a variable number of ethnic groups according to the era in which it was drawn up (the list totaled more than 100, because of the large number of minor peoples in the Caucasus and Siberia).[22] In 1953, there were 53 administrative entities: the RSFSR (the only federal entity, thus not founded on the nation-state, making it a USSR in miniature); 14 SSRs; 20 ASSRs (one of these, Karakalpakia, is included in Uzbekistan; another, Nakhichevan, is attached to Azerbaijan; and 16 are attached to Russia); eight ARs (of which one, Gorno-Badakhshan, was included in Tajikistan and another, Nagorno-Karabakh, in Azerbaijan); and ten NTs (all included in Russia).

The principle according to which a nationality was defined by a language and a territory leads to well-documented anomalies resulting simply from the extension of this bureaucratic logic. Since the Jews were recognised as a nationality, it was decided that their language is Yiddish and a territory was invented for them – Birobijan, in deepest Siberia. Recognising Hebrew as a language of the Jews would involve defining them as a religious group, which was not acceptable in the theory of nationality. As a consequence, the Jews of Bukhara and Azerbaijan, who have a strong identity and speak respectively Persian and Tat, are not recognised as 'Jews' and are obliged to describe themselves as Azeris, Tajiks or Uzbeks.[23]

The Strategic Logic of the Territorial Realignments

But there are anomalies even within the official framework of the theory of nationalities. Among the Muslims, two administrative entities, the ASSR of Daghestan and the AR of Gorno-Badakhshan, existed without there being a corresponding nationality. Daghestan officially contained about 30 ethnic groups; it was a kind of catch-all republic. The real specificity of the Autonomous Region of Gorno-Badakhshan, Ismailism, could not be recognised as such, because it was a religious phenomenon, as was the case with Judaism. But the state also did not recognise the other specificity – the Pamiris – despite the fact that they meet the official criteria of having a language of their own. 'Shughni', the vehicular language, was already recognised as the national language of Gorno-Badakhshan in the 1920s, but it was subsequently 'purged', as were Pamiri cadres in Tajikistan, in 1937. The language followed the political fate of those who spoke it. The 'Pamiri' nationality was not taken into account in censuses (even though they numbered between 200,000 and 400,000). They were not mentioned as such in the Soviet atlas of Tajikistan published in 1968, although they had been several years previously (in 1964, in an ethnic map of peoples of the world, destined for more general use). From 1937 onwards, the Pamiris were obliged to describe themselves as Tajiks, but their administrative entity was not abolished. The reason for this was that the three other border zones of Pamir (China, Pakistan and Afghanistan) were also peopled with Ismailis, and a showcase of good Soviet Ismailis could be useful. Here the principal motive was strategic.

The true logic of administrative realignment was not in its proclaimed intentions. It was strategic and political.

The first purpose, apart from the determination to curb Russian nationalism, was to block the possibility of pan-Islamic and pan-Turkic movements developing. This meant differentiating individual ethnic groups from each other and rooting them within the framework of a nation-state, following the same logic of ethnicisation which was in operation in the late tsarist period. But this general principle does not explain all the concrete choices which were made. These were geared to a variety of strategic and political considerations which were liable to alter through time.

In 1919, the urgent question was how to break the Tatars' pretensions to being the vanguard of Muslim identity within the empire: the first autonomous republic to be created in that year was that of the Bashkirs, who were linguistically very close to Tatars and still used Tatar as a written language. One year later saw the creation of the Republic of Tatars and the Chuvash, Udmot and Mari Autonomous Regions, which completely encircled the Tatars and thus downgraded them from élite status to that of one small people among others. In order to make the Bashkirs a nationality in the full sense, a literary language was fabricated for them. In Central Asia it was the idea of Turkestan which Moscow wanted to eradicate.[24] Therefore, specific nationalities were developed among the Turcophone populations, accentuating existing linguistic differences.

However, there was another strategic consideration underlying partition: the trans-frontier factor. Nationalities were created as a function of the principle of the dual bridgehead,[25] the idea being to favour ethnic groups which might serve as a bridgehead to enable the USSR to extend beyond its frontiers and, inversely, to break up those which might function as bridgeheads for another power. The potential adversaries were Turkey in the Caucasus, and Iran in relation to Azerbaijan and Tajikistan. The Soviets favoured ethnic groups which were in a minority situation on the other side of their borders, all the more so since the establishment of the nation-state model of Atatürk in Turkey and the Shah in Iran led to resentment among those who linguistically fell outside the official state language. So the Soviets were to favour Azeri, Turkmen, Kurdish and Laz identities to the detriment of Persian or Turkish ones. Since there were no Azeri, Turkmen or Uzbek states outside the USSR, the development of these national identities would inevitably suit Moscow's interests. On the other hand, there could be no question of developing a 'Persian' identity which might be fostered by a rising Iran. Thus the Tajiks were broken up in 1924, to the benefit of the Uzbeks. As for the Azeris, they were favoured by being given priority over the Armenians (Nagorno-Karabakh, with its majority Armenian population, was given only the status of an autonomous region, whereas Nakhichevan, peopled by Azeris, was a republic).

But the international context can change. In 1928, the overthrow of Afghanistan's King Amanullah briefly brought Bacha-i Saqqao, a Tajik, to power in Kabul. The NKVD, precursor of the KGB, pushed for the Tajik card to be played, contrary to the inclinations of the Ministry of Foreign Affairs, which was pro-Pashtun.[26] It was probably this event which contributed to the promotion of Tajikistan to the status of soviet republic in 1929. This card was played in relation to Afghanistan, and not Iran; it remained an open option right up till the withdrawal of Soviet troops from Afghanistan in 1989, which accounts for the hesitancy over the linguistic status of Afghan Persian, as noted above. A similar logic came into play with the creation of the Autonomous Republic of Gorno-Badakhshan; after the purge of the Pamiri cadres in 1937, one might have expected this autonomous region to have disappeared, but the presence of a sizeable Ismaili population on Pamir's four frontiers (Afghanistan, British India, China and the USSR) must have convinced Moscow to keep an Ismaili card in reserve; and, as it turned out, this proved useful on the occasion of the invasion of Afghanistan.

Soviet theoreticians still had a job to do: to explain in 'scientific' terms how it was that between 1924 and 1929 the Tajiks had suddenly acquired characteristics which enabled them to make the transition from the status of a 'feudal society' to that of 'nation', which presupposed entry into the capitalist sphere (which would have had to have taken place during the five years of Sovietisation). We have already looked at the scientists' efforts in this field.[27] Most of the time, changes of status were announced simply by the publication of decrees from the various soviets concerned.

The principle of the dual bridgehead explains why some groups were punished and others promoted: the Meskhetians, who were Turcophone Sunnis, were deported in 1944 because they were thought to favour Turkey; the Taleshis and the Tats were merged with the Azeris because they were suspected of being too Persian. On the other hand, the several tens of thousands of Kurds living (some of them as refugees) in the USSR were treated favourably (with newspapers, schools and radio stations) because they were a card in a potential power-play with Turkey and Iran. In the same way, the several hundred Lazes living along the Black Sea coast on the border with Turkey found themselves being furnished with a literary language.

The Uzbeks were relatively favoured: they were given Samarkand, a Tajik city, and Khiva, which had a sizeable Uzbek population but had formerly been the capital of an emirate which ruled over a majority Turkmen population. They were not given Osh, despite its Uzbek population, which was given to Kyrgyzia. This latter case shows how elements of weakness and friction are always built in, even within favoured republics.

Frontiers and Minorities

Partition also serves one final principle: it ensures that none of the new republics is really viable on its own, and thus capable of independence. Here the elements of fragility relate to frontiers, minorities and enclaves.

The frontiers of the various countries of Central Asia have no rationality, whether geographic, economic or ethnic. The valley of the Syr Darya begins in Kyrgyzstan in a district populated basically by Uzbeks (Osh), and then passes through to Uzbekistan in the Ferghana. Then it passes through Tajikistan (Khojent), returns to Uzbekistan, and ends up in Kazakhstan. The direct road linking Tashkent, the capital of Uzbekistan, to the Uzbek province of Ferghana thus has to pass through Tajikistan (Khojent); there is another route which does not involve leaving Uzbekistan, but it involves crossing a mountain pass and is far more difficult. Similarly, the viable all-weather roads that link Dushanbe, capital of Tajikistan, to Khojent and Khorog (the capital of Gorno-Badakhshan) pass respectively through Uzbekistan and Kyrgyzstan, while the direct roads, in Tajik territory, are closed by snow between October and May. The south and north of Kyrgyzstan are also cut off in winter. When one travels from Dushanbe to Tashkent in summer, taking the Ura-Teppe route, one has to cross the border between the two countries twice.

These anomalous frontiers cannot even be argued to reflect ethnic spaces. The ethnic groups were so extensively intermingled that no frontier could ever have been entirely rational. But even in this area the Soviets amused themselves by making things more complicated. The town of Chimkent, close to Uzbekistan, is majority Uzbek. However it was attached to Kazakhstan, in the same way that the town of Osh was attached to Kyrgyzstan. The Tajik city of Samarkand remained in Uzbekistan, even though it is less than 70 kilometres from the Tajik border. And when you cross this border, going from Samarkand, the population of Tajikistan is Uzbek right through to the town of Penjikent. Why was the frontier not fixed higher up? An ethnic inversion of this kind is also to be found in the south: the district of Sukhan-Darya in Uzbekistan is majority Tajik-speaking, while the district of Tajikistan which faces it, Hissar, has a large percentage of Uzbek-speakers. Was it a Machiavellian calculation in order to make independence impossible, or bureaucratic incompetence, or the power interests of local factions at work? The real history of the writing of these borders is still to be written.

★   ★   ★

The artificiality of both states and borders becomes a machine for creating ethnic minorities. These minorities come under various different headings. On the one hand there are the 'Europeans' (Russian-speakers from the north, including Slavs, Armenians, Ashkenazi Jews and Tatars) who, up until independence, considered themselves representatives of a higher political entity, the USSR, and in no sense saw themselves as minorities – although that was what they were shortly about to become. One sub-category consists of Germans and Koreans, whose status is curiously similar: both are present in considerable numbers (1.9 million for the former, and 400,000 for the latter). They have not become assimilated with the 'Russians' and preserve their own identities and their own economic niches (specialist *kolkhoz* for both, and construction technician work for the Germans). They never enter into competition with local ethnic groups, whether over land, employment or political power (which they carefullly avoid). They are therefore accepted and respected.[28] In almost all cases conflicts in Central Asia involve Muslim groups fighting among themselves. There are no conflicts between religious communities (Christians against Muslims, for instance). A religious reading of ethnic conflict in Asia Minor and the Caucasus would be totally mistaken, because the alignments have nothing to do with religion. The Russians may support the Christian Armenians against the Muslim Azeris, but they also support the Muslim Abkhaz against the Orthodox Christian Georgians, while the Armenians receive aid from the Iranians, and relations between Azeris and the Israelis are close. The only location of potential conflict between 'Russian-speaking' populations and Muslims today's in Kazakhstan.

The second category is that of people who were left out of the overall division into nations: the groups which have no republics, whether soviet or autonomous, like the people who were punished and sent into exile, Tatars from the Crimea, Meskhetians, Chechens (from 1944 to 1956), who were to establish themselves in specific and lucrative economic niches, thereby exposing themselves to the rancour of the Muslim 'majorities' (for example, the Ferghana riots in the spring of 1989). But in this second category one also finds indigenous groups that have been ignored by censuses and forced by statistics and the logic of internal passports to merge with a recognised ethnic group (Yaghnobis and Pamiris, for instance, who were recognised in the census of 1926, but who disappeared from that of 1937, assimilated with Tajiks). Finally, one finds non-Muslim (or only superficially Muslim) groups that have always lived with a minority status (the Jews of Bukhara, and the Gypsies, or 'Joggi'). This second category plays no political role: the most recent arrivals for the most part had to flee after independence (Crimea Tatars and Meskhetians); the Jews of Bukhara and Samarkand left for Israel or New York, for reasons which were principally economic (notably in the 1970s, when they benefited from the Jackson Amendment, which gave them the right to emigrate).

Finally, there is a third category, covering titular nationalities living outside the territory of their eponymous republics (Tajiks in Uzbekistan and Uzbeks in Kyrgyzstan, for instance). Leaving aside Kazakhstan, this has been the most important breeding-ground for potential conflicts. This category really only involves Uzbeks and Tajiks. One does find Kyrgyz in Tajikistan (in Isfara district, and northeast of Gorno-Badakhshan), but Uzbekistan has ethnic Uzbeks living on the other side of each of its five frontiers: Osh in Kyrgyzstan, Tashauz and Charju in Turkmenistan, Chimkent and Jambul in Kazakhstan, Hissar and Khojent in Tajikistan, and finally Kunduz and Mazar-i Sharif in Afghanistan. When one realises that the main Tajik minorities are to be found in Uzbekistan, the question of Muslim ethnic minorities in Central Asia relates mainly to Uzbekistan's relations with its neighbours, particularly Tajikistan.

Uzbekistan contains a number of Tajiks, ranging from 4 to 10 percent of its population, depending on which sources you take. They are divided into two fairly different groups: the Tajiks of Samarkand and Bukhara, and those of the foothills. These latter, about whom not much has been written, often speak highly Uzbekised dialects, but they have schools in the areas where they are in a majority; they live in the valleys which run down into the plains of Uzbekistan, and thus have little lateral communication between them. From west to east, going clockwise from Tashkent, one has the Tajiks of Borjmollah, then in the Ferghana those of Chadak, Chust, Kasansoy, Marhamat (Andijan), Sukh and Rishtan; then, after Tajikistan, Sukhan-Darya. These Tajiks have almost no solidarity links with the Tajiks of Samarkand and Tajikistan.

A similar pattern is found in Azerbaijan. Leaving aside the question of Karabakh, one finds in the north of the country a sizeable Lezghin minority backing onto Daghestan, where they are one of the largest groups after the Avars.

One final characteristic of Central Asia is the presence of enclaves, such as Nagorno-Karabakh, which are completely at odds in ethnic terms. For instance, the district of Sukh is attached to Uzbekistan, enclaved within Kyrgyzstan, but with a population that is 95 percent Tajik, 5 percent Kyrgyz, and with not one single Uzbek.

★   ★   ★

The list of nationalities is subject to a constant process of emendation. Sometimes the changes involve just the names: in 1925 the 'Kyrgyz' were renamed Kazakhs, and Kara-Kyrgyz became 'Kyrgyz', to bring their name into line with local usage. Some nationalities, such as the Karluks, disappeared. In the census of 1926, the Qipchaks of Ferghana, politically linked to the Uzbeks but with a dialect closer to Kazakh, were classified in the census lists as a 'nationality'. In 1937, they were classed as 'Uzbeks', and the term 'Qipchak' disappeared from official lists;[29] however, the term is still used locally as the name of a *qawm*. In the same way, the 'Turki' – in other words the descendants of the Turcophone populations who settled in Central Asia before the time of the Uzbeks – were classified first as a nationality as such, and then as Uzbeks. The Yaghnobis of the Upper Zarfshan Valley (Tajikistan), who speak an East Iranian language deriving directly from Sogdian, were classified as a nation up until 1926, but then disappeared from the lists to become 'Tajiks', and were finally deported to the plains of North Tajikistan in 1970 (this was the last mass deportation of the Soviet era). In Azerbaijan two populations speaking Iranian languages, the Talesh and the Tats (the latter including a Jewish group) were redefined as Azeris back in the 1920s.

This assimilation to the dominant ethnic group also applies to recognised nationalities. The Tajiks of Uzbekistan were the object of a discreet but persistent policy of Uzbekisation. This was launched by F. Khojayev in 1924 and was based on a notion employed in Russification: since the Uzbeks were at a more advanced stage of development (they were already officially a nation in 1924, whereas Tajikistan was only an autonomous republic), it was seen as progressive to declare oneself an Uzbek when one was Tajik (a similar argument applied in Azerbaijan)[30]. During the 1970s and 1980s the Samarkand Tajiks complained that they were constantly being required to refer to themselves as Uzbeks.

The intention of these rearrangements is clear: they were an attempt to homogenise the republics and to contribute to the merging of small groups into the dominant ethnic group.

Other groups, on the other hand, were promoted to the status of nationality: the Karakalpaks, settled in the area southeast of the Aral Sea, spoke a Kazakh dialect, but they lived under the suzerainty of Bukhara. Logically, they ought to have been assimilated with the Kazakhs, particularly because, then as now, they never developed any hint of national spirit. However, they were elevated to the status of having an autonomous republic, with its own 'literary' language, and were finally attached to Uzbekistan, after having first been attached to Russia. What was the aim of the operation? One might conjecture that it was an attempt at divide-and-rule in order to weaken the Kazakhs, of whom Moscow was particularly suspicious; or a way of rewarding the Uzbeks for their loyalty; and also perhaps to compensate them for the fact of Tajikistan's elevation to the status of soviet republic.

Acceptance of the Division Into Nations

While it is certainly the case that the territorial realignments under Stalin were arbitrary, were they also entirely artificial, or did they merely systematise in something of a caricature fashion tendencies that were already at work? Notions of Uzbeks, Tajiks, Turkmens, Kazakhs and Kyrgyz certainly existed at the time. But they were far from covering the whole field of possible identities, as we saw in the first part of this book. Many did not recognise themselves in the official list of nationalities offered by the authorities, and had difficulty in choosing. *Mushtum*, a pro-reform satirical newspaper published in Soviet Turkestan, printed a cartoon to illustrate this confusion. It showed a Kazakh signing up as a Tajik, and vice versa.[31] The concept of 'Uzbek' in 1924 was not that of a nationality conscious of itself: there was no Uzbek 'national movement', and what predominated were localist, tribal and infra-ethnic identities.[32] The borders between these identities were vague, in particular between Uzbeks and Tajiks, as we have seen (this remains true to the present day). Finally, there was no symmetry between the 'nationalities'. A Turkmen is first and foremost a Tekke or a Jomud, and there has never been any great desire for the creation of a Turkmen state. Azerbaijan's leading writer, Mirza Fath Ali Akhunzade (1812–78), who wrote his plays in the vernacular and campaigned for a simplified and adapted Arab alphabet, used to refer to himself as a Persian.[33] He called the language that he used 'Turki' rather than Azeri. The notion of 'Azeris', or rather Azerbaijanis, emerged as a result of the brief period of independence in 1919–20. The Karakalpaks had absolutely no national pretensions. The Kazakhs, on the other hand, despite being divided into tribes, had a sense of collective belonging that had been forged through their resistance to Russian settlement and their attempts to create a political party (Alash Orda) in the early part of the century.

However, the principle of national division found support among many Jadid intellectuals, who only contested the mode of its implementation, to the benefit of neighbouring nationalities. The debate (should one privilege a greater Turkestan, a new Bukharia, or the concept of Uzbekistan?) was limited to intellectuals and hardly affected the masses, who were attached to their regional and infra-ethnic identities.

On the one hand, as we have seen, the process of 'ethnicisation' of various Muslim groups was already under way during the tsarist period. On the other hand, the 1920s saw the creation of nation-states in place of empires in Turkey, Iran and Afghanistan. In 1924, the last supporters of a Greater Turkestan (Sultan Galiev and Turar Ryskulov) lost the battle. The debate was then focussed between those who approved of the creation of Uzbekistan and those who wanted the creation of a Greater Bukharia. But both effectively operated within the same perspective: a principally Turcophone state, with an aim of becoming hegemonic in Central Asia. One of the first actions of the People's Republic of Bukharia, under Jadid leadership, was to impose Uzbek as the official language in place of Persian.

When the decision was taken to create national states, the Jadids of Bukhara were endlessly trying to turn Soviet Uzbekistan into a Greater Bukharia. Fayzullah Khojayev (born in Bukhara in 1898) played an important role in this, in his position as president of the Bukhara Sovnarkom (1920–24) and later as president of the Executive Comittee of Sovnarkom (the Soviet of People's Commissars) of the SSR of Uzbekistan (up until 1937). The reaction of the 'Tajik' intellectuals was interesting: many, such as Abdurrauf Fitrat and Biktâsh, defended this 'Turkish' project, as if they were actually incapable of conceiving their 'Tajik' identity in terms of nation.[34] Even Sadruddin Ayni, the founder of 'modern Tajik literature', was never to leave his city of Bukhara to go and live in Tajikistan. The only campaigning for the promotion of Tajikistan to the status of Soviet Republic was among minor intellectuals such as Abdullah Muhiddinov, a Bukhara Tajik who was president of the first Tajikistan Sovnarkom from 1924 to 1929 (he disappeared in 1933). This remained a very live polemic up until 1929, and rumbled on in the background right through the Soviet era. The proponents of Tajikistan were recruited from among the new intelligentsia, emerging from the Soviet system. However, this struggle was conducted in Samarkand, via the magazines *Dânesh wa Amuzegâr* and *Âvâz-i Tajik-e kambaghal*, and it had no effect on the main peoples concerned – those who lived in the territory of the Autonomous Republic of Tajikistan. This Tajik nationalist intellectual élite was something completely new, as if the unavoidability of the division into nationalities was forcing universalist intellectuals to defend a territory and an administrative status in order to preserve their language and culture. Thus the very principle of territorial division into nationalities was very quickly taken on board by intellectuals. Stalin's great victory was to have brought the intellectuals of Central Asia to a position of defending their language and their 'nation' against their neighbours, and not against Moscow, whom they then called upon to assist in the mediation of conflicts.

There was no popular resistance to partition because there were no alternative identitities operating at an identical level, in other words national. Partition left infra-ethnic solidarities intact, and in a rural society these were the basic building blocks of identity. What the great national division did destroy was the pan-Islamist vision, which, as the *basmachi* movement had shown in negative form, had been the province of intellectuals and city-dwellers.

The logic of the definition of nationalities was above all political, but for all its opportunism it was nevertheless based on a theoretical and 'scientific' conception of ethnic group. This conception was to outlive the purely political usage that had been made of it. It filtered through to the heart of ethnographic teaching, and one was to find it emerging in the policies of the independent states. Thus we need to look at this before going on to look at the histories of the individual republics.

Language Policy

The invention of national identities was by no means a phenomenon restricted to the USSR. It was the major characteristic of the nineteenth century in both Europe and Latin America. It also has to be seen in a regional context: after 1920, in Turkey, Iran and, to a lesser extent, Afghanisation, the heads of those countries pushed through a redefinition of the relationship between the citizen and the state (an end to the status of *dhimmi*, or non-Muslim, the emancipation of women, and attacks on traditional solidarities), and forged a nationalist identity model which broke with the logic of empires (the importation of a juridical system, language reform, rewriting of history and an emphasis on the pre-Islamic past). In each of these countries, compulsory schooling provided the main channel for the popularisation of this model and for a homogenisation of society. There were particular attacks on anything that could be seen as a universalist Muslim cultural model (this meant a shift from the Arabic alphabet to the Latin alphabet, campaigns against traditional clothing and the veil, the imposition of new forms of names etc). One might even say that in some ways reform was less radical in the USSR than in Turkey. For instance there was no attempt to secularise people's names: people continued calling their children Muhiddin (he who revives religion) and Islam (the name of the present Uzbek president), and the use of the suffix '-ov' had also become customary among the educated classes during the tsarist period.

What was new in the Soviet method was that it was imposed by a leadership that was 'European' and external, and that it was not conceived within a continuity of a project of national independence, as in Latin America, Serbia and Turkey. The desire to enact social engineering, to manufacture not only a national identity but also a new society, was another specific characteristic. By means of collectivisation, purges and the imposition of an ideological model, an attempt was being made to redefine society. The idea of nation was created above all by a set of administrative measures which had the effect of creating a reality.

The idea of nation was first and foremost a political creation, the result of the territorial administrative realignments of 1924, subsequently revised in 1929 and 1936. This administrative product (frontiers, institutions, laws etc) subsequently saw itself enhanced by the addition of cultural expressions (language and literature), by scientific formulations (history, ethnography and archaeology) and finally by a sociological reality (élites, social differentiation and competition within the new republics).

The social sciences were not simply invoked in order to justify policy, nor were they simply influenced by the personal ideological choices of the scientists (as in the history of France in the nineteenth century); they had an explicit role in this process of manufacture. Soviet linguistics manufactured languages to meet the requirements of political directives. The Soviet ethnographer was charged with manufacturing rites in order better to anchor Sovietism in the social reality which he was studying.[35] The work of scientific observation was only a first step: the linguists went out and identified a series of dialects, while ethnographers made inventories of rituals and customs. These taxonomic labours, which were often of high quality, were then used as materials in order to construct a new language or new rites. Historical studies were obviously more problematical: political censorship intervened here even in the process of seeking sources and facts. Historical research was thus limited and tended to concern itself with the relatively distant past.

★   ★   ★

Officially, the aim of language policy was to enable each 'nationality' to use its spoken language, and to create from it a written language. The problem was that there was no clear delineation between dialects belonging to the same family (Turkish or Persian). For both Turkish and Persian, the geographical space of Central Asia is actually a continuum in which there is seldom a clear-cut linguistic border separating two dialects, for example Iranian Persian from Central Asian Tajik. This dialectisation means that one has always to select a particular vehicular language, and that it should correspond either to a local usage (the Tatar of Kazan) or to a major cultural language (Persian or Chaghatay). Since the Soviet system had decided that a nation was defined by the existence of a language, a language thus had to be selected each time it was decided that there should be a nation. But the problems of the choice of criteria enabling one to fix this language were considerable. A precise condition had to be fulfilled: it had to accentuate the dialect differences between the populations of a single linguistic area. The nation was constructed on the basis of difference.

The most notorious case is the separation engineered between 'Tajik' and Persian. The Tajiks used literary Persian as their written language – and still today there is perfect comprehensibility between the literary languages current in Iran, Afghanistan and Tajikistan. Needless to say, in their daily lives the Persian-speakers of Central Asia use dialects which vary considerably: those of Ferghana are very Uzbekised, not only in their vocabulary which contains a higher proportion of Turkish words than one finds in Iran (such as *tinj*, 'peace'), but also as regards identifiable influences on grammar (postposition instead of preposition, as in *shahr-be* instead of *be shahr*, 'towards the city'). As for the pronunciation, it is very close to that of classical Persian, which is very different from Iranian Persian (Tajik maintains the distinction between the long 'é' and the long 'i', between 'q' and 'gh' etc). The relationship between Iranian and Tajik Persian is akin to the relationship between Parisian French and Québecois. Russian linguists were required to formalise and fix differences and to invent a 'modern literary Tajik language' known as 'Tâjik'. Instead of taking as their standard one of the existing Tajik dialects, an artificial language was manufactured combining characteristics from different regions: they kept the phonological system of Old Persian, but adopted grammatical variations which heightened the difference with Iran. For example, Persian has a subjunctive prefix 'be-', which does not exist in some Tajik dialects, although it is considered the norm in literary language: this prefix disappears in 'modern literary Tajik'.

Since it is obviously not possible to deny that the two languages are related, it was proposed that the two had diverged in the sixteenth century,[36] which made it possible to appropriate classical Persian literature, from Rudaki to Sa'adi, under the rubric of 'Farsi-Tajik'. It was claimed that all the Persian-speaking writers born between Tus and Dushanbe in Greater Khorasan were specifically Tajik. Rudaki, the first poet of modern classical Persian (d. 940) thus became the founder of Tajik literature. The problem was that he was also the founder of Persian literature as a whole. As a result of this operation, all the Persian-speakers of Central Asia, past or present, thus found themselves defined as members of a 'Tajik ethnic group'.

The agents of this 'Tajikisation' were rarely Tajiks. Iranian communists in exile (Monafzade, Deylami and Lahuti) played a major role in Latinisation of the alphabet, and Abbas Aliev, head of the education comissariat in Tajikistan from 1924 to 1927, seems not to have been a true Tajik (born in Bukhara, he died at Alma-Ata and had a Shiite name, which made him presumably an 'Irani'). The case of Sadruddin Ayni (1878–1954) was particularly instructive: he was an authentic Persian writer who defended the creation of literary Tajik, of which he was considered the founder, but when he wrote, he always used the Arabo-Persian alphabet.

Uzbek too was the subject of manipulations. In the name of ethnic authenticity, an initial attempt was made in the Ferghana to work on an Uzbek language close to Qipchak, in other words to the linguistic group to which Kazakh and Tatar belong. Then, in 1929, at the time of the first change of alphabet, the linguistic experts (a profession almost as dangerous under Stalin as that of poet) received orders to take as their basic language the more Iranianised model, that of Tashkent, which is in fact the descendant of Chaghatay. The reason was that this model was the most distanced both from Qipchak and from the Oghuz spoken in Turkmenistan and Turkey. This was the only dialect to have lost vowel harmonisation (a basic characteristic of Turkic languages in which the first syllable of a word determines the timbre of the others). This explains why today a number of different dialects are spoken under the name of Uzbek, closer to Turkmen in Khwarezm and to Kazakh in Ferghana.

*   *   *

The invention of languages goes hand in hand with changes in alphabets. Here the trajectory was particularly chaotic. The changes went from a reformed Arabic alphabet (1923–29), still to be found today in Chinese Sinkiang, to Latin (1929–40), then to Cyrillic (1940), and finally, today, back to Latin (Azerbaijan, Turkmenistan and Uzbekistan), or to Arabic-Persian (Tajikistan). At the time of the final change to Cyrillic, the Soviet linguists carefully avoided the common alphabet for Turkic languages that had been perfected by the Academy of Sciences a century previously, and one finds a similar avoidance after independence, at the time of the return to the Latin alphabet.

With the new alphabet, 'small dialect differences' become fixed, in the sense that the Arabic alphabet does not represent the short vowels (so that the word 'mlt' may be pronounced variously as 'millet', 'millat' or 'mellat'), and it consolidated the differences that were introduced in ways that were often artificial. For example, Tajik and Uzbek share a sizeable common vocabulary (probably about 60 percent of Uzbek words come from the Persian). The words held in common are pronounced identically in many different regions. Now the linguists seek to introduce artificial differences of transcription and alphabet. Both Tajik and Uzbek have in common the sound 'j'; in the former case it is transcribed with the Russian character 'tch' augmented with a cedilla; in the second it is written with the Russian character 'zh' (with the risk of a confusion between the sounds 'zh' and 'j'). As a result, the word *tâjik* comes to be written differently in the two languages. A softening diacritical was introduced into Tajik spelling in words of Persian origin, such as *dar'yâ* ('river' or 'sea'), which disappears in the Uzbek writing of the same word (which, needless to say, has exactly the same pronunciation and meaning). One could show how this game is played in all the alphabets invented in this period.

The change of alphabets also had another function: it prevented new generations having access to the writings of previous generations. The alphabet reform in Turkey had the same effect, but there publishers were free to retranscribe Ottoman works into the Latin alphabet; in the USSR, on the other hand, the absolute control exercised by the censors over any printed production meant that younger generations could only read what they were permitted to read (in Tajik, the classical works of Firdawsi and Sa'adi, but not Iranian authors of the nineteenth century). In particular, the large number of religious books, which were to be found everywhere in the countryside, could no longer be read without a special education that had to be undertaken clandestinely. Thus by the simple act of permitting or refusing transcription it became possible to select from the works of the past those which would be permitted to be seen as precursors or foundations of the new national literatures. Each culture was to see itself assigned a founding ancestor, in general a poet, which reduced the problems of content: Makhtum Quli for the Turkmens, Ali Shir Nava'i for the Uzbeks and Rudaki for the Tajiks.

Change of alphabet went alongside mass literacy campaigns. Not only did school students learn solely the new language, but it is only through that language that they have access to knowledge, to writing and to social promotion. Only the old would say that they spoke Turki. Young people know only the name of Uzbek to describe the language which is taught them at school. However there was relatively little intellectual production in local languages: this consisted of the small inheritance from the past which was agreed, translations of Russian works, a literature that was 'national' but Soviet, and various didactic works (for example an *Ateistik entsiklopedik loghat*, an atheist encyclopaedic dictionary written in Uzbek and published in 1985). The scarcity of publications in local languages is striking, particularly in Tajik. Contrary to other projects of inventing languages, the new Soviet languages were not designed to be the chosen channel for the distribution of new intellectual or cultural models.[37] National identity is established on the basis of a weak content, on a code, and not on the reconstruction or promotion of a real culture. The real content is Soviet literature or Russian culture; national culture needs to be kept in a position of inferiority, and it should not be capable of meeting the demand for culture, so that those seeking to educate themselves have to pass through Russian culture.

The Cyrillic alphabet is also a channel of Russification. While signs were invented for sounds that were properly 'Turkic' ('gh', 'q') it was required that the Russian alphabet be taken on board wholesale, including the letters for the sounds which are solely Russian ('ts', 'shch'), so that Russian borrowings were written according to the Russian orthography and never retranscribed according to the local pronunciation. The penetration of Russian words was encouraged in everything to do with ideology, administration (*vilayat* becomes *oblast* in the local languages from the 1930s), science, and even technology (*poyezd*, 'train', *samoliot*, 'aircraft'). Even without being forced, Russian words penetrated into everyday life in the same way as French words did in Turkey and Iran, and English words in Afghanistan.

Finally, as regards divisions at the administrative level, there was hardly any longer any multi-lingualism between 'Muslim' languages. People were bilingual in the sense of having their local language plus Russian, except in local situations of ethnic mixing, as with the Tajiks in Uzbekistan. But here one finds a constant of multi-lingualism: it always functioned in a hierarchised manner. Not everybody needed to speak all languages: a Tajik from Ferghana speaks Uzbek, but the reverse was no longer true. The dominant groups (not only demographically but also politically) had no need to learn the languages of the dominated. This asymmetry in multi-lingualism leads to a marginalisation of the languages of the dominated.

SOCIAL AND DEMOGRAPHIC EVOLUTION IN THE SOVIET PERIOD

To what extent did Sovietisation lead to major changes in Central Asian society? The project of social engineering that the Soviets were so keen to impose clearly had its limits.[38] The continuation of traditional behaviours was obvious throughout (the importance of family and network links, the subordinate social role of women, demographic structures etc). But this was not simply the leftovers from the past. The Soviet period obviously saw a major reordering of society, as in any revolution. Traditional society came under attack at various levels. The first was pure and simple destruction – by war, famine, purges, the arrests of kulaks and beys, the closure of mosques, and finally by collectivisation. The second was the use of the law against traditional Islamic customs such as veiling and polygamy. The third was the embedding of a new ideology by means of schooling and propaganda. Soviet élites were rarely drawn from within the old élites (although there were exceptions to this, particularly among religious families, in Azerbaijan for example, or among the *ashraf* of Leninabad in Tajikistan).[39]

I shall now look at the attempted transformations of society and demographic developments during the Soviet epoch, in order to identify the sense in which one can speak of a perpetuation of traditional society.

Laws Against Traditional Customs: The Emancipation of Women

In 1927 and 1928, the Soviets launched a direct attack on traditional customs, concentrating on the status of women, which was seen as the keystone of a closed family system which operated as a screen to block the ideological and cultural influence of the Russian model.

Changes were made in the system of lawcourts (September 1927) and the penal code (April 1928). *Sharia* courts were banned. The new code, initially promulgated in Russia, was part of the fight against 'Oriental' societies in the Soviet Union. It punished 'crimes constituting survivals from the past',[40] and targeted specifically Muslim practices: dowry (*kalym*), child marriage, forced marriage, polygamy etc. A major campaign, known as the 'assault' (*hujum*), was launched for the emancipation of women. It focussed principally on Uzbekistan. On 8 March 1927, public unveiling ceremonies were held throughout the republic. Cadres were required to attend and to bring their wives (some brought substitute women). Thus far, the USSR was following Kemalist Turkey, which had implemented forced unveiling between 1925 and 1927. As in the case of alphabet reform, socialism was not the first in the field.

More radically, the Soviets made efforts to get women into the labour market and into the structures of the party. It was hoped that this would modify family forms of behaviour, by bringing women out of *purdah* ('seclusion') and by giving them an income. It was also hoped that women cadres would be able to impose a new model of modern womanhood and end the hegemony of male cadres, who were still seeking to preserve a special place within Soviet society. Here women played a role of 'substitute proletariat', in the absence of a proper proletariat.

Female candidates were thus favoured throughout the 1930s. In the 1950s, a new offensive enabled several hundred young Tajik and Uzbek women to go to study in Moscow and Leningrad, and to return afterwards as cadres within regional governing structures.

What was the impact of this policy? As always, Asia put up a quiet resistance. Moscow was not opposed, but people quietly undid what had been done, and waited for the campaign of the moment to be replaced by another (campaigns on virgin lands, or the bettering of plan targets).

The statistics show the limits of the operation. While there was certainly an increase in the number of women in the parties in the republics, the increase was illusory. The percentage of women was often inversely proportional to the percentage of Muslims, which indicates that the more indigenous people made their way up through the apparatus, the fewer women there were, or at least Muslim women. In Tajikistan, the percentage of women in the party rose from 9 percent to 15 percent between 1933 and 1938; at the same time the number of Muslims (Tajiks and Uzbeks) of both sexes fell from 75 percent to 58 percent. One can conclude from this that many of the women were non-Muslims. The greatest percentage of women in the party was reached between 1942 and 1945, when it went from 20 percent to 28 percent, but it had fallen back to 19 percent by 1947 – in other words when the men came back from war. In Dushanbe in 1944, only 10 percent of women in the Communist Party were Muslims, less than the percentage of Muslims living in the town.[41] In Kazakhstan, women made up one third of members of the Communist Party in 1944, but then this figure fell to 20 percent, and stayed there.[42] In Uzbekistan, figures for the Communist Party registered 30 percent women in 1945, 13 percent in 1962 and 20 percent in 1970. Indigenisation took place at the expense of feminisation. This rule was confirmed after independence: ethnic Uzbeks in Parliament went from 77 percent in 1990 to 86 percent in the Parliament of 1994, and over the same period the presence of women fell from 9 percent to 6 percent.

The results of women's access to the labour market were more spectacular, but the statistics show that they still occupy positions inferior to those of Muslim men and European women.[43] All it takes is a walk through a *kolkhoz* to see that the work groups in the fields are made up mainly of women. It is also noticeable that girls leave school much earlier (at 14 years old) in the rural districts of Ferghana (personal observation, 1993).

The statistics dealing with marriage show that traditional practices are being maintained. In Uzbekistan, a demographic survey based on the 1989 census, under the auspices of INED, shows that more than 20 percent of married women were married to a cousin or a close relation. Curiously, the city of Tashkent seems not to have broken with the traditional form of the couple, which shows that the town-country split does not necessarily apply there. Marriages take place mainly within the same nationality (ranging between 94 percent and 98 percent, depending on sex and republic); only Russian women have a significant percentage marrying outside their nationality (73 percent of married Russian women living in Uzbekistan in 1988 were homogams), and the figures suggest a societal reticence to marriages between 'Muslim' women and European men.[44]

The marriage age is also younger than in the rest of the USSR, except among the Kazakhs: for the generation of women born between 1952 and 1957, 44.8 percent of Tajik women married before the age of 20, 35.3 percent of Uzbeks and 19.3 percent of Kazakhs, compared with 30.2 percent of Russian women. However, the figures show that early marriage is becoming less common everywhere, having peaked with the generation born between 1937 and 1942. Kazakh women of the present generation marry even later than Russian women (while the proportion for the generation of 1937–42 was 45.5 percent for Kazakh women and 28.5 percent for Russians, this should be compared with 61.2 percent of Tajik women of the same generation marrying before the age of 20).[45]

Certainly, in the new middle classes, women are studying and working in modern sectors (schools and hospitals), and they are more often to be found living in apartments, in other words in smaller families. However, 'traditionalism' remains the order of the day: there is a marked preference for the traditional style of house (hawâli), with a courtyard and an awning, where the family lives, while richer families may have a guestroom, reserved for males and guests. The separation into interior (the women's domain) and the exterior (men's domain) is strong (disheri/içeri in Turkish, and birun/andarun in Persian). Women who are in contact with the public (waitresses in restaurants, floor women in hotels) are for the most part Russian. In the countryside, but also often in cities such as Dushanbe, women wear traditional costume (long dresses worn over trousers) and a headscarf over hair which is not cut.

The Soviet press carried articles about the continued existence of polygamy. The debate on polygamy is making an interesting comeback: in Dushanbe in 1993, at meetings organised by the Union of Women, calls were made for its conditional legalisation (personal observation).

Traditions and Lifestyles

People's unwillingness to adopt the Russian model can be read in other things. All the censuses point to a continued maintenance of 'national' languages. The number of people giving their national language as their mother tongue is considerable, and remains at a high level (between 97 percent and 98 percent for the five Republics between 1959 and 1989), even if it is probable that the Kazakhs were not telling the whole truth (this indicates their attachment to a language which the majority of them speak rather badly). More significant is the fall (between 1979 and 1989) in the number of those who claim to be proficient in Russian: among Uzbeks and Tajiks, these fall from 49.3 percent to 23.8 percent and from 29.6 percent to 27.7 percent respectively. Such a fall among the Uzbeks seems rather unlikely: one should take into account what the person being interviewed may be trying to express, and not necessarily their real level of ability. During the 1970s, it was considered good form to speak Russian; during the 1980s, there was resentment against 'Big Brother'.

The continued existence of traditional lifestyles can also be read in the high rate of private ownership of housing, including in towns (which rules out the rural factor): in 1986 the rate was 40.7 percent in Uzbekistan, 31.6 percent in Tajikistan, and 40.8 percent in Kyrgyzstan, as compared with 16.4 percent in Russia.[46] It is also apparent in the preservation of customs strongly marked by the influence of Islam, even in urban and apparently cultured environments. Muslim rites of passage such as circumcision are respected, and burials and weddings are always accompanied by prayer. These rites are celebrated with big festivals, involving ostentatious expenditure, the *tuy*, to which the *mahalla* is invited. Religious practices are very much alive, albeit in watered-down form (people don't eat pork, but they do drink vodka). Names given to children are massively Muslim, even in the families of Russified cadres. Contrary to the situation in Turkey (and to a lesser extent in the Shah's Iran), there was no serious attempt to replace Muslim names with more Soviet ones. Even among apparatchiks entirely trained and educated in the Russo-Soviet style, there were very few Russian forenames: all the present presidents have Muslim forenames (Islam Karimov, Imamali Rahmanov, Saparmurad Nyazov, Gaydar or Haydar Aliev). The only known exception is the Turkmen minister for foreign affairs, Boris Sheikhmuhamed. This says much about people's attachment to traditional culture.

Traditional clothing continues to be worn by women; men, in both Tajikistan and Uzbekistan, mostly wear the skull-cap (*doppi*), including at the university. Traditional music remains very popular, even if disco music began to make a noisy and ostentatious entry in the 1980s (together with *rai*-style fusions, which were less successful). Classical European culture, which was favoured during the Russian period (an opera house was built in Tashkent, with almost daily performances), extends only to audiences that are either European or very Russified. In everyday contacts one still finds local customs and habits presented as more socially suitable than those of the Russians: hospitality, cooking, the use of carpets and cushions, respect for the elderly, reservations about accepting tobacco among young people etc. Strong views are held on morality and good behaviour, particularly for young people and women.

However, does this mean that there are two societies living separate lives (as in former French Algeria)? Not at all. First, because political equality had been won. Also, there are opportunities for intermingling (work, the party, official ceremonies, the shared life of apartment blocks for the middle classes); people meet and talk, but within the 'European' space. The European, for his or her part, hardly 'orientalises' at all. In short, it is indigenous people who live their lives according to a double code, but without schizophrenia, because there really are two social lives. The élites have a double culture, a double code, and pass from one to the other with no problem.

Demography and Society

Two basic facts characterised the Muslims of Central Asia during the late Soviet period (1959–89): strong demographic growth and the absence of any real rural exodus. The region's towns (in particular its capitals) were established through European immigration, and were to remain European up until 1980.

Tajiks (or people who declare themselves to be Tajiks) hold the record for rising birth rates: 35.7 percent between 1970 and 1979, 45.4 percent between 1979 and 1989. Over these same two periods, Uzbeks, Kyrgyz and Turkmens experienced growth rates of between 31 percent and 35 percent. Such a development threatened the ethnic equilibrium of the USSR, to the detriment of Russians, whose demographic growth for the period 1979–89 was around 5.6 percent, a decline compared with the preceding decade.[47]

However, Central Asia was not really the USSR's Third World. If one compares it with countries of the Third World which enjoyed similar growth rates over the same period (broadly between 1960 and 1980), there are two uncharacteristic features in Central Asia: the absence of emigration to the north, and the absence of rural migration to towns. The 1989 census indicates a low rate of urbanisation: 38 percent in Kyrgyzstan, 57 percent in Kazakhstan, 41 percent in Uzbekistan, 45 percent in Turkmenistan and 32 percent in Tajikistan. In comparison, the population of Russia was 74 percent town–dwelling. Since all the capitals have a majority of 'non-nationals', this means that the majority of nationals live in the countryside, and they are over-populated in relation to the land available.[48] One consequence of this is that the division of labour is very much along ethnic lines, particularly in Transoxiania: the peasants are 'Muslim', while technical professions such as pilots, doctors and engineers are massively European, and the administration is mixed (although with Europeans over-represented in relation to their ethnic presence).

In Tajikistan and Turkmenistan, there was even a reduction of the urban population between 1979 and 1989.[49] This reduction is explained by the departure of Europeans prior to independence. Migration from south to north began at the end of the 1970s,[50] and involved principally Russians, Europeans (Germans and Jews) or marginalised nationalities such as the Tatars. There was no indigenous emigration, despite encouragement to this end in the 1980s. Even after independence, there was nothing to indicate a beginning of this kind of emigration from south to north, such as has been seen in Mexico and the Maghreb.

The consequences of this demographic situation are manifold. For a start, it led to ethnic homogenisation. In all the Muslim republics, the 1959 census indicates that the demographic weight of each ethnic group in its own republic had reached its lowest level in relation to the Russians. However the censuses of 1969, 1979 and 1989 reveal a spectacular demographic advance of the national ethnic group in each republic. The Kazakhs move from 30 percent to 39 percent of the population of their republic between 1959 and 1989; the Uzbeks from 62 percent to 71 percent; the Tajiks from 53 percent to 62 percent; the Turkmens from 65 percent to 71 percent, and the Kyrgyz from 40 percent to 52 percent. This process of homogenisation leaves a category of marginalised peoples: ethnically mixed families, Russians and ethnic groups with no eponymous republic. But it favours ethnic nationalism and makes the republics more politically viable. It also deprives Moscow of one of its traditional cards: the manipulation of minorities. Ethnic homogenisation also has another effect: the great majority of titular ethnic groups live in their own republics. Figures for the 1989 census show that 80.3 percent of Kazakhs lived in Kazakhstan, 88 percent of Kyrgyz in Kyrgyzstan, 93.3 percent of Turkmens in Turkmenistan, 84.6 percent of Uzbeks in Uzbekistan and 75.1 percent of Tajiks in Tajikistan. Even though the frontiers are curiously arranged, there was a broad match between any given ethnic group and its nation-state. This may be principally a product of Soviet reclassifications, but it is a solid and concrete fact.

The second consequence is that the societies of Central Asia are mainly rural, and therefore the mechanics of politics cannot be understood without looking at their roots in the *kolkhoz*.

However, the third consequence is a pressure on land, and growing poverty, which became very apparent during the 1980s. Independence certainly made the pauperisation and land pressure more dramatic, but they were not caused by independence. The poorest countries in the USSR were already the republics of Central Asia, in particular Tajikistan.[51] Basic social provision here had long been inferior to the rest of the USSR: Central Asia was at the bottom of the pile as regards the number of inhabitants per doctor, dispensary and sanatorium.[52] At the same time, though, the region was better provided than neighbouring Afghanistan and Pakistan.

However, the societies of Central Asia have entered a phase of demographic transition, in other words the phase of falling fertility rates. The transition began with the Kazakhs during the 1960s, and has now reached the last group, the Tajiks.[53] But given even more rapidly falling birth rates among Russians, and the departure of Russians from the region, the indigenisation of the Muslim republics had already become irreversible by the 1960s. The place to watch nowadays is Kazakhstan: figures for age of marriage (which comes later for Kazakh than for Russian women) show that Kazakhstan is likely to see a very abrupt demographic transition, which would re-establish demographic equilibrium with the Russians, unless there were to be considerable emigration among the latter.

5

The Recomposition of
Solidarity Groups During
the Soviet Period

One of the paradoxes of the Soviet system was that the project of destroying traditional society and the implementation of 'social engineering' with a view to creating a new society translated, at least in the Muslim republics, into a recomposition of solidarity groups within the framework imposed by this system, and also into the creation of a two-level political culture: on the one hand an appearance of conformity with the social project imposed by the authorities; on the other, a subversion of that project by practices of factionalism and clientism. These latter were exacerbated by the disappearance of most of the protagonists and most of the issues at stake in the preceding society, leaving a state which was at once weak and omnipresent. The political scene was reduced to a few basic issues: land, administrative division and power in the republics.

The apparent traditionalism of the cadres of Central Asia was due not so much to remnants of old cultures as to the adoption by the Soviet system of a tradition of indirect management of solidarity groups. If the new élites tended to function in ways that were traditional, this was because kinship and clan networks were recomposed on the basis of the territorial and administrative structures put in place by the Soviets. This process produced leaders by the same logic as the traditional system: a rather distant state administered solidarity groups by installing a category of leader whose role was to serve as interface between the state and the communities in question. The function of the Communist Party was then to guarantee circulation between the upper and lower reaches of society: a function of control, but also of representation of civil society in the absence of a strong state apparatus in rural areas.

As Massel predicted,[1] the destruction of the traditional élites did not break the structure of the solidarity groups, because these élites did not form a separate 'class' with its own interests. The function of bey, like that of the khan in Afghanistan, was a status constructed as much as inherited. The logic behind a solidarity group's connection to the state was to produce leaders whose power derived from this function of interface, and not from the way in which they are able to use the group as a way of extracting extra reward. Since the Soviets had preserved the solidarity groups within the units of production that emerged from collectivisation, and had imposed the state as the sole body of control, distribution and promotion, while at the same time leaving the countryside under-administered, they automatically produced these leaders – the new beys and khans.

The *kolkhoz* and districts were the places where these Soviet notables had their power base, and where factions and political networks were set up. This was a result of the low level of urbanisation of the Muslim republics, the weakness of the urban élites, and the correlation between the structure of the Communist Party – the only political power – and the administrative structure (soviets at village, district, regional and republic level). Since the independences of 1991, urbanisation and the emergence of a national political scene have gradually led to a further development of this system, already noticeable in the establishment of allegiance networks which are no longer territorially based. But we have to look at the system as it was set up if we want to understand the present political and social set-up.

Two elements are fundamental: the generalised territorialisation brought about by collectivisation and the administrative territorial re-alignment; factionalism within the party, which is an automatic consequence of the fact of a single-party system and which, in the republics of Central Asia, was built on the basis of the geographical origins of apparatchiks.

TERRITORIALISATION AND 'LOCALISM'
Tied to the Land: *Kolkhoz* and Territorialisation

The first effect of collectivisation was to terminate all forms of nomadism and semi-nomadism, and to bind rural communities to the land, while at the same time limiting the possibilities for rural exodus. In the Soviet system, one's social existence was constructed around belonging to a 'collective' (*khwajegi* in Tajik, *khwajalik* in Uzbek, both being translations of the Russian *khoziestvo*), and this obliged the individual to identify with a group (in the countryside this group was the *kolkhoz*). The group acted as a social mediator for the individual: one's administrative existence (internal passport), the availability of basic social services, and the right to housing and travel were conducted through this group. In Central Asia, contrary to the position in the rest of the Near East, the rural exodus was particularly weak, and urbanisation has involved principally European immigrants. As a result, political identity was forged by the rural system. It is thus fairly natural to find the Soviet 'collectives' moulded on the basis of pre-existing solidarity groups.

But was this a simple translation of a traditional order into a new system? At the very local level (neighbourhood or village), one can speak of a translation; this is also true in the zones where there were no displacements of population

(Turkmenistan). However, even in the regions where there were massive population transfers (Tajikistan), it is clear that Sovietism did little to disturb the basic cores (kinship structures, *qawm*, *awlad*, as well as the *mahallas*, the neighbourhoods inhabited by one solidarity grouping). These transfers, whether due to civil war or to the opening up of new land for cotton cultivation, brought about new ethnic intermixing; but since they were collectives, the base groups preserved their structure during the transfer.

Collectivisation, initiated with the start of the first Five-Year Plan (1928–32), in all cases involved a systematic territorialisation of solidarity groupings within the framework of the *kolkhoz*. The *awlad*, the *mahalla*, and (in the tribal zones) lineage segments[2] were reincarnated in the sub-divisions of the *kolkhoz* (the *uchatska* or *kolkhoz* section, which was itself divided into brigades, with each division having its own territory and its own separate habitat, called a *khutur*). There were three possibilities. Either all of these segments fitted in with an entity which had already been a solidarity group before the Revolution, for instance some of the tribal *kolkhoz* (in Turkmenistan, or the Lakays in Tajikistan). Or the *kolkhoz*, by the fact of having gathered together different groups, was itself constituted as a solidarity group. This was automatically the case with mono-ethnic *kolkhoz* in a foreign alien environment, for example the German and Korean kolkhoz, but it was also the case with the Ismailis in southern Tajikistan.[3] In far rarer cases, the displaced groups transferred their conflicts into the *kolkhoz*. This was what happened with the mixed Gharmi and Kulabi *kolkhoz* in southern Tajikistan, and it led to the civil war in June 1992.[4] But in all cases it is clear that it is the logic of the solidarity group, whether pre-existent or reconstituted, which creates the kolkhozian identity.

In tribal zones, the effect of translation is particularly evident, even if the functions and the meanings have changed. Bertrand Bouchet has studied this continuity and recomposition of lineage segments in the Turkmen *kolkhoz*.[5] Given that sedentarisation of the Turkmens had begun before Sovietisation, the occupation of space took place as a function of lineage segments, around an oasis and its irrigation networks. Since the *kolkhoz* has no choice other than to organise around the same irrigation network, unless it extends it, it quite naturally takes on the structure already in place, to such an extent that the same word (*yap*) is used for both the secondary irrigation channel and the tribal fraction. In the case of Kazakhstan, the nomad cultivators grouped themselves into *awl*, or camps encampments, which also resembled a lineage segment.[6] Some Kazakh leaders in the early 1920s even claimed that tribalism offered a type of community which was perfectly compatible with socialism,[7] an analysis which arose in connection with demands over lands occupied by Russian settlers. However, unlike the situation in Kazakhstan, in Turkmenistan sedentarisation was carried out relatively gently, because the Turkmen groups were already sedentarised and organised around oases (and also there was no colonisation process involving settlement by Russians). In Kazakhstan, on the other hand, sedentarisation was carried out (in 1925) with huge costs in human tragedy: the drastic reduction in levels of livestock ruined the economic base of the beys and the lineages, and it is estimated that around 40 percent of the 4.12 million Kazakhs featured in the censuses disappeared between 1930 and 1939 after the launch of collectivisation in 1928. While the fact of belonging to one of the three hordes makes sense, because they corresponded to a geographical space, the reality of the tribal system at the level of the Kazakh *kolkhoz* still remains to be evaluated. The translation effect was perhaps less evident than in Turkmenistan, but it is clear that the result was the same: the *kolkhoz* functions as a new tribe, whatever its relations to the former tribes.

★   ★   ★

The Soviets several times took steps to break these solidarities. The authorities made efforts to concentrate the number of *kolkhoz* and embarked on an authoritarian regroupings of habitats in order to break the structure of the *awlad*. The most determined campaign on this front took place in 1954 and 1955, to be taken up later under Brezhnev. In Tajikistan, for instance, the number of *kolkhoz* fell from 2,695 in 1959 to 453 in 1955.[8] In Uzbekistan, first secretary Rashidov announced to a 1964 plenary the abolition of the *khutur* system, which in fact corresponded to the *mahallas* of the solidarity groups. Similarly, a decision was taken to combine numbers of *kholkozes* whose elected presidents represented principally traditional society into single groupings. In these new *sovkhozes*, since they were larger entities, the managers were appointed by the state. But even when these kinds of recomposition were imposed, the *kholkoz* itself turned into a solidarity group, and the *mahallas* did not disappear. The communities had a reality which survived bureaucratic manipulation. The old *kolkhoz* became *uchatskas* or brigades of the new *sovkhoz* and thus preserved their specific identities, albeit with less autonomy. However there were often instances during the 1980s of a dismantling of new *sovkhozes* to the benefit of the old *kolkhoz*. As regards the authoritarian modification of habitats (the replacement of *khutur* consisting of family houses by apartments grouped together in small towns), this was generally a failure because all the various forces of inertia conspired together. Administrative reform was carried out on paper but actually achieved little in terms of changing social realities.

Once the *kolkhoz* became a recomposed solidarity group, it benefited from an administrative, economic, social and even political institutionalisation within in the framework of the Soviet system. This *kolkhoz* was relatively autonomous. The state was not represented within the *kolkhoz*, but only at the level of the 'village-based soviet', which combined a number of villages and corresponded to a single or several *kolkhoz*. The president of the *kolkhoz* was elected, and operated as an interface with the state. The *kolkhoz* functioned as a global collectivity: it took care of work, administrative identity, social welfare, the sharing out of incomes, and public works (irrigation, etc). But it also sought to provide protection for its members beyond the confines of its territory, for example when they migrated to the towns. A member of a *kolkhoz* could always rely on *kolkhoz* solidarity, or on the *kolkhoz* president's networks within the party or administration, as a way of finding work, or resolving difficult situations. The kolkhozian identity was preserved even when people left the *kolkhoz*, so the *kolkhoz* became something more than a purely functional institution.

KOLKHOZ AND NOTABLES
The *Kolkhoz* as a New Tribe

A single *kolkhoz* may bring together several villages, either pre-existing or created at the time of population displacements. In the latter case, at the time of independence villages tended to keep their Soviet names (eg Lenin Yolu, or Lenin's Way), whereas the traditional villages reverted to their former names if they had been changed. The village as such has no administrative structures; one would certainly have found a party cell, but as institutions these had no reality: they were always absorbed or undermined by the informal self-organisation of the village, around the council of elders and the new notables. People met among themselves, with the representatives of the different *awlad* and *qawm* (the Turkmen *maslahat* and the Tajik *gap*) in order to discuss issues. State organisation only appears at the next administrative level up the hierarchy: the soviet, consisting of a number of villages (the *shure-yé dehât* in Tajik); the district soviet; the provincial soviet. The institutions of state power (militia and KGB) often exist only at district level (*rayon* in Russian, or *nahye* in Tajik).

The *kolkhoz*, the interface between the state and the peasantry, is not a collective of peasants with apparatchiks as managers. It is not an anchorage point of the state within the peasantry, but, rather, an autonomous community which reaches out its branches towards the town and state. This power of the *kolkhoz* is possible because the countryside is under-administered by the state. Here we need to revise the image of the Soviet state as totalitarian and all-embracing. In Ferghana and Tajikistan, it is possible to see how weak this state presence was. In the village soviet of Chadak in 1993, there were only about ten militiamen for 18,000 inhabitants; the KGB was only to be found in the main town in the district, Pap. The soviet consisted of eight members, theoretically elected, all of whom originated in the villages. The district of Kasansoy had 100 militiamen for 120,000 inhabitants; the entire administration, including the *hâkim* (in this case a woman) were local to the region. Everywhere you go the cadres are local, and below the level of *hâkim* or president of the soviet district they were virtually unshiftable. They run things not so much by administrative power as by means of networks and informal meetings. They themselves operate via a logic of networks: if they are suspected of favouritism to their own people, they have to move fast to smoothe things out with the other groups so as to avoid incidents which might be reported back to the authorities at the centre and compromise their position. Rotation of cadres is a punishment, and therefore temporary.

The living space of a *kolkhoz* consists of small houses surrounded by private plots of land, following the 'Muslim' model: the house (*hawâli*) is built on a single level. It extends onto a terrace, protected by a canopy, which opens onto a courtyard, and all this is surrounded by a closed garden. One may find several houses built within a single private enclosure, each of which is destined for a married son. The extension of this living space takes place within the structure of the patrilinear and patrilocal extended family: houses are built for married sons either on the father's plot, or, once this has been filled (which happens fast), on new land close by. This is similar to the main land system existing in Afghanistan, where brothers stay on the land of their deceased father for a long time and the land remains in joint ownership, with the new division taking place only with a third generation arriving at marrying age. Houses nowadays are private property, either bought from the *kolkhoz* (at what appear to be low prices) or recently built by their owner on land given by the *kolkhoz*.

The extended family remains a key element of the *kolkhoz*, but these families are grouped into solidarity groupings at various levels; one *kolkhoz* will thus be divided into several *mahallas*, each of which will have had a mosque since 1991. The *kolkhoz* is often managed by a dominant faction, from which the president will be chosen. Although the *kolkhoz* functions as a 'solidarity group', it is not exempt from division, hierarchy and conflict, and is itself located within a more general interplay of antagonisms and alliances. But *kolkhoz* solidarity makes sense at the economic and social level.

The internal factionalism of *kolkhoz* is often manifested in the geography of mosques, the construction of which is determined not by the number of believers but by the power relations between solidarity groupings. During the 70 years of Soviet rule, all mosques were closed, but each village and each *kolkhoz* had its parallel mullah(s), who were generally registered as workers; the *kolkhoz* protected its members and did not act as a relay for the state's anti-religious policies. Today, each *kolkhoz* has built its own mosque, which is not exclusive of other mosques. In fact the presence of mosques is a good indication of segmentation into factions: the *kolkhoz* mosque may be matched by the presence of an independent mosque, controlled by mullahs who are more critical of the regime. But these 'oppositional' mosques also generally express the existence of kinship relations (*awlad*) which see themselves as excluded or marginalised by the factions or big families within the *kolkhoz* who hold the power because they played the Soviet card at the moment of collectivisation. Opposition factions thus tend to identify with Islam as one way of consolidating their opposition to others – although of course everyone would claim to be Muslim.

The *kolkhoz* is not simply a unit of production; it is a socio-economic community. The fact that its workforce is under-employed and over-populated has been known for a long time; however, there is no question of 'slimming down' a *kolkhoz*, because one is a member of it by birth (all *kolkhoz*ian children have the right to be considered *kolkhoz*ians); it is a place of residence, a society. As a result, there is some discrepancy between the number of '*kolkhoz* workers' and actual members of the *kolkhoz* (who can go from one to ten, and can also include children and retired people). The economic activities of the *kolkhoz* extend directly or indirectly into the different sectors in which its members are involved (small units of production, marketing networks in the towns, and also trading).

The *kolkhoz* extend towards the town. Take for example the Lenin *kolkhoz* in Dushanbe, capital of Tajikistan (studied in 1990 and 1994). Located in the suburbs, it numbers 24,000 people, but, as its president pointed out, 7,000 of these have to work in the town. The *kolkhoz* has 1,300 hectares of irrigated land and 4,000 non-irrigated. In the view of this president, the several thousand who work in the town are still members of the *kolkhoz*. However, unlike the Turkmen case, this *kolkhoz* is not the expression of a pre-existing solidarity group. It was founded in 1931 in a region that had been depopulated as a result of the war against the *basmachis* and repopulated by populations brought in from elsewhere, in particular Uzbeks from Ferghana. At the time of our research, the founding president, Abdul Fâteh Otanazarov (an Uzbek) still lived on *kolkhoz* land, with 58 grandchildren which he had by his four sons and five daughters. Every meeting with the young new president, Hamdanov (a close relative of the founder), presupposed a protocol visit to the founder. This man, who was both beneficiary and agent of Sovietisation, behaved in the manner of a traditional notable: he kept open house, and pronounced the blessing after each meal; he said he was a Muslim, and made no reference either to the party or to communism. A '*kolkhoz*ian identity' had thus been created, but based on the traditional mode of group solidarity. In other *kolkhoz* further away from the capital, families which had gone to live in town returned to the *kolkhoz* in order to stock up on food in the event of shortages, or to seek refuge at times of political threat. They provided help and hospitality for young people from the *kolkhoz* coming to town looking for work. The child of the *kolkhoz* who succeeded in town was expected to find jobs for his *kolkhoz*'s candidates in the administration where he had authority.

It is not particularly important for our study whether this *kolkhoz* identity expressed the continued existence of former factionalisms (for example tribalism in Turkmenistan), or was the reconstitution of traditional modes of power via a sociological upheaval and the creation of new élites (as is the case in Tajikistan). What matters is what this sociology of the *kolkhoz* means for the economic evolution of the rural economy in Central Asia. In effect, in the south of the ex-USSR, which is under-industrialised, notably unurbanised and subject to significant demographic growth, the *kolkhoz* is the key locus of all in-depth economic development. The modes of sociological structuring referred to above have led to the creation of a category of notable who are the leading actors in the economic arena.

Kolkhoz Cadres: From Apparatchiks to Notables

In Russia apparatchiks belong to a caste that exists separately from the population for which they are responsible. There is a substantial turnover among management personnel; the job is a step en route to something else; promotion generally involves geographical transfer, sometimes to the other end of the country. The power network within which the apparatchik operates is not territorially based. Basically, the Russian president of a *kolkhoz* has no need of support from the peasants of a *kolkhoz*; while waiting for his next promotion, he cultivates horizontal relationships with his peers; his vertical relations with members of the *kolkhoz* are not politically significant, but only temporary and administrative.

In Central Asia, on the other hand, *kolkhoz* presidents always originate from within the district in which the *kolkhoz* is situated. There is very little turnover: people's careers are made in their local districts. Management positions in *kolkhoz* tend to be handed down within the same local factions, even within the same families: increasing numbers of presidents are the sons of their predecessors. When a president leaves his *kolkhoz* and his district it is generally to go to the capital, where his career will depend on support from his district or province, and where he will certainly be perceived as representing the interests of his region of origin. In the event of conflict, he will mobilise his supporters in his district of origin, and it is to that district that he will retire in the event of setbacks. This was a familiar scene during the 1992 civil war in Tajikistan: the supporters of the two camps in question ('Islamists' and 'communists') descended on the capital in trucks from their respective *kolkhoz*, with their apparatchiks and their mullahs in tow. All of which, incidentally, provided the unusual spectacle of a 'Red October *kolkhoz*', obviously proud of its name, but also waving a green flag emblazoned with the Islamic declaration of faith.

An official of a *kolkhoz* in Central Asia is directly engaged with the population of the *kolkhoz*. He cultivates this relationship, because his political power depends on solidarity networks originating within his district. The networks are therefore first and foremost vertical: upwards from the *kolkhoz* to the higher reaches of the state. In the event of conflicts of interest, horizontal solidarity (caste solidarity) between apparatchiks does not mean that the protagonists will abandon the prime loyalty, which is regionalist. The *kolkhoz* is the territorial basis of all power, the first connecting point with the state apparatus. The split between the world of the peasantry and the world of the city which is so marked in Russia does not exist here.

This political importance of the *kolkhoz* and the countryside explains why the president cannot operate as a simple bureaucrat or as a predator. The recognition of his power and authority by *kolkhoz* members rests on mutual interest: the president's job is to ensure the provisioning and outgoings of the *kolkhoz*. It is he who provides work for people, negotiates the price of agro-industrial produce with the state etc. This political requirement has an obvious economic consequence: in a situation where the planned economy collapses and the state falls short, the *kolkhoz* notable has to transform himself into an economic agent.

This class of rural notable is very much in evidence. The main symbol of social status is one's house – how large it is (how many storeys) and whether or not it is able to offer hospitality to guests. So how do the managers of *kolkhoz* become rich? Obviously, things on this front are not always entirely clear. The wealth of the *kolkhoz* notables is self-evident, and often ostentatious. In the villages they live in large, beautiful houses, they have cars, and they spend lavishly on social functions such as *tuys*. Relations, friends and neighbours are invited; the duty of a notable is to offer hospitality to the whole village: on such occasions he maintains open house, providing dishes that are rich in meat and fat, a contrast with the frugality of people's everyday fare, and the vodka (which is expensive nowadays) flows. Here one should note that the Muslim kolkhozian notable consumes and displays his wealth within the context of the village, unlike the Russian apparatchik, who prefers distant *dachas*, private clubs, and restaurants behind closed doors. This ostentatious expenditure is an integral part of the relation of clientelism which he maintains with those whom he administers.

Managers of *kolkhoz* like to present themselves as simple paid officials elected by their peers. This is true in formal terms. However, as in French agricultural cooperatives, the real nature of power (and wealth) cannot be understood just from reading the organisation's statutes. The wealth of these notables bears no relation to the official salaries which they are paid by the *kolkhoz*. As in the case of the peasant, the salary is more a mark of belonging to a solidarity group than a distribution of wealth. So, is the wealth of the notables therefore founded on predation (percentages, bribes and the sale of collective property) as in Russia? If so, then the managers' role would be anti-economic. However, while corruption cannot be excluded, there is a fundamental difference between the notable of a *kolkhoz* in Central Asia and his Russian counterpart. The former has every interest in the peasantry working, producing and becoming rich. He derives his wealth from the fortunes of the *kolkhoz*, and knows that the privileges that he enjoys will not be contested by the majority of peasants as long as he adequately fulfils his functions as a notable: defending the *kolkhoz* in its dealings with the state apparatus, taking care of supplies, and redistributing part of his wealth in the form of ostentatious expenditure, which thereby further reinforces his prestige. The prime source of wealth is very much what the *kolkhoz* produces, and not what can be acquired via the state apparatus (which has anyway been bled dry since independence). The state is no longer a *milch cow*. For a *kolkhoz* notable to become rich, the *kolkhoz* has to produce. The main aim of *kolkhoz* managers has been, and remains, that of improving production.

During the Soviet period, these notables were necessarily members of the Communist Party, but after independence they joined whatever the single ruling party happened to be. They are not ideologically communists, and behave more as beys and khans than apparatchiks. But the Soviet past is an integral part of their legitimacy. The external signs of their status as notables come in two forms: the Soviet one is represented by things that hang on walls (medals, official credentials, photos and certificates commemorating official trips to Moscow), and the traditional one is seen in situations where people sit on carpets, and where status is expressed in gesture and dress, and individuals' rank and position in the guestroom where the notable receives them and offers hospitality. They are simultaneously traditional notables concerned with ostentation and good living (keeping open house, marrying young wives, returning in some instances to polygamy) and enterprise managers intent on achieving prosperity for their *kolkhoz*. Their economic function is to place the *kolkhoz* into a semi-market system where the roles are all played by former apparatchiks, who may or may not be independent from the state apparatus. The political role of the notable is inseparable from his economic role.

One sign of this symbiosis between notables and their *kolkhoz* is the fact that after independence many *kolkhoz* abandoned their Soviet names and took instead that of their founders. In Kulab the Shatalof *kolkhoz* (founded in 1938 and named after an officer in the Red Army) was renamed the Safarali Zarifov *kolkhoz* in around 1991, after the man who had been its president for 40 years. The people of Kulab were conservatives, so the change was not done for ideological reasons. In the district of Kumsangir in Tajikistan, the Hassanov *kolkhoz* also bears the name of its former director, who came from Fayzabad in 1949 along with the *kolkhoz*'s present population. At the time of its founding, it was called the Stalin *kolkhoz*. New élites are created, which transmit their power to their descendants and fit themselves into the framework of politics which opened after independence. In May 1994, Imamali Rahmanov, the president of Tajikistan, summoned the diplomatic corps and the chiefs of staff of the Russian army to celebrate the eightieth birthday of Mirali Mahmadaliev, formerly chairman of the Krupskaya and Lenin *kolkhoz* in the district of Vose, Kulab province. More than 5,000 people attended the ceremony, which involved banquets and *buzkachi*. This man had become a local potentate and was the godfather (in all senses) of the team currently in government.

The War of the *Kolkhoz* (Tajikistan)

The tribalisation of the *kolkhoz* has also led them to engage in tribal wars. A particularly violent instance was the civil war in Tajikistan. The problem derives from the fact that the *kolkhoz* are new recompositions of solidarity groups resulting from sedentarisation or population transfers. Identities are thus reconstituted in antagonistic mode. Systematic sedentarisation results in groups being plucked out of their ecological niches and placed in competition with other groups with which they had coexisted collaboratively up until that point. Substantial demographic growth leads to food resource shortages and competition over land. In 1940, Tajikistan had 0.6 hectares of cultivated land per inhabitant; by 1989, the figure was 0.17 hectares.[9]

Collective transfers of populations of different origins within one same zone of development do not in fact lead to intermixings of peoples. They lead to identities becoming fixed in a communitarian mode. Thus the displacement of Gharmi, Kulabi and Pamiri mountain-dwellers in the region of Kurgan-Teppe (in two waves, in the 1930s and the 1950s) created an antagonism between the three groups, and accentuated both endogamous practices and cultural divergences. All these groups previously lived in valleys that were separated by hills, and were not in competition for land: here one can not talk of previously existing and long-standing antagonisms. Similarly, these cultural divergences did not necessarily exist before the displacements. The Gharmis became 'religious' and the Kulabis 'secular' recently, while at a time when, during the 1920s, both groups were equally present within the fundamentalist Muslim resistance. Today, Gharmi men wear beards and Kulabis are clean-shaven or have moustaches. There is little intermarriage between Kulabis and Gharmis, and various distinguishing signs (the styles of embroidery on skullcaps or robes) are preserved.

The fact that this war was far from ideological can be seen by the way in which apparatchiks reacted in terms of clan membership. In the district of Vakhsh, the Noruz *sovkhoz* (specialising in vegetables) was created in 1986 as an offshoot of the Turkmenistan *kolkhoz*. Its director (Shâdi Kabirovich) was an apparatchik of Gharmi origin. He, like all his group, turned Islamist and fled to Afghanistan (in 1994, after the 1992 war, 1,500 of its 4,000 inhabitants did not return). The new director is a Kulabi. As for the Turkmenistan *kolkhoz* (which was renamed the Haqiqat, or 'truth', *kolkhoz* after the civil war), it was set up in 1953 with immigrant Gharmis and Kulabis. The Gharmis were in the majority and the *kolkhoz* was an opposition stronghold (Mullah Nuri had a mosque there). The Kulabis, who were in the minority, lived in the *mahalla* of Maskinabad. In June 1992, the Gharmis expelled the Kulabis, who went over to the Moskwa *kolkhoz*, which was majority Kulabi. The territorial limits of the two *kolkhoz* became the front line in the fighting that lasted from June to November 1992, with the digging of trenches and the mounting of ambushes, until Kulabi troops arrived from the north and retook the Turkmenistan *kolkhoz* in November. In 1993, the new managers were all Kulabis and, of course, originally from the *mahalla* of Maskinabad. The Gharmis who were not expelled became simply agricultural workers of the *kolkhoz*. In several instances, Gharmi refugees returning under the auspices of the UN High Commission for Refugees were taken on with this status of *declassé* waged workers, while the victorious Kulabis took possession of good-quality housing and land. After the victory, a number of Kulabi families came from overpopulated *kolkhoz* in the province of Kulab and installed themselves, together with their tractors and livestock, in the newly conquered *kolkhoz*. Thus what one had here was the reconstitution of a social differentiation arising out of the combined effects of war, predation and neo-tribalism.

This social defeat of the Gharmis can be observed in other collective farms. In the district of Bakhtar, which contains the town of Kurgan-Teppe, is the Safarali *kolkhoz*, named after the Kulabi warlord buried there. The minority Gharmis came in 1948 and took up residence in the village of Sar-i sang. The Lenin *kolkhoz* in the village of Rah-i Lenin ('Lenin's way') contains only Darwazis, who have been in the area for two generations and who are allied to the Gharmis.

FACTIONALISM AND POWER NETWORKS
Regionalist Factions

With the *kolkhoz* we still have a purely local solidarity group which, as we have seen, only rarely becomes politicised. At a higher demographic level, identities then crystallise within the Soviet territorial and administrative structure of districts and provinces (*rayon* and *oblast*). Now, this framework is the complex product of a number of invariables ('Pamiris' have always lived in Pamir) and of forced population transfers during the Soviet period. Sovietisation brought with it a recomposition of human groupings around a general territorialisation of which the twin axes were administrative territorial realignment and the system of *kolkhoz* and *sovkhozes*. The end result of sedentarisation and forced population transfers was often to create competition between groups which had not hitherto been in competition. The systematic territorialisation implemented by the Soviets also had the consequence of creating antagonisms between ethnic groups where they had not existed before. The Kyrgyz nomads of northern Tajikistan existed within an economy which was complementary with that of the Tajik peasants. However once they were sedentarised they found themselves competing with them for water and land,[10] as were the Tajiks with the Uzbek Lakay, Kungrat and Durman tribes of southern Tajikistan (province of Kurgan-Teppe). In the same way, the Tajiks of the foothills and the Pamiris of the mountains had no reason to be in a state of conflict. But the population transfers of the 1950s brought them into contact and then into competition with each other: for instance, displaced Pamiris came to make up the population of the small town of Kalininabad in the Tajik district of Bakhtar, in the midst of Kulabis, Gharmis and Uzbeks (they were to flee the town in 1992, whereupon it became entirely Kulabi). The groups caught up in this process went on to develop antagonistic identities and worked at playing the Soviet system (the party and regional power bodies) as a way of advancing their respective interests.

Although generalised territorialisation had been achieved in 1929, forced population transfers continued right through until 1970 (eg the transfer of the Yaghnobis from South to North Tajikistan). Thus territorialisation is not the expression of some preceding traditional society, of rural society, but is actually a recomposition carried out by the state. Regional tensions are exacerbated not in the original zones of derivation of the various groups, but in the areas where they are forcibly placed into contact with each other and find themselves having to share land. At that point, there is a reactive effect of a crystallisation of identities relating back to their valleys of origin.

Population transfers reduce the oppositions between lineages and consolidate essentially geographical identities (one's place of origin) as primary identities. Paradoxically, transfer reinforces territorial identity. Thus the refugees of Central Asia in Afghanistan (Mohajer) are defined not on the basis of their ethnicity but by their place of origin (Samarqandi, Ferghana'y etc). The term 'Gharmi' develops in Tajikistan among transferred populations in the province of Kurgan-Teppe. But in order to play a political role at the national level, or simply to connect with the state apparatus, solidarity groups are obliged to operate within the state's official categories of district and province. Thus they have to operate at a demographic level higher than that of simple lineage.

Administrative realignment makes the territorialised group the necessary basis for any power strategy related to the apparatus of the Communist Party. The Communist Party, as we know, held a monopoly of power: it was only through the party that an individual could pursue a career. The increasing number of indigenous cadres from the 1940s onwards created a situation in which, at the local level, the party soon ceased to be an externally imposed structure and became the place in which local élites were formed and expressed. Now, the party apparatus was territorially based: on the *rayon* and *oblast*. In order to operate as a party notable one needed to have such a base. In this first stage, local power issues may result in conflicts between groups (as with the Gharmis and Kulabis in Kurgan-Teppe), but more often a solidarity and a district and provincial identity emerge. The administrative structure imposed by the system crystallises and politicises former solidarities deriving from history and geography (irrigation networks in the Turkmen oases and the Tajik and Kyrgyz valleys). In Kyrgyzstan, the country's geographic fragmentation has meant that the imposition of a tight administrative framework has solidified and institutionalised very long-standing oppositions between the more Islamicised south and a north that was closer to Kazakhstan – a kind of north-south split that one also finds in Tajikistan.

This crystallisation of solidarities around issues arising out of administrational realignments is known as localism in Russian (*mestnichestvo*, which in Tajik translates as the neologism *mahalgera'y*). A new word had to be invented because the old terms designating solidarity groups (*qawm* and *awlad*) referred to networks and not to territories. Territorialisation is an effect of Sovietism, and paradoxically it makes a reality of words such as 'feof' and 'feudal', which previously in Central Asia were not a historical reality, despite the claims of the Marxist vulgate.

All of a sudden, administrative realignment became a power issue unto itself. It may have been artificial in terms of previous ethnic, geographic and tribal realities, but it soon took on a reality. The dominant factions thus try to break up their adversaries' territorial power base and to strengthen their own by means of new administrative realignments. The case of Tajikistan is a caricature of the process. In 1929, the country had nine *vilayat*, or provinces (*oblast*), corresponding to 'solidarity spaces' which still make sense today (from north to south these were: Khojent, Ura-Teppe, Penjikent, Hissar, Dushanbe, Gharm, Kurgan-Teppe, Kulab and Gorno-Badakhshan, or Pamir). Progressively they were almost all abolished as the faction from Khojent (renamed Leninabad) proceeded to take power: In 1953, the provinces of Dushanbe, Kulab and Gharm disappeared; in 1956, the only provinces left were Leninabad-Khojent and Gorno-Badakhshan. Leninabad annexed Ura-Teppe and Penjikent, while the districts around Dushanbe were 'attached to the republic', in other words to the faction currently in power. But Kulab was re-established as a province in 1973, followed by Kurgan-Teppe (1977) at the moment that the alliance between Leninabadis and Kulabis emerged. After their victory the Kulabis annexed the province of Kurgan-Teppe in 1993 and created a new entity called Khatlan, which was the old name of Kulab. Two 'provinces', Kulab and Leninabad, vied for central power, while the regionalist group within which the opposition recruited lost its entire administrative existence (with the exception of the Autonomous Region of Gorno-Badakhshan).

In Uzbekistan, one finds a similar correspondence between administrative divisions and 'solidarity groups', at least at provincial level:[11] Tashkent, Ferghana, Khwarezm, Karakalpakia, Bukhara, Samarkand, Sukhan-Darya and Kashka-Darya. Here the re-creations of administrative entities are also indicative of power balances: in 1973, two years after the victory of the Jizak clan over that of Tashkent-Ferghana, the small town of Jizak was raised to the status of *oblast*. This status was cancelled in 1988, and then re-established at the time of independence, decisions depending on whether the Samarkand group or the Ferghana Tashkent group was in power. Behind such administrative decisions in the Soviet system lay struggles between regionalist factions.

From Solidarity Group to Network

Political networks are still rooted in regionalist factions, but operating within different modalities – namely communitarianism or deterritorialised networks.

In the former case, the regionalist group became community-based and almost turned into an ethnic group, as was the case with the Kulabis and the Gharmis: here the fact of belonging to the group, which is decided by birth, automatically implies a political solidarity which, even if it is rejected by the individual concerned, will be assumed in him by others. Thus one is Kulabi or Gharmi in the same way that one is Maronite or Druze in Lebanon. This kind of infra-ethnic communitarian crystallisation includes *qawm*, *awlad* and lineages that are external to each other. It may even include ethnic sub-categories (for instance 'Turki' among the Kulabis). One finds this phenomenon in Afghanistan, with the Panjshiris. In Central Asia, it seems limited to Tajikistan, where it broadly explains the ruthless nature of the warfare. When the Gharmis held Dushanbe, all Kulabis were suspect (in the language used by the mullahs, the words *kafir*, infidel and Kulabi were often interchangeable); when the Kulabis retook power, people were being shot on the basis of their identity cards (to have originated from Gorno-Badakhshan, an indication of belonging to the Pamiri group, was tantamount to a death sentence).

But in the rest of Central Asia this kind of communitarianism is much less marked. The network counts more than the group. This network begins initially on a regionalist basis. People of Khwarezm who come to Tashkent count on the solidarity, and also the suport, of their 'fellow countrymen', and tend to group together in the same *mahalla*. An individual goes looking for a well-connected Khwarezmian in order to advance his cause. Thus networks interlock: from the *kolkhoz* to the regional soviet, then to the regionalist network as it has transferred to the capital. These networks are not necessarily political, let alone ideological. Nor are they exclusive of other forms of social-ising and political allegiance. But they may also become independent of their region of origin and transform into political factions. Here, what counts is solidarity between apparatchiks rather than their popular base in the region of origin.

Power struggles can often be explained in terms of such networks, even though there may also be other issues at stake. The Rashidov clan is the expression not of a previously existing clan but of just such a recomposition of solidarities, between cadres originally from Samarkand.[12] In fact, the population of that city, which is rather Tajik, feels itself somewhat external to the system of politics in which the so-called Samarkand faction is rising. In the same way, in Azerbaijan political power is traditionally held by Azeris deriving from Nakhichevan or Armenia (the 'Yeraz', or Erevan Azeris). Elchibey, Rassul Gouliev (president of the parliament in 1994) and Abbasov (head of the KGB) are from Nakhichevan; Aliyev is originally from Armenia. One cannot say that Armenia was a popular base for Azeri nationalism. Thus one is dealing with networks created on the basis of a common origin, rather than the expression of a regional demographic group.

But whatever the method of their constitution these regionalist factions are a major key to politics in Central Asia, as we shall see in the chapter that follows.

★   ★   ★

At the same time, these regionalist groups are not the whole story as regards the concept of network. Beyond the upper reaches of the state, interpersonal networks are created around leading public figures or important families. While these networks are often originally region-based, they then separate off from the region and create alliances along other lines (marriage, exchange of services etc). Purely social solidarity networks thus come into being, bringing together people from different regions, and they are often built on a hierarchical differentiation among their members (for example, the teachers in an institute and their director, members of a particular administration, former fellow students etc). Here the clan is no longer endogamous, as is the tradition among rural 'solidarity groups'. On the contrary, exogamy now comes into play as a means of making links. The fact that a son of Rashidov married the daughter of the first secretary of Karakalpakia, Kalibek Kamalov (purged in 1984) creates a relationship of alliance between two different groups, partly in ethnic terms and partly through the power that they hold, but the one aspect is clearly subsidiary to the other.[13] This relationship explains why there is no Karakalpak question in Uzbekistan, because that particular link is maintained via the neo-Rashidovian Karimov, whose minister for foreign affairs, Kamilov, is himself the son-in-law of Rashidov. The links between politics and marriage are close in governing circles: for example, in the Tajik clan of the Leninabadis in 1993 Governor (*ispalkom*) Abduljallil Hamidov was the son-in-law of the son of Prime Minister Abdulmalik Abdullajanov, both of whom were allies of the Kulabis in 1992 and were subsequently ejected from their posts in December 1993. But when Hamidov rallied the Kulabis in summer 1994, at the time when Abdullajanov went over into open opposition, the children divorced.

The place where these networks become manifest is the *tuy*. It is the duty of the patron to attend the social events of the people who are his clients. Here marriage plays a major role. The network is something constructed and maintained. In this case it is more personal. Today, for example, professional *tuys* exist, bringing together groups of colleagues from work.[14] This system is very developed in Kazakhstan, where exogamy was the rule in the tribal system (even though by preference people married within their horde and their social category – the so-called 'white bones' and 'black bones'). Here solidarity groupings were defined more by systems of alliances than by a relation to a given place, particularly because the sedentarisation process was far more traumatic here than elsewhere.

Nowadays, networks founded on regionalism and the extended family tend, in the city, to give way to purely relational networks built around an individual or a family. Here one finds the Iranian-style concept of *dowre*, a 'circle' of people of different origins around a particular person, which brings them into membership of a particular political, social or even intellectual register to which they would not otherwise have access.

At this level, the much-decried mafia can be seen as just a solidarity group oriented towards 'business'. The war in Tajikistan has shown the inter-relatedness of these different kinds of networks: Sangak Safarov, head of the Kulabi militias, and Yakub Salimov, minister of the interior from 1993 to 1994, were 'mafia' figures allegedly involved in smuggling and racketeering during the Soviet era, but they immediately became military leaders of the Kulabi faction, because their mafia was simply the expression of Kulabi solidarity networks, with access to arms and money.

6

Political Factionalism and National Affirmation During the Soviet Era

MOSCOW AND SOVIET CADRE POLICY

We have already seen the difficulties that the Bolshevik authorities had in finding indigenous transmission channels in situ. The first Communist organisations had practically no Muslims: the first Tashkent soviet had none, as did the Turkestan Commission and the first Congress of Communists of Siberia (which included the governorate of the Steppes); in the Baku commune, out of 27 commissars only two were Muslims; the Communist Parties of Bukhara and Khiva were created artificially in Tashkent in 1918, with a handful of minority Jadids. When sections of the Russian Communist Party began to be established in various places from 1918 onwards, those who joined were basically Europeans.

In the initial period, Moscow relied on Jadids and fellow travellers who joined the Communist Party after 1917. They were almost all to disappear in the purges of 1937. Some disappeared even before this (in Kazakhstan, for instance), at the same time as the old Bolsheviks of European origin. The Bolsheviks' fellow travellers during the 1920s generally came from leading families and the urban intelligentsia. The family of Fayzullah Khojayev was one of the richest in Bukhara, and he himself was educated in Saint Petersburg. In Azerbaijan, Narimanov was an aristocrat, and a number of cadres came from religious families (as can be seen from their names, for example Sheikhulislamzadeh and Ruholla Akhundov). In Kazakhstan, the members of Alash Orda came from the tribal aristocracy. In Tajikistan, there was no élite, since the Persian-speaking Jadids of Samarkand and Bukhara were rather pan-Turkist in 1920 (for instance, Abdurrauf Fitrat), and because they did not go and settle in Dushanbe after partition in 1929.

The destruction of the old Bolshevik élites began with the members of the Kazakh Alash Orda party in 1923. The Kazakh leadership's calls for the return of land taken by Russian settlers prompted the purge. It continued with the Tatars of Crimea, who were also in conflict with the Russians over the question of land (Veli-Ibrahimov was executed in 1928). The key question was how to assess the Russian colonialism of the tsarist era. In 1934, the Seventeenth Congress of the CPSU decided that the colonial period could be seen as positive: this gave the green light for colonising settlement policies, effectively ending attempts by Kazakhs and Tatars to get back their lands in the name of anti-colonialism. The repression subsequently extended to more recently acquired territories, still in the name of the struggle against nationalism. The ex-president of the Tajik Sovnarkom from 1925 to 1929, A. Muhiddinov, disappeared in 1933. The president of the Supreme Soviet of Turkmenistan, Naderbey Aitakov, was executed in 1936. The elimination was completed with the purges of 1937–8. Among those who disappeared were the Uzbeks F. Khojayev and A. Ikramov, the Kazakhs Ahmed Baytursun and Ryskulov, and the Tajiks Shahtimur (president of the Supreme Soviet) and Rahimbeyzade (prime minister). The Azeri Narimanov, who died in 1933, was sentenced posthumously in 1937. However, this strictly political repression conceals a far broader repression against the former notables, who had become very widely present within the state apparatus. In 1926, a decision was taken in Moscow to eliminate them,[1] a move which was facilitated by collectivisation, since it deprived the notables of their economic base (this ended up with the destruction of their flocks) and by the repression of 'kulaks'.

At the time, the beys were deliberately viewed as the same as the kulaks, even though their social framework was different: the kulak was an individual entrepreneur, whereas the bey was the head of a network of patronage and solidarity.[2] In 1927 a massive wave of deportations and disappearances hit the rural élites. Combined with the *hujum* campaign designed to emancipate women, and with a systematic attack on religion, the aim of the 1927 collectivisation was the destruction of traditional society.

In order to create a new transmission belt, in 1921 the Tenth Congress of the CPSU launched the policy of *korenizatsya* ('indigenisation', 'nativization') implemented mainly between 1921 and 1934 (when there was a pause as a result of the purges) and then resumed after the Second World War. Since the intention was to replace the old élites, recruitment took place principally among the poorest elements of traditional society: ex-nomads who were now sedentarised as a result of having no flocks; sharecroppers; seasonal workers; shepherds etc. The first attempt at the mass introduction of indigenous local people in 1920 was a failure: equally massive purges took place in 1921 when it became obvious that the new members had no education in, or even any real interest in, communism and were simply attempting to gain entry into the power apparatus.[3] The purges of 1937 mark a clear distinction between the educated cadres, who were generally eliminated (Khojayev, for instance), and the relatively uneducated cadres, who survived (Y. Akhundbabayev) or were promoted. It took about 20 years after the purges of 1937 for the system to arrive at a degree of stability. The turnover of cadres was very marked right through till the late 1950s.[4] But this generation of 1937 took power in the 1950s, setting up what were effectively satrapies sanctioned by Brezhnev (1964–82), which unwillingly established the conditions necessary for independence. The Brezhnev period was marked by a stabilisation of the Communist apparatus in Central Asia and by the continued power of the first secretaries of the parties in the republics: the Kazakh Kunayev was in his post from 1959 to 1986, the Uzbek Rashidov from 1959 to 1983, the Turkmen Gapurov from 1969 to 1986, the Tajik Rassulov from 1961 to 1982, and the Kyrgyz Usulbayev from 1961 to 1985. The present rulers of the independent republics came directly out of the entourages of the first three; their formative years were under Khrushchev, and their progression through the apparatus took place under Brezhnev. Such a continuity presupposes an alleviation of the threat of rotation or replacement, unlike previous periods. The framework of political life was stable. A political culture and a system had been given the time to become established, in an atmosphere of assured security and impunity that was a complete break with preceding periods. Far from destabilising the republics, the crisis of 1983 left their apparatuses relatively unaffected, except at the highest level, and turned out to be the beginning of the divorce between the local nomenklaturas and Moscow.

The result of indigenisation was that the social base of the party cadres transferred from the town to the countryside. The communist parties of Central Asia were rural parties, all the more so since urbanisation tended to operate mainly in favour of 'Europeans'. This rurality came to be a dominant characteristic of their political culture. It goes hand in hand with the establishment of territorialised solidarity groups. Regionalist factionalism is explained by this double transformation: the recomposition of solidarity groups, and the ruralisation of the party's cadres. Even when, in the 1950s, the educational level of cadres rose significantly (at that time they were all engineers), the fact of their rural origins, of rootedness in their district, and their links with the structure of the *kolkhoz* remained very strong.

A fundamental characteristic of the emergence of this new political élite is the role of regionalist factionalism. As we have seen, the paradox of Sovietisation was that it led simultaneously to a homogenisation of the national space and the crystallisation of a regionally-based political factionalism. The factions were never constituted on the basis of ideological criteria (reformers versus conservatives, nationalists against 'sovietists' etc). The cadres were all loyal to the Soviet system and conformist to the point of being model blockheads; they all founded their strategy for power on Moscow's (or some leading personality's) support for their faction, and they all discreetly promoted the interests of their republic, not so much to the detriment of the USSR as to the detriment of neighbouring republics. The central powers in Moscow, after having made an attempt to find a 'substitute proletariat'[5] – women, labouring masses, etc – rapidly settled for manipulating political factionalism, either by supporting one faction against another or by maintaining a balance between them. Purges were easy to operate: all it needed was to recruit prosecutors and successors from within the rival faction that was eager for power. Each faction worked on finding and keeping support in Moscow, and Moscow acted as a referee. Thus a patron-client relationship came to be established between key members of the apparatus in Moscow (the general secretary himself, post–1937) and the leaders of the republics. In the case of Uzbekistan, the pairings were Fayzullah Khojayev-Kuibishev (who oversaw Central Asian affairs from 1920 until his death in 1935), followed by Muhitdinov-Khrushchev in 1957, Rashidov-Khrushchev in 1959 (Rashidov was a member of a delegation that Khrushchev took to India in 1955), Rashidov-Brezhnev in 1964, and finally Osmankhojayev-Andropov in 1983. The concern of the General Secretary in Moscow was to have his man heading the local republic's party; he was not particularly concerned whether he represented one faction or another. But each of these pairs necessarily relates to a faction: in 1937, following the purges, all the important positions in Uzbekistan were occupied by the Ferghana faction, which (in the 1960s) lost power to the Samarkand faction supported by Brezhnev. In 1983, Andropov ousted the Samarkand faction and once again replaced it with the Ferghana faction.

Needless to say, Moscow always officially condemned regionalist factionalism: throughout the 1920s, one of the centre's abiding concerns was a critique of the continued existence of traditional power practices among the cadres of Central Asia. This was in fact the justification for the high degree of turnover of cadres before the 1960s. But Soviet power was perfectly capable of reaching an accommodation with this style of politics, which it was adept at manipulating.[6] This pragmatic politics sanctioned factionalism and exacerbated conflicts between groups who were intent on playing the Soviet apparatus against their rivals. In protecting one's own group, one plays by the traditional rules, and in promoting it one plays by Soviet rules.

Thus the centre practised a form of indirect administration. All Moscow had to do was to keep control of certain key mechanisms: the top levels of the KGB, the army, frontier guards, and control of top cadres within the party. The various general secretaries of the CPSU contented themselves with directly overseeing the first secretaries of the parties in the republics, leaving the business of controlling the apparatus in those republics up to them. One effect of these personal relationships was to short-circuit the Soviet apparatus and to reinforce the real power of the first secretaries. Here one should temper what people have said about the contradiction between the apparent autonomy of the republics and the reality of power, which is depicted as always having been in the hands of Moscow. In fact, the system was more complex. Each side had what they considered to be the basic essentials: Moscow had control of ideology, security and strategy; the local Communists had rotation of lower-ranking cadres, the distribution of emoluments, administration of the population, which was mainly rural, and the reality of economic power. In order to guarantee their independence at the local level, the local communists zealously carried out the Moscow line in all things relating to the politics and the big spectacular campaigns that passed down to them from the centre: Rashidov's kowtowing to Brezhnev was proverbial, and a 'national' campaign such as the struggle against alcoholism launched by Gorbachev promptly led to the destruction of vineyards in the south (but not to any diminution in the consumption of alcohol). Needless to say, this tail-ending brought with it certain contradictions: in 1986–7, the first secretaries took up the anti-religion campaign that had been launched by Gorbachev one year before the great liberalisation; and the Uzbek authorities called for the traditional skullcap to be replaced by the trilby hat etc. But these kinds of campaigns left the population indifferent anyway.

Even the control exercised by Moscow via the medium of the party's second secretary and the person responsible for cadres, who were always Russians, was illusory. As Rywkin notes, 'The Second Secretary is rather a junior partner with a great deal of clout and ability to intervene in case of nationalist deviation or gross economic shortcoming, but it is the First Secretary who remains the *khoziain* ("the boss")'.[7] In the same way, the mobility of cadres, at least up until the 1960s, was more apparent than real: often a change meant only a temporary setting aside, and left intact the functioning of the solidarity networks actually within the party.[8]

This compromise between Moscow and the parties in the republics was possible because the generation of cadres which came to power in the 1950s was a product of the Soviet system, and shared both its appearances and its technical know-how: they spoke Russian fluently, and they were all graduates, which had not been the case previously. This élite was thus more presentable, but its methods had not really changed.

★   ★   ★

What is striking is that Moscow never contributed to setting in place a locally resident Russian élite, at a time when (in 1990) there were almost five million Russians living in what was termed Central Asia *stricto-sensu*, and seven million in Kazakhstan, of whom a large percentage had also been born there. The Russians who occupied important positions in Central Asia were almost always from the metropolis. They did a stay in the south in the course of a *curriculum vitae* which was mainly Moscow-based, as in the case of Brezhnev himself. This was beginning already in the 1920s: Moscow distrusted the Russian settlers, who were, at the time of the revolution, Menshevik and Socialist Revolutionary rather than Bolsheviks. Hundreds of European cadres were then sent to the south for indeterminate periods. In 1925, the first secretary of the Kazakh Communist Party was a Russian, Goloshcheskin, who was replaced in 1932 by the Armenian Mirzoyan. In Tajikistan, the three first secretaries from 1933 to 1946 were Broïdo (a Lithuanian Jew), Shaduntz (an Armenian from Azerbaijan) and Protopopov (a Russian from Voronej). In 1983, the first secretary of Tashkent, the Russian B. Satin, was sent from Moscow. One of the rare counter-examples was G.M. Orlov, a deputy member of the political bureau of the Uzbek Communist Party from 1973 to 1981; he was originally from the republic. The Russian community of Central Asia was never represented within the political apparatus, a fact which explains why there was no appearance of a 'pieds-noirs' phenomenon as a result of the lack of a local political class.

Since the Russian leaderships were in a sense only passing through, the local Muslim apparatchiks were able to consolidate their political culture as an ongoing fact. Furthermore, the Russian populations almost never learned the local languages. Russian civil servants, whether of local origin or expatriate, were thus cut off from the local society. All their information came via their Muslim colleagues. The handful of rare 'Europeans' who had a good working knowledge of the country were often outcasts in their own way: deportees or voluntary exiles fleeing the purges prior to 1937, refugees during the war (Poles and Jews), or scientists who could not abide the central bureaucracy and who could make a local career without too many constraints (archaeologists etc). They were the kind of people who were not much in favour.

Within the security organisations (the KGB and the ministry of the interior, or MVD), the divide between Muslims and Russians who did not speak local languages was of no little importance. Some information failed to reach the centre because dissident figures were 'covered' by their personal solidarity networks, outside any ideological connivance.[9] Up until the 1960s, there was some impermeability between the security services on the one hand and the party and the administration on the other.[10] Unable to exert vertical control on the security apparatus, Moscow played the card of regionalist factionalism in at least two instances. In Tajikistan in the 1980s, one notes a massive entry of Badakhshan Pamiris (Ismailis) into the KGB and MVD. They were sufficiently numerous in 1992 to paralyse the Communist authorities in dealing with the Islamic-democratic opposition to which they are close. This recruitment appears to have been linked to the war in Afghanistan: Moscow was nervous about solidarity between Soviet Uzbeks and Tajiks and their Mujahedin Afghan cousins, but trusted the Ismailis, whose Afghan counterparts supported the Communist regime. It appears that the Taleshis (an Iranian-speaking group, but not Persian) held key posts in the Azeri MVD. It just so happened that these were the two republics in which the Communist Party apparatus was not able to make a significant mark after independence, because its leaders did not belong to the same regionalist faction as the people who ran security.

Finally, as we have seen, the countryside of Central Asia was underadministered. Russian cadres and representatives of security bodies were to be found only in the district capitals; *kolkhoz* and village soviets were entirely in the hands of local apparatchiks, functioning on a logic of group solidarity and not state control.

★   ★   ★

How do we explain this particularity of the Muslim Republics? The easy answer would be to explain it by a continuity of a pre-Soviet traditional culture. However, while, as we have seen, belonging to a solidarity group is a key to political loyalty, one cannot say that power before the Bolshevik revolution was defined by regionalist factionalism. The ruling dynasties had nothing 'regionalist' about them. In fact, the institutionalisation of regionalism was largely a product of the Soviet system, first because the societies of Central Asia are above all rural. The great majority of cadres had a father, or at least a grandfather, who came from a village. As President Islam Karimov said in a speech in Tashkent on 15 July 1994, 'We were all born in a *mahalla*'. The environment in which cadres are educated is the *kolkhoz*, and the environment within which they are promoted is the district. Then, and most importantly, the Muslim cadres in the Soviet era were almost all condemned to pursue their careers within their own republics, either going from one *rayon* to another or pursuing their whole career in their own rayon or province of origin.[11] Unlike the career of a Russian or European, the career of a Muslim cadre was limited to the confines of his republic.

European cadres, and Russians in particular, pursued a career that was deterritorialised. For a young cadre initially appointed to a distant district, the ideal was to hitch his wagon to the engine of a more senior cadre and follow him in his ascent, something which presupposed a large degree of geographical mobility (thus Brezhnev had been first secretary of Kazakhstan, a republic that was unknown to him). One would find a Russian, a Ukrainian, an Armenian or a Jew (Ashkenazi) in positions in a Muslim republic, but the reverse did not hold. A Tajik cadre would never be appointed to Leningrad, or even to Kyrgyzia. So his strategy was to get himself appointed in his district of origin, and to work for the collective elevation of his regionalist faction within the state apparatus of his given republic. At worst, he would be sent in exile to a district of this same republic, where he would sit and wait for a promotion either towards the capital or towards his original 'home ground'. There he would perhaps remain as a powerful and respected local notable. At best, he would find his way to the capital, where he would be in a position to ensure the promotion of younger members of his regionalist faction, whether he himself was first secretary of the party or the director of the bus service. This phenomenon of rotation within a single republic strengthened both national sentiment and regionalist loyalty.

The number of Muslim cadres who succeeded in making their mark at the centre is small, and limited to a brief period during the reign of Khrushchev and Brezhnev. Their promotion was clearly a result of both men's Third World policy, which was intent on using the Muslim part of the Soviet world as a showcase. The first Muslim from Central Asia to enter ruling circles in Moscow was the Uzbek N. Muhitdinov, who became a member of the secretariat of the CPSU in 1958. The Brezhnev period was exceptional, because there were three Muslims in the Politburo of the CPSU until 1983: Aliyev, Kunayev and Rashidov. One year later, there was not a single one.

In the army, with only a few exceptions (such as the Chechen Johar Dudayev), there were no Muslim generals in the élite corps, and the few Muslim generals in the rest of the armed forces were more Russian than local (for example the Tajik Ashurov who commanded the 201st Division at Dushanbe in 1992 and who chose to remain within the Russian army rather than join the Tajik army). In 1978, Muslim officers made up no more than 3.06 percent of Soviet forces, at a time when Muslims were 16.5 percent of the Soviet population as a whole.[12] In the period 1961–90, the greatest presence of Muslims was to be found in the diplomatic corps (as ambassadors: the Uzbeks Muhitdinov in Damascus and Nishanov in Lebanon and Sri Lanka; the Azeri Mutalibov in Pakistan and the Tatar Tabiev in Kabul), but they would all be serving in Third World, and particularly Muslim, countries.

Given that Muslims were excluded from central functions, they gradually took over the administration of their own republics. This was possible thanks to the policy of indigenisation of cadres which had been launched in 1921, and then blocked, or resumed in chaotic manner, because of fears of nationalism. Even in Kazakhstan, which was closely watched because of the deep antagonism between Russians and Kazakhs, the proportion of Kazakhs in the Communist Party rose from 29.1 percent in 1925 to an average of 50 percent between 1932 and 1942, before falling abruptly in 1943, and subsequently stabilising at 40 percent, which tallied with the percentage of Kazakhs living in the republic. At the Tashkent's Congress of the Intelligentsia in 1956, ethnic Uzbeks were only 51 percent of those present, even though in the 1959 census they were shown as representing 62.2 percent of the population. However, by the end of the Soviet period it was clear that indigenisation had become a reality, and not only at the level of the party. The percentage of 'national' cadres within industry, management, transport and communications corresponded to the representation of their group within the total population, in other words 67.6 percent in Uzbekistan as a whole.[13] Significantly, the number of Muslims increased even more in educational institutions. This, incidentally, led the Russians and some observers to speak of a kind of Soviet-style 'affirmative action', discriminating in favour of native populations. Nancy Lubin shows how, during the 1970s, Central Asian institutions of higher education allocated a quota of between 66 percent and 80 percent of their places to students belonging to the national ethnic group. In 1978, the figures for admission to the teacher-training institute in Bukhara show that one out of every three native-born candidates was admitted, compared with only one in seven for non-natives – and there is nothing to suggest that the latter were in any way inferior candidates. It is also noteworthy that institutions of higher education in the province of Jizak, from where the first secretary hails, have the republic's highest rate of acceptance of candidates, thereby combining, as often happens, ethnic nationalism and regionalist factionalism.[14] This reverse discrimination was to play a role when Russian prosecutors went onto the offensive between 1983 and 1987 against 'mafia' activity, clientelism and nepotism in the south.

Muslim cadres thus found themselves existing within a double culture which they lived without any apparent schizophrenia. The Brezhnev period (1964–82) was the period in which the system of regionalism and clientelism became established and functioned without intervention from Moscow. But it was also the era that saw a major campaign for the 'fusion of peoples' (in other words Russification), launched in 1956. For cadres, this Russification was something to be taken seriously: Rashidov required his collaborators to have perfect mastery of the Russian language, and having a Russian wife was a definite plus in career terms. The nomenklatura sent their children to the Russian school, in other words the school where Russian was the language of teaching, and where the level was consistently higher than that of schools teaching in national languages. They increasingly spoke Russian at home, keeping the national language as a kind of patois which was used for speaking to grandma or peasants in the *kolkhoz*. Russification and 're-traditionalisation' go hand in hand, and involve the same protagonists. The latent nationalism of the cadres in the republics did not derive from some former society reasserting its existence, but began when Russia started to threaten the advantages acquired from Sovietism, as well as this compromise between a power politics which local people had learned to master and access to a universality which was available through the fact of belonging to the Soviet system.

What we see emerging in the Brezhnev era was a cultural nationalism that was actually searching for compromise with Moscow.

REGIONALIST FACTIONS AND THE STATE APPARATUS

The reality of power in the Soviet republics turned on three positions: the first secretary of the Communist Party, who had the real power; the president of the Supreme Soviet, who functioned as head of state, often the next step on the road before becoming first secretary; and the prime minister. The allocation of these three positions in terms of clan interests is indicative of how the power balance worked. Traditionally, the post of second secretary was reserved for a Russian (it was given to a Muslim in the event – rare after 1947 – of the first secretaryship being given to a Russian). In order to illustrate the history of political factionalism in the various republics prior to independence, I shall give some examples of how the mechanism worked.

Uzbekistan

Uzbekistan has always been ruled by native-born cadres, unlike all the other republics of Central Asia. For reasons that were essentially strategic, it was given favoured treatment in the 1920s.

In Uzbekistan between 1925 and 1937, Bolshevik power rested on a trio consisting of Fayzullah Khojayev, the prime minister, who hailed originally from Bukhara; Akmal Ikramov, first secretary of the party and originally from Tashkent; and Yoldash Akhundbabayev, president of the Supreme Soviet, who was from Margellan in the Ferghana Valley.[15] The first two disappeared in 1937, with the customary accusation of nationalism and pan-Turkism. The third became president of the Supreme Soviet (he died in 1943). He was a man with little education and was not part of the Jadid élite; he also came from Ferghana, which was a rising region after 1937, and this presumably played a part in his success.

The relative balance between regions disappears with the new team of 1937: now the Ferghana faction takes charge. The following key figures all had a Ferghana background: Osman Yussupov, first secretary of the party (1937–50); Amin Nyazov, president of the Supreme Soviet from 1947 to 1950 and then first secretary of the Communist Party from 1950 to 1955; two successive presidents of the Council of Ministers, S. Segizbayev (1937–8) and A. Abdurrahmanov (1938–50); and the man who was the president of the Supreme Soviet up until 1943, Akhundbabayev. Such a homogeneity cannot be purely fortuitous. The Ferghana group established an alliance with the group from Tashkent, an alliance which still makes sense today; so it was that Siraj Nuritdinov entered the seraglio (born in Tashkent in 1911, he became first secretary of the province of Tashkent in 1947 and joined the Politburo of the Uzbek Communist Party in 1949). This is not the expression of a 'traditional' alliance. One can only say that these two regions embody the most 'Uzbek' and least Persian part of the country. But they are not the bearers of a more Uzbek vision of nationalism: the Bukhara and Samarkand factions, albeit more 'Persian' (Khojayev spoke Tajik, as does the present president, Karimov), pursued a policy of Uzbekisation to the detriment of the Tajik identity, in rather the same way that the unification of Italy was built around the most French and French-speaking part of the country, Savoy and Piedmont.

The Tashkent-Ferghana axis maintained power up until 1959, after a hand-over to a new generation, which saw the arrival of apparatchiks who were pure products of the Soviet system. N.A. Muhitdinov, first secretary from 1955 to 1957, was born in Tashkent in 1917. He began his career in Namangan in Ferghana, in 1950 becoming first secretary of the province of Tashkent. He then became president of the Council of Ministers in 1951, and subsequently deputy prime minister. In December 1955, when Khrushchev returned from his Asia tour and stopped over in Tashkent, Muhitdinov was promoted to first secretary, before then going on to Moscow to become secretary of the CPSU in 1957 (the first person from Central Asia to occupy such a post). His successor as first secretary from 1957 until March 1959, Sabir Kamalov, was also born in Tashkent (in 1910), came up through the Komsomol, and also began his career in Ferghana (in 1938, as second secretary of the district of Ferghana) and went on to become president of the Council of Ministers from 1955 to 1957. Their two routes are almost identical: from Tashkent to Tashkent, passing via Ferghana.

This hegemony was broken by the rise of an outsider: Sharaf Rashidov, born in 1917 in Jizak near Samarkand, where he began his career. From 1944 to 1947, he was in charge of cadres for the province, going on to become editor first of *Lenin Yolu* in Samarkand, and then of *Qizil Uzbekistan* ('red Uzbekistan') in Tashkent (1947–50). He became president of the Union of Writers (1950–1), then president of the Praesidium of the Supreme Soviet in 1951, and finally first secretary of the Communist Party in 1959. While it is clear that his career was initially launched by a relation (Olimjan, editor of *Qizil Uzbekistan* and president of the Union of Writers from 1938 to 1944, the year of his death), his rise was manifestly due to the protection of Muhitdinov. By bringing Samarkand people into positions of power, Muhitdinov was hoping to hold off rivals within his own regionalist faction (Nuritdinov, his wife Nasriddinova, Sabir Kamalov and Mirza-Ahmedov). It is also probable that Moscow, where Muhitdinov was now located, wanted to avoid any single faction gaining hegemony. It seems that it was Khrushchev who came down in favour of Rashidov. In 1959, Rashidov became first secretary of the Uzbek Communist Party, while Iadgar Nasriddinova, the wife of Nuritdinov and an adversary of Rashidov, became head of state in his place.

When Muhitdinov was removed from the Politburo of the CPSU in 1961, Rashidov joined as a deputy member. This presumably reflected Khrushchev's desire, at the time of his charm offensive in relation to the Third World, to open high-ranking offices in the USSR to Muslim apparatchiks (Muhitdinov was subsequently appointed ambassador to Damascus). This required that there be a quota of Muslims within the Politburo, regardless of factional struggles at the base.

This new position gave Rashidov a certain power, but the Uzbek apparatus was still largely in the hands of the Tashkent-Ferghana faction, represented by Sabir Kamalov, Nishanov and Rahmankul Kurbanov (the president of the Council of Ministers, originally from Bukhara, but who had spent his entire career in Ferghana), with Iadgar Nasruddinova as head of state. After the firing of Muhitdinov from the Politburo, the Tashkent-Ferghana faction once again became homogeneous and closed ranks against Rashidov the intruder. He, however, then found an incident which he was able to use. In 1969, on the occasion of a football match between the Pakhtakâr ('cotton worker') Uzbek team and a Russian team, the crowd demonstrated against the Russians. The compromise on which the north-south relation was based (a broad autonomy of action in exchange for loyalty and anti-nationalism) was threatened. Rashidov succeeded in convincing Moscow that it was all the fault of the Nasruddinova group, and she lost her position. Kurbanov was sentenced to six years in prison. Rafiq Nishanov, originally from Tashkent, who had entered the Politburo in 1966, remained there until he was thrown out in 1970. Associates of Rashidov took control of two other key positions in the state apparatus between 1969 and 1971: N. Khodaberdayev became president of the Council of Ministers and Nazar Machanov the head of state. The former was from Jizak, like Rashidov himself, and the second was born in Samarkand in 1923. In 1971, a new group held hegemonic power: the Samarkand-Jizak faction.

However, as in 1959, Moscow wanted to avoid the development of hegemonies, and discreetly began pushing other pawns into place: Machanov was replaced in 1978 by Inamjan Osmankhojayev, who was born in Ferghana and had pursued his whole career there (among other positions as director of Ferghana's canal).[16]

Brezhnev's death and the accession of Andropov changed the situation. In 1983, the 'cotton scandal' opened the way for a Moscow-directed clean-up. Rashidov died in November 1983. Inamjan Osmankhojayev was thereupon appointed first secretary. He allied himself with A.U. Salimov, the new head of state, and G.H. Khaydarov (born in 1939), the new president of the Council of Ministers in 1985. All three had been either students or teachers at the Polytechnic Institute of Tashkent, and they represented the Ferghana-Tashkent faction. A purge subsequently decimated the ranks of the party cadres: in January 1985, 40 of the 65 provincial secretaries were relieved of their posts (including 10 out of 13 first secretaries). In January 1986 the Congress of the Uzbek Communist Party attacked Rashidov, and Salimov lost his position in that same year to Rafiq Nishanov, who was even more fiercely anti-Rashidov. Unexpectedly, in 1988 Osmankhojayev was accused of corruption, sent for trial and found guilty. Nishanov became first secretary in January 1988, and Habibulayev, a Samarkandi, became head of state. Nishanov waged war on Rashidov's ghost: he abolished the district of Jizak, which had been created by Rashidov; he engineered the replacement of Habibulayev, who refused to speak against Rashidov, by Ibrahimov, a Ferghanite. The Tashkent-Ferghana faction was in power once again.

In the middle of 1989, Moscow was backing the hitherto almost unknown Islam Karimov, who had not had much of a career in the party. Karimov was born in Samarkand in 1938. An orphan, he began his career as an official in charge of the plan and became finance minister in 1986. However, in December of that year he was exiled to Kashka-Darya (as provincial first secretary), an exile which lasted until 1989. Evidently, Moscow was once again trying to play a balancing act between regionalist factions. But times had changed.

Islam Karimov was elected first secretary in June 1989, to replace Nishanov, who again became head of state. Power had transferred once again to the Samarkand-Jizak faction. Karimov was to capitalise on the rancour fuelled by Moscow's actions since 1983. He turned Rashidov into a symbol of Uzbek nationalism, and made himself champion of his country's independence. Nationalism became the new legitimacy for the same goal: power.

Tajikistan

The drama of Tajikistan is that potential élites could not be drawn from the territory which the country had been allocated, because the Tajik intelligentsia had always been based in either Samarkand or Bukhara. The first president of the Sovnarkom of Tajikistan (1925–29, when it was still attached to Uzbekistan) was a Samarkand Tajik, Abdullah Muhiddinov. As we have already seen, his successors came from Russia. The Persian-speaking cadres were either from Samarkand and Ferghana (for example, Urunbey Ashurov), or Afghan (for example, Nissam Muhamedov, the minister of education).

An initial élite was recruited from among the Pamiris (for instance Shirinshah Shahtimur, born in 1899, who was president of the soviet from 1933 to 1937). The explanation of this may have been that the Pamiris, being poor, not very religious, looked down on by the Sunnis and under Russian domination since the 1870s, had played the Russian card. However, the Pamiris were purged in 1937.[17]

Babajan Ghafurovich Ghafurov (1909–77, born in Isfara, Leninabad province) was second secretary of the Tajik Communist Party from 1944 to 1946, and first secretary from 1946 to 1956. His secretaryship inaugurated the uninterrupted power of the Leninabad faction over a period which was to last right through to 1992. He was to be followed by Tursunbey Uljabayev (first secretary from 1956 to 1961), Jabbar Rassulov (1956 to 1982, the year of his death), Nabiyev (1982–5) and Kahhar Mahkamov (born in Khojent in 1932) from December 1985 to August 1991. Thus in Tajikistan Moscow did not switch factions in 1983. This hegemony is explained by the fact that the town of Khojent-Leninabad, conquered by the Russians back in 1864, is more developed, more Russified, and also more 'Uzbekised' than the rest of Tajikistan. These were people that Moscow could trust.

The four main regionalist groupings in Tajikistan were as follows: Leninabadis, Kulabis, Gharmis (originating from the region of Karategin) and Pamiris. To this, one should add the internal divisions: the district of Ura-Teppe in the province of Leninabad tends to maintain an identity of its own, while the valley of Zarafshan (Penjikent) avoided involvement in the competition but supplied a number of democrat intellectuals. The district of Hissar to the west of Dushanbe defends its independence and at the same time allies itself with the Kulabis: here one has a real regionalist identity, going beyond ethnicity, because the district's population is comprised of roughly 60 percent Uzbeks and 40 percent Tajiks who are not divided by political differences. The Darwazis are assimilated with the Gharmis.

We have seen how the hegemony of the Leninabadis in the period 1946–92 translated into the disappearance of all the other provinces, except the Autonomous Region of Gorno-Badakhshan, whose status could only be changed by Moscow. However, the situation became tense at the start of the 1970s. Kulab was re-established as a province in 1973: Leninabad had to ease off. The president of the Kulab soviet, a Leninabadi, was assassinated in 1974 and replaced by a Kulabi. But two years later the adjoining region of Kurgan-Teppe was upgraded to province status to act as a counterweight to Kulab. It was populated principally by Gharmis who had been transferred in the 1950s and by Uzbeks. Thus one can see how the interplay of politics gives an administrative reality to regionalist groups as a function of power struggles.

The Leninabadis then conceded positions to other groups. While the first secretary was from Leninabad, the president of the Council of Ministers was a Kulabi from 1985 onwards (Khayayev between 1985 and 1990) and the president of the Assembly (an honorary position) was a Gharmi from Fayzabad, the Gharmi town closest to the power élites. The war in Afghanistan put the Pamiris back in the saddle, because Moscow was nervous of possible collusion between the Tajiks and the Afghan Muhajedin, and decided to give the Pamiris the MVD and part of the KGB. Thus the only ones to be excluded from power were the Gharmis, and they went on to become politicised under the banner of Islam.

The stage was all set for civil war: unlike the situation in the other republics, the dominant faction controlled neither the security apparatuses nor the apparatus in the countryside. It controlled only the central political apparatus and its own province.

The Other Republics

Studies on the political life of the other republics are rare.

In Kazakhstan, the direct political hold of the Russians was obviously stronger, and this meant that tribal oppositions were less pertinent. The allocation of power positions is seen in ethnic (Russian versus Kazakh) rather than regionalist or tribal terms. Members of Alash Orda were thrown out of the party in 1923. In 1925, the first secretary, the Russian Goloshcheskin and the president of the Sovnarkom, U. Isayev, took a hard line: sovietise the *awls* ('encampments') and combat the beys. In 1932, following on collectivisation, the nomads killed their flocks. Goloshcheskin and Isayev were removed; the new first secretary was to be Mirzoyan (an Armenian), with S. Nurpeysov as his second-in-command. In 1936, Kazakhstan became a Soviet republic; in 1937, the first congress of the new Communist Party was accompanied by purges which worked to the advantage of those who had joined the party in the late 1920s. Turar Ryskulov was tried in 1937 and subsequently executed; the following year, those who had succeeded Alash Orda members in the Communist Party were eliminated (S. Seyfulin).

By 1939, a new duo was ruling the country: N. Skortsev became first secretary, and Jumabey Shayakhmetov second secretary; in 1946 he was to become the first Kazakh first secretary (in this he was to be followed by Brezhnev (1954–6), Yakovlev (1956–9) and finally Kunayev, through to 1986). The key to Kazakh politics as regards the allocation of power positions is very much the ethnic opposition between Russians and Kazakhs. However, it is clear that the Great Horde, established in the south and south-east of the country, was the predominant political power within the Kazakh apparatus. The current president, Nazarbayev, is a member of the Great Horde.

In Azerbaijan, the political élite recruits among people from Nakhichevan and the town of Erevan. Here the regionalist faction has no social base. It is a pure apparatus faction, like the Samarkand-Jizak faction. But this is not the only criterion dictating solidarities, because rivals may be of the same regional origin. Abulfaz Elchibey, the leader of the Popular Front after independence, was from Nakhichevan, as was Rassul Gouliev (the parliamentary president under Aliyev) and Abbasov (head of the KGB). Aliyev was born in Armenia. This way of imposing a political élite that comes from outside accentuates the centrifugal tendencies of the various regions, in a sense returning to the logic of the khanates which existed before the tsarist administrative reform unified Azerbaijan in the last century.

In Kyrgyzstan, the political system is built on an opposition between north and south. The current president, Akayev, and his whole team, are from the north, from the valleys of Talas, Jui and Kemin (his birthplace), while the valleys of Issik Kul and Nahrin remain outside their control. These regionalist oppositions do not translate into a struggle for central power, as in Tajikistan, but rather into a determination to neutralise and ignore that power. Behind the various labels ('conservative', 'progressive', etc) the nature of the political struggles reflects these regional conflicts. In 1995 there was a crisis in Osh, between the *hâkim* ('governor'), Janish Rustambekov, who was from the north and appointed by Akayev, and the *kenesh* ('local soviet'), presided over by Bekmamat Osmonov.

In Turkmenistan, it is the faction originating from within the Tekke tribe and from the town of Ashkhabad which holds power. The president, Nyazov, was born in Ashkhabad in 1940. In 1980, he became first secretary of the Communist Party at town level, and then subsequently at the level of the republic. In 1995, all the local *hâkim* were drawn from the locally dominant tribe. Despite his autocratic behaviour, Nyazov is maintaining a balance between the various tribes.

But while regionalism is a key factor on the domestic political scene, it has not prevented the emergence of a national political scene (which, moreover, it needed). Any struggle for power presupposes that there is power to be won. Factionalism needs the state, given that it defines itself in relation to a central point, a source of power and of possible revenues over and above those deriving from its own region. This strong stamp of the state left by sovietism explains why autonomy and regional independence are of interest to none of the regionalist factions, except the Ismailis of Pamir, who at a certain point (in 1993) dreamed that the Aga Khan Foundation would help them to become independent of a Tajikistan which was rejecting them as a result of their alliance with the Islamic-democratic opposition.

THE REALITY EFFECT OF A STATE STRUCTURE

At the moment of independence, the republics already had virtually all the attributes of independent states: a head of state, a parliament, a party and a ministry of foreign affairs. Symbolic sovereignty preceded and made possible real sovereignty, particularly since sovietism had also installed the beneficiaries of these nations: ie 'nationality', the people whose name the republic bore, the nation. The Soviet system was a remarkably effective machine for ethnicisation and ethnic homogenisation. It obliged people to choose their 'nationality' and encouraged the merging of small groups into larger groups. All people speaking a Turkic dialect in the terrritory of Uzbekistan, as long as they were not members of a recognised titular nationality (Kyrgyz, Kazakh or Karakalpak) were invited to declare themselves Uzbeks. The function of censuses was not to describe society: it forced people to choose an identity from the list of possible identities laid down by the state.[18] The multi-ethnic category 'Sarts' disappeared in the 1926 census to be replaced by Tajiks and Uzbeks. We have seen how the system created an ethnic homogenisation (Qipchaks and Turki were registered as Uzbeks, and Yaghnobis and Pamiris as Tajiks). The very concept of nation suggests that people should belong exclusively to either one or another. If one follows certain rules, one has the right to change to another ethnic group, but one cannot belong to several at the same time.[19] The system turns identity into an administrative category, of which the highest is that of nation.

For all that they were artificial, the Soviet republics transformed into realities. This reality effect comes into play at several levels: the manufacture of a national imaginary; the creation of a bureaucratic élite which owes everything to this national framework; and finally the setting in place of a state context which generates a national habitus. The 'Soviet' republics provided the framework for literacy programmes, for intellectual formation and for the political and social promotion not only of the élites currently in power, but of the whole intelligentsia. The Communist Party in the republics manufactured a national political class, even if it was not yet nationalist, not least because the apparatchiks did not have the option of making a career outside the republic.[20] And leaving aside regional factionalism, the rotation of cadres within the republic also created a sense of national identity. The political scene creates its own protagonist: a political élite. There are now identities which are Uzbek, Turkmen, Kyrgyz and Kazakh. These are linked to the rise to power of local apparatchiks who owe their promotion in the face of the Russians to the national framework of their republic. But in order to guarantee themselves a power base by traditional methods (clanism and clientism), these people were able to, and had to, retain very close links with their rural society, 'nationalising' this to a certain extent, even if the establishment of identities and local solidarities was dictated by other principles.

The social transformation imposed by sovietism took place after the national division of 1924 (the reform of law courts and codes of law in 1927 and 1928, collectivisation from 1927 to 1932, and the change of alphabet). The new societies thus know only this frame of reference. These reforms were matched by the emergence of institutions which were all organised within the framework of the nation in question – schools, universities, academies etc – with a cohort of beneficiaries and promotees who from now on were tied to this framework.

However, some key attributes of sovereignty were missing: the most important of these was the army, and everything to do with transportation and communication (which was maintained as a monopoly of the centre, as in the case of Aeroflot). But in the republics these domains were in the hands of Europeans. As a result, there were relatively few natives of the republics whose social and professional status was intrinsically tied to the continued existence of the USSR (a few generals, perhaps, and diplomats not belonging to the dominant faction of their country of origin – people such as as General Ashurov, who commanded the 201st Division in Dushanbe in 1992).

The manufacture of nationality also requires the existence of institutions able to deal with questions of language, history, ethnology, archaeology etc. The need for the administrative management of a body of knowledge creates a core of intellectual state employees, of 'literati', whose social existence is tied to the existence of this body of knowledge. Why do intellectuals play this role? Because their job is to manage this imaginary. They reflect back on the Soviet censor, the concept of 'national culture' which the Soviets had invented in order to get people to believe in the existence of their nations, but this time with a flavour of authenticity. Of course, the promotion of these intellectual state employees was dictated by other factors (conformism and clientism), but they also had other motivations, particularly since promotion was limited to the space of the given republic. The national science academies sponsored works that were designed to make these nationalities exist. Academics and experts also owe their status to these new nations. After the purges of 1937, the intelligentsias of the various republics reappropriated to themselves the concept of nation and national culture, initially against their neighbours, but subsequently also against Moscow. The reality effect created by the nationalities policy is that everyone fought to defend their own territory, their own heritage and their own access to the Soviet 'market'. Moscow's response was ambiguous: over-enthusiastic outbursts of 'nationalism' were repressed, sporadically, particularly when they threatened Russian superiority, but Moscow was far more permissive in the face of conflicts between 'nationalities'. These conflicts between 'nationalities' in the Soviet era were a consequence of national division, but were also part of the way in which they took root.

Literature and the humanities became sources of contention. In archaeology, nationalist Tajiks were searching for Sogdians or perhaps Zoroastrians, while Uzbeks were looking for Turks and were interested in Tamerlane (whose tomb was to be discovered by Russian archaeologists).[21] There were battles over nationalising key figures of the Muslim era: the Azeris took Nezami, born in Ganja in 1141, and turned him into a Turk, while the Tajiks said he was a Persian. These arguments were low-key and expressed themselves in coded form in journals and reviews within the individual republics, but everybody knew what was going on. All you need do is to read the article under the heading 'Nava'i' in the *Tajik Soviet Encyclopaedia* to see how a latent polemic can slip under the wire of apparent Soviet normalisation. As we know, Nava'i wrote equally well in 'Turki' and Persian, but the Soviets turned him into the founder of Uzbek literature, and thus left out his whole Persian aspect, which is unknown to Uzbeks. The *Tajik Soviet Encyclopaedia* therefore carries the official definition, 'the founder of classical Uzbek literature' and then, a few lines later on, quotes in Persian a verse which the poet had written in that language: 'The sensation of sugar and of colour is for me without limits in Turkish/I consider Persian as rubies and white pearls/One would say that when I speak in the alley of the bazaar/On one side there is a confectioner's shop, and on the other a jewellery shop'. The text discreetly rehabilitates this bilingual Turko-Persian literature, and wipes out the myth of Nava'i as founder of the Uzbek language, a term which incidentally he never used. In the same way, the *Tajik Soviet Encyclopaedia* includes, on the slightest pretext, names and quotations in the Arabic-Persian alphabet (for authors preceding the Soviet period). This is a way of keeping the memory of these things alive, but also of signalling that Tajik and Persian literatures are in fact one.

More importantly, intellectuals in the republics had to defend themselves against the inquisitions, criticisms or simply contempt of their 'European' colleagues. These conflicts, which had the appearance of being scientific or ideological, counterpose two groups: the 'Russian' academics, who were concerned to keep the most interesting areas of work for themselves (medieval archaeological excavations, for example), and local scientists concerned to defend their section of the 'market'. The national argument is also an argument over appropriation of the market of intellectual labour.

The labours of these intellectuals receive a degree of support from the apparatchiks in power, although they may find deviations being condemned on the orders of Moscow. Broadly speaking, the apparatus protects the local intelligentsia. Ghafurov, the first secretary of the Tajik Communist Party from 1947 to 1957, was the author of a book, *The Tajiks*, which, while accepting the Soviet concept of nation, laid out a defence and illustration of the Persian nature of Central Asia. He himself had tried, at the time of the population transfers of the 1950s, to get Tajiks from Ferghana to come and settle in the region of Kurgan-Teppe, which up until then had been majority Uzbek. By the same token, Tashkent opposed the separation from Tajikistan, and the inclusion of districts of Chimkent into Kazakhstan.

But the nationalisms thus created were also capable of entering into open conflict with Moscow. In the early 1950s, the microcosm of Russian censorship had a field day in the so-called 'Manas affair'. This related to the traditional epic of the Kyrgyz, which Moscow had suddenly decided was suspect.[22] At the same time, the Kazakhs were attempting to rehabilitate the Kazakh revolts of the nineteenth century.[23] In both these cases the warning shots fired by Moscow had hardly any effect, and the authors under investigation were discreetly protected by their peers.

★   ★   ★

But when we talk about national culture, what exactly are we talking about? Leaving aside the Tajiks, who are able to draw on a rich Persian literature, the other nationalities are limited in their quest for a culture of their own by the national division, which bans them from drawing on anything which has not explicitly been defined as belonging to their 'modern national literature'.

The Soviet system defines a national culture, reduced to some minimal elements, which was folklorised, codified, and limited by the requirements of 'internationalism' (that is by the primacy of Russia), and by the concept of 'form and content': the 'form' (language, style, location) could be national, but the content should be 'international'. Moscow spent its time keeping a close watch on these limits (polemics about folk epics, and on the reactionary character of various national heroes), and lost sight of the fact that the very maintaining of a 'national culture', however narrow, was creating a core of administrators of that culture, an intelligentsia which had no hope of recognition at the Soviet level, and who owed its social status to the management of that national body of culture, however poor it may have been.

Bureaucracy produced not so much control as social categories that were charged with managing the spaces which the state wished to appropriate unto itself. Ethnography, folklore and poetry were there in order to transform all content into a simple code. This folklorisation of social content was initially conceived as a way of opening the road for the installation of a new content, which would be Sovietist. The national element was turned into a remnant, a historical leftover, by mummifying it in advance. But as it happened, there was a social dynamic attached to the running of that mummy (rather more alive than the mummy of Lenin), because behind it lay the existence of a whole society. The people concerned thus picked up on the vision of themselves that they had been given and reappropriated their national folklore, which had been defined and appropriately sanitised by the Soviets. They then proceeded systematically to emphazise the 'small differences' that had been authorised: horse meat on the menu of all Kazakh banquets; the *chapan* ('long coat') which is offered as a matter of course to all foreign delegations visiting Turkmenistan. The fixing of ethnic identities is reinforced by ethnography: the split between Kazakhs and Kyrgyz on the one hand and Uzbeks and Tajiks on the other is expressed by hats (the Kyrgyz *kalpak*, as against the *tupi*).

Mass education turns the country's language into a reality. That language is one of the preconditions for acquiring knowledge, even if its status is inferior to that of Russian. But the pre-eminence of Russian, which is incarnated in the twin system of teaching (ie either in Russian or in the local language) has perverse effects: those who are excluded from the Russian schools develop a reactive national identity, and for them imposing the national language becomes a way of taking the place of the Russian-speaking élites. Spontaneous language reform began before independence; already by 1960 one was beginning to see a tendency to replace Russian borrowings with local words, beginning in Uzbekistan.[24] Foreign archaeologists working in Tajikistan after 1985 discovered that their Tajik workers were imposing a small fine every time anyone used a Russian word. In the same way, from the 1960s onwards there is a tendency for the suffixes -ov and -ev in surnames to disappear.[25]

There was the old slogan about the role of national cultures: 'The form is national, the content is socialist'. Now the form was getting the upper hand over the content, because there was no content in the socialist system. Socialist ideology had nothing to say to the peoples of the south. There was none of the political imaginary which is associated with it in European societies that had been powerfully politicised and marked by a history of revolutions. The 1917 revolution is not part of the imaginary of Muslims, and while it may be the case that the memory of the *basmachis* has been erased or minimised, or even provides no identity support whatever, it has not been replaced by a Soviet imaginary. For the south, sovietism was a code not a culture.

Thus it was the national form which created the national *habitus*. Language prevailed over the message, administrative territorial realignments over internationalism, and the apparatus over ideology.

There is almost no national cultural *corpus*, apart from officially aproved poems, and collections of proverbs, because nobody is writing anything new in the national language. What one has is a national praxis designed to show differentness, conceived within registers which are not only authorised but promoted by the Soviet system: cookery, folklore, ostentatious hospitality etc. Ethnography takes the upper hand over sociology, and even over ethnology: it sets about defining a repertoire of national culture made up solely of materials and segments of a literary *corpus* that are fossilised and basically limited to to poetry, as a decorative art based on worn-out clichés.[26]

Thus people draw on the authorised folklore registers to find themselves new identity sources which they then present to the outside world. These function rather like a mask for more complex and traditional social practices. In defending a folklorised national culture, one defends a body of practices, a social reality, that particular civil society which has been recreated, in the realm of the unspoken, behind the Soviet appearance.

This register is all the more folklorised because the Soviets did what they could to conceal anything that might attach it to any broader area of civilisation (Islam, Central Asia, the Turkic-Persian world etc). All of a sudden anything traditional (customs and beliefs) is presented as the expression of a 'national culture' and helps to promote and root a fabricated national identity. People talk about Uzbek clothing, Uzbek cooking, Uzbek customs, Uzbek hospitality etc, even though most of the elements involved actually relate to Islam and Central Asia in general. Rashidov rehabilitated Newruz in 1981 and presented it as an Uzbek festival even though it is a Persian tradition widely observed by people, from the Kurds to the Baluchs.

The isolation of the republics from broader regional entities, whether cultural or political, tended to reinforce the national identity rather than accelerate a fusion with the Russian world. The republics' relations with each other passed through Moscow in matters such as the economy or transportation, and this lessened any possibility of regional solidarities. The fact that Russian was the language of communication made it pointless to go looking for a 'common Turkic language': Uzbek and Turkmen officials communicated in Russian.

So, when the relationship with Russia began to become increasingly tense, independence came to be a possibility, precisely on the foundations that had been laid by the Soviet system.

The Dilemma of the Tajiks: Between Culture and Ethnicity

However, in this embedding of nationalities we have a paradoxical case: that of a group whose identity has a strong historic rooting, and which completely failed to appropriate the model of nation-state as the Soviets had formalised it. This was very much a sign that Soviet nation-making worked on the basis of a deculturation. The Soviets made a determined attempt at deculturation in the case of Tajikistan – by cutting off the new country from its urban élites and its Persian past. The ethnicisation of the Tajiks as a precondition of their elevation to the status of 'nationality' required their centre of gravity to be transferred away from the old historic towns towards the rural populations, who were less marked by Persian culture.

The drama of Tajikistan is that it was created without the historic Tajik cities, and on the basis of a rural and mountain-dwelling population that lacked élites and also lacked a sense of nationalism. There was a fundamental division between the Tajiks of the cities, Samarkand and Bukhara, who were interested in fighting for a Greater Uzbekistan or a Greater Turkestan, even Turkified, and the Tajiks of the foothills and mountains, who were known as Ghalcha[27] and who saw themselves landed with a republic that they had not asked for, but which regionalist factions then tried to appropriate for themselves. The events of 1992 in both camps were the retribution of the peasants and mountain peoples against an intelligentsia that had no localist rooting.

There was no transfer of élites from Samarkand and Bukhara to Tajikistan: like Sadruddin Ayni, the 'father of modern Tajik literature', they chose to remain in their towns of origin, thus marginalising themselves equally in respect of both Uzbekistan and Tajikistan. The few families who did relocate staffed the university and the media, but they never either wanted or were able to create their own political faction. Regionalism was thus able to function fully on the basis of rural power bases which were all of a sudden mutually competitive in relation to a central power that had been created artificially, but which was still the main source for delivering the goods. The paradox here is that the heirs of an old urban civilisation that was accustomed to being in the service of a state controlled by others after national division suddenly found themselves represented by rural factions who lack any vision of either state or nation.[28]

The Tajik élite of Samarkand and Bukhara was, as we have seen, inclined to notions of a new Greater Bukharia. Abdullah Rahimbayev, president of the Tajik Sovnarkom in the 1920s, registered himself as Uzbek by nationality (which in his view presumably meant 'Bukharian').[29] The secretary of the Communist Party of Bukhara, Ahmed Mawlanbeg, the president of the economic council of the Popular Republic of Bukhara, Abdulqader Muhitdinov, and the Tajiks' representative at the partition commission, Shinar Imamov (who was to become secretary of the organising committee of the Tajik Communist Party) all rejected the idea of creating a Greater Tajikistan. They preferred a Tajik identity within the framework of a federal Uzbekistan, with an autonomous Tajik region for the mountain dwellers from whom they felt themselves to be distant (Pamir, Mastsha, Kulab and Kurgan-Teppe).

The Soviets did everything they could to prevent the crystallisation of a Tajik national sentiment. The Tajik State University was only created in 1948, and the Academy of Sciences in 1951. This systematic devaluation, compared with the treatment accorded to their Uzbek neighbours, created resentment among Tajik nationalists, who are obsessed by the Uzbek threat, and today paradoxically seek some support from Moscow, which established this very assymetry in favour of Tashkent.[30]

How might one define 'Tajik nationalism'? There are two possible approaches: one is to take, as elsewhere, the Soviet ethnic view. Here the Tajiks are defined as the descendants of the Sogdians, formerly masters of Central Asia, who were then conquered by the Arabs, Persianised and subsequently Turkified. Occasionally it is noted that Uzbeks are often Turkified Tajiks, and people nurture a dream of a Greater Central Asia, reconnecting with the heritage of the Samanid emirate in the tenth century. At the moment of independence, many Tajik intellectuals developed a megalomaniac vision of 'Tajicity'. However, this maximalist position found little echo among the 'Turkified' populations in question, and left open the question of relations with Iran and the Persian-speaking populations of Afghanistan: if Tajik identity derives from language, then where are the limits of the Tajik world among Persian-speakers? In Bukhara, Kabul or Shiraz? As for the 'Sogdian theory', one would have a hard job resuscitating Sogdian. It is, incidentally, significant that nobody is trying to restore to pride of place the Yaghnobis, who are the only descendants of the Sogdians in linguistic terms. Soviet ethnographic theory, which was easily taken on board by the Uzbeks, does not work for the Tajiks, because the language (Persian) is wider in extent than the nation.

The second approach involves viewing the Tajiks as the heirs not of a nation, but of the great Persian and Sunni civilisation of Central Asia more broadly defined. What is stressed here is the universality of this culture, against all ethnic particularities (while at the same time it is admitted that Uzbeks are only Turkified Tajiks). This time one has a common denominator: the Islamic-Persian synthesis in its Sunni form. This was the position of Qazi Turajanzade, expressed in an article that he wrote in 1995.[31] He stresses language (Persian, not Tajik), culture and history, rather than the *sharia* and the Islamic state. Such an alliance between Islamists and nationalists is rather rare in Central Asia. Islamism becomes the expression of a national identity that was reduced by the ethnicisation set in motion at the time of Soviet division. The common point is the defence of language: no longer 'Tajiki', but Persian. Tajik nationalism crystallises around language in affirming its Persian-ness, and calls for a return to the Arabic-Persian alphabet.

Defence of the language is a popular theme in Tajikistan because it reconnects with a glorious past which neither Turkmenistan or Kazakhstan can claim. This defence is to be found as much in the popular milieux as among the Soviet élite. A typical example might be someone such as Mohamed Assimov (or Assimi), president of the Academy of Sciences, who came from an *ashraf* family of Khojent and served under all the regimes from 1960 to 1996 (the year of his assassination). He travelled regularly to Communist Afghanistan to help in the development of an Academy of Sciences on the Soviet model. In a sense, he recuperated the Soviet invasion of Afghanistan in order to strengthen the common elements between the two cultures, a double game typical of the national apparatchiks. But he is a fierce defender of the Persian language, if necessary against Iran too (a country which he reproached for having dialectised the classical heritage). He himself published in 1980 a work in the Arabic-Persian alphabet, evidently officially destined for Afghanistan, but which was distributed in Tajikistan (*Tashkil o takamol afkâr-i felsefi* – the formation and evolution of philosophical concepts). He reconciled his twin loyalties (to Persian and to Soviet 'Tajikism') by seeing in Tajik the best of Persian as regards pronunciation, while at the same time resisting Russification and Uzbekisation.

Even people who express themselves better in Russian than in Tajik regret that their language became corrupt (*zaban ganda shod*) and ask a foreigner for the 'correct' word in Persian (and are very disappointed to hear that the word 'lift' is rendered as *asansor* in Iranian Persian). The ability to speak properly remains a badge of prestige: for instance, the mullahs used to maintain a very classical Persian in order to stress an Islamo-Persian identity.

The Rastakhiz nationalist and democratic movement (led by Tahir Abduljabbar) and the Democratic Party (led by Shadman Yusuf), initially rather inclined to an 'ethnic' quest for the origins of Tajik nationalism (stressing in particular Zoroastrianism and the Sogdian heritage), allied themselves with the Islamist movement, with which they shared the desire for a return to Persian. This was also the case for the group of poets and intellectuals who came from the valley of Zarafshan (one of the popular strongholds as regards preservation of the language), who were little inclined to Islamism.

Iran, whose identity is more Shiite than Persian, was unable to use the common linguistic heritage in order to achieve a bridgehead into Tajikistan. The contacts which were made – intense during the course of 1992 – soon revealed the cultural gap. The arrogance of the Iranians towards the Tajiks ('Hey, do you speak Persian?', or 'How do you say such-and-such in your dialect?'), the heavy ideology of TV broadcasts to Tajikistan, and the Iranians' lack of interest in anything that may have been written in Persian outside Iran and the Shiite world, broke the myth of Iran. Persian-ness in Tajikistan is defended outside the terms of the Iranian model. But this literary and universalist vision proves incapable of being embodied into a concrete national project.

In the mountainous republic which the Tajiks were given, the form taken by politics is that of localism, a spontaneous vision of the presidents of the *kolkhoz*. The localist groups use the political scene as a way of defending their particular interests, even through predation. The idea of the Tajik nation, given that it lacked an urban élite, was paradoxically defended by the Pamiris. It gave them a chance to escape from their traditional marginality. They supplied political leaders (up until 1937), poets and musicians. But in the eyes of others they were always seen as a regionalist faction, and their attachment to the cause was inevitably seen as concealing other ambitions.

Nevertheless, the peace agreement of June 1997 between the warring factions, the threat of an Uzbek intervention, and the polarization of Afghanistan between the Pashtun Taliban and the Tajik Masud, gave a new incentive for a fledgling Tajik nationalism, this time reduced to the defence of the republic, mainly against Uzbek encroachment.

7

From Nationalism to Independence

THE RISE OF NATIONALISM: THE DIVORCE WITH MOSCOW (THE 1983 CRISIS AND *PERESTROIKA*)

When Andropov came to power in November 1982, his accession translated into a serious crisis between Moscow and the Muslim republics, in particular Uzbekistan. Having decided to denounce the economic stagnation and the scandals of the Brezhnev era, Andropov took as his example the 'cotton scandal'. The Uzbek authorities, in collusion with Brezhnev's entourage and his son-in-law in particular, were accused of having falsified figures for the cotton harvest in order to acquire massive sums of money on the basis of fictional sales. The 'Uzbek mafia' became the archetype for the mafias of the south. Sharaf Rashidov, the first secretary of the Communist Party, opportunely died in November 1983 and was replaced by the Moscow candidate, a Ferghana man, Osmankhojayev. The period between 1983 and 1987 marked the divorce of Moscow from the republics of the south, preparing the terrain for the proclamations of independence in 1991.

The three Muslim members of the Politbureau of the CPSU were removed in 1983. Over a three-year period, all the first secretaries of the Muslim republics were replaced. In Kyrgyzstan, first secretary Turdakun Usulbayev was stood down in December 1985, replaced by Absamat Masaliyev, and the Tajik Nabiyev by Mahkamov. In 1983, for the first time since the war, a Russian (Satin) was the first secretary of the Gorkom of Tashkent (he lasted through to 1990). Ninety percent of the nomenklatura of the Central Committee in Uzbekistan was changed between 1984 and 1987. Worse, Gorbachev replaced the Kazakh Kunayev with a Russian, Kolbin, a decision which unleashed the Alma Ata riots in December 1986, which can be seen as the real starting point for the dissolution of the USSR.

Even though the struggle against corruption involved all sectors of Soviet society, the Muslim republics were particularly targeted, and the line

125

separating the good guys (uncorruptible judges, all Russians, such as Gdilian and Ivanov, who had been sent to Uzbekistan) from the 'bad' (Uzbek and Azeri mafiosi such as Rashidov or Adilov) was clearly ethnic. Thus the 4 October 1987 *Moscow News* (a newspaper designed for foreign or Muscovite consumption) announced the authoritarian closure of an Azerbaijani university institute in which the students were enrolled on the basis of recommendation, and bought their diplomas. This kind of thing was not rare in the USSR. The article began as follows: 'This is the first time that such an event [the closure of an institute] has happened in the history of establishments of higher learning in the Soviet Union'. The state inspector in charge of the closure, a Russian, gave as his justification, in addition to the corruption, the fact that 'the republic needed only half the number of specialists who were being trained in the Institute'. This was a double insult to the Muslims: they were the only ones seen to have been buying their diplomas, and they were also seen as producing too many graduates. Behind the big words one can also read the nervousness of many Russians at what was happening with the policy of promoting indigenous cadres: it was translating not into their Russification, as had been hoped, but into a surreptitious exclusion of Russians from the region.

In pure Stalinist style, Moscow found a new name for the political deviation based on local traditions of clanism and clientelism: 'Rashidovism' (*rashidovshchina*). The attack was not only political. It was cultural and almost sociological, because the finger was being pointed at the ways that a whole society worked. With the advent of *perestroika* the Russian 'free' press began launching attacks on mafiosi and feudalism in the south. A typical example appeared from the pen of V. Sokolov in the *Literaturnaya Gazeta* ('Zona molshanaya', 20 January 1988) describing the vices of a minor Uzbek feudal *seigneur*, namely Adilov. Tashkent was depicted as a city at the mercy of organised crime.[1] Anyone who eight years later had the opportunity to compare security in Tashkent with security in Moscow, and the role of the mafia in the two cities, would agree about the 'exotic', in fact openly racist, nature of the Russian media's view of the south. Coupled with the contempt with which Muscovites treat the southerners (known as 'black-arses'), this kind of denunciation goes a long way to explaining why opinion in the south ended up favouring divorce from the rest of the USSR: what one has here is no longer a simple settling of accounts between apparatchiks, but a cultural and political split between north and south. This was something that was understood immediately by rulers such as Islam Karimov.

Perestroika was also a threat to the economy of the south. This was firstly because restrictions were placed on economic practices that had previously been widely practised. It was also because the south had enjoyed special attention from the centre during the Brezhnev era. The war in Afghanistan had strengthened the position of Central Asia within the Soviet system – partly as a showcase, and partly as a strategic hinterland (a fact which brought it, for example, electrification and the establishment of a good road network along the Afghan border, and also subsidies in energy and money). Young Tajik and Uzbek graduates were sent as experts and volunteers to Afghanistan and to Muslim countries, on high salaries. The Orientalist Institutes of Tashkent, Baku and Moscow taught hundreds of young Soviet Muslims Arabic and Persian with a view to sending them abroad. The muftiyya of Tashkent played a public relations role in relation to conservative Arabic countries. In short, the republics of Central Asia achieved an access to the rest of the world thanks to a helping hand from the USSR. Contrary to what some have claimed, none of the thousands of young Soviet Uzbeks and Tajiks employed as overseas aid staff and experts in Afghanistan joined the Mujahedin (and such desertions as there were involved Slavs). The withdrawal from Afghanistan, the retrenchment from involvement in the Third World, and the low regard in which all Muslims were held all contributed to under-mining the kind of collective promotion which the republics of the south had found in their belonging to the USSR.

The scale of demographic growth in the south was becoming a real problem, because it was hard to create jobs to match. There were two possible solutions: either develop local industry and agriculture, or encourage the workforce to be more mobile, in other words promote emigration northwards. The preference of the peoples of the south was obviously for the former option, which was what Brezhnev had intended with the Sibaral Project, which was based on diverting a number of Siberian rivers towards Central Asia. The project was officially abandoned in August 1986 on account of its lack of economic rationality, a decision based on a report by a Russian economic expert, Aganbekian, one of Gorbachev's economic advisors. When one recalls that opposition to this project (as well as to the project of diverting rivers in European Russia) created a common front between eco-nomic experts and Greater Russian nationalists, it is easier to understand the bitterness of the Muslim populations, particularly with the worsening of the ecological situation in the south (for example, the drop in the water levels of the Aral Sea and increasing levels of drought). Instead, Moscow's economic experts began preparing projects for the transfer of workers from the south to Siberia, which caused revulsion among Muslims, who were very attached to their land.

At the same time, there was an abrupt and very noticeable drop in Central Asia in the amount of investment coming from the centre: per capita investment from the centre was two thirds lower than in the rest of the USSR.[2] There was a generalised state of economic crisis, but the Russian withdrawal from the economy of the south did not date solely from the period of independence. For the first time Uzbek intellectuals were to be found writing in the Soviet press denouncing the colonial nature of eco-nomic relations between Russia and the south.[3]

Gorbachev contributed to this political and economic ferment with a note of cultural contempt. In Tashkent in November 1986, he made a violently anti-Islamic speech which was perceived as discriminatory because unlike

Khrushchev, he steered clear of attacking Christianity (preparations were being made for the celebration on the thousandth anniversary of Russia's conversion to Orthodox Christianity). In the same year, an Uzbek official in the new team proposed abandoning the Uzbek skullcap in favour of the trilby. Leaving aside questions of aesthetics, such a message was poorly received.

Finally, there were two other factors that added to the tension and increased the mobilisation of a population which in normal circumstances was not very political: the situation of Muslim conscripts in the Soviet army, and the ecological catastrophe affecting the region. Harassment of Muslims was nothing new, but from the 1970s onwards it seemed to be on the increase, perhaps as a result of a crisis of morale and discipline within the ex-Red Army.[4] There were reports of ethnic polarisation within units: young soldiers from the south were having to stick together to defend themselves against persecution by 'European' conscripts. A protest movement began in 1989 and spread to all the Muslim republics, demanding the right for conscripts to serve in the republics from which they came, which was tantamount to the setting up of national armies. As for the ecological issues, they were not new, but it had now become possible to talk about them, so they too played a role in the mobilisation of an intelligentsia that had become better informed and more critical. The issues included the pollution created by the Sumgait industrial complex in Azerbaijan, with its generation of deformed children, the ecological disaster of the Aral Sea, the nuclear firing range at Semi-Palatinsk etc. Curiously, such ecological issues suddenly became secondary during the debates post-independence.

★   ★   ★

The aim of the offensives launched by Andropov and Gorbachev was to break the satrapies set up under Brezhnev, and to open the way for the emergence of reforming cadres. The idea was to take the regionalist factions which had been sidelined and kept away from the levers of power, and play them against the established 'mafias', following a method tried and tested since the purges of 1937. Thus in 1983 the Samarkand-Jizak faction in Uzbekistan was replaced by the Ferghana one; the Kazakh Great Horde was replaced by its two 'rivals'; Pamiris were brought into the Tajik security apparatus in order to control the Leninabadis etc.

Here, however, Moscow made its biggest mistake (which it was to repeat with the Chechens). Clan and regional conflicts were undoubtedly real enough, but that did not prevent the development of a national political space and the creation of a solidarity against Moscow. From then on, clan struggles took place behind closed doors, and anyone who went seeking advancement in Moscow was seen as being in breech of an implicit understanding. The Russians did not understand that regionalist or clan factionalism was not at all contradictory with the rise of modern nationalism (except in the case of Tajikistan). The purge of 1983–7 created a set of common interests between the political class and the population. It also led the Muslim apparatchiks to play the nationalist card against Moscow. Of course, for them the issue was never one of independence. It was still a contractual relationship between the centre and the periphery. But the apparatchiks of the south reproached Moscow for no longer wanting to create mutually profitable relations, *á la* Brezhnev: a devolution of local power, with all its various perks, in return for political and ideological loyalty. The complicity had been broken. Both the campaign against corruption and *perestroika* were seen as instruments of Russification and an imposition of discipline.

The political culture of the south was seen as an obstacle to *glasnost* (having formerly been identified under Stalin as an obstacle to the building of socialism), and was targeted by Moscow. However, this political culture was also seen by those involved as a defence of their own identities.[5] The purges of 1983 generated an ethnic solidarity between cadres who up until that point had lived their lives entirely as Soviets. These cadres now saw the Muscovite élite no longer as comrades in arms, but as the expression of a chauvinist current operating classic Stalinist techniques and using the argument about corruption as a means to other ends. The psychological break between Asiatic and Moscow nomenklaturas dates from this era. Moscow was seen as betraying Sovietism in the interests of Russian nationalism. Andropov and Gorbachev were seen by the south as Russian nationalists and traitors to the Soviet ideal as it had been implicitly defined by Brezhnev. Yeltsin was to be seen in precisely the same light, but with him at least things would be clearer.

Thus it was not that the apparatchiks of the south suddenly became intent on independence. They simply no longer recognised themselves in a Soviet model that had become exclusively Slavic. Moscow's attacks on them failed in their intention of making them unpopular, because Muslim public opinion was perfectly well aware of what was at stake: the loss of the few advantages that had accrued to them under 70 years of Sovietism, and a loss of honour too. This explains the paradox: the majority of leaders in the south approved the *putsch* of August 1991, and dissolved their communist parties in the two months that followed. There was no opportunism in all this: they may have wanted Brezhnev's USSR, or they may have wanted independence, but they certainly did not want a Soviet system which worked only for the advantage of Russians. The attitude of the Azeri Mutalibov, who had been imposed by Moscow as first secretary in January 1990, was typical. He was a soulless apparatchik who, as ambassador to Pakistan, had defended Soviet policy over Afghanistan. But no sooner had he been appointed than he set about defending the rights of Azeris against those of the Armenians, and advancing arguments that were almost as nationalist as his opponent in the Popular Front, Elchibey. He was to approve the Moscow *putsch*, and then dissolve the Communist Party one month later. Moscow and Sovietism were no longer of any use if they did not defend 'national' interests.

This crystallisation of nationalism does not cancel out the interplay of factions and regionalism, but it limits the possibility of them being manipulated by a foreign power. In fact, it was only in Tajikistan, and to far less an extent in Azerbaijan, that Russia found itself in a position to set one faction against another. Everywhere else the titular ethnic group succeeded in creating a bloc against what was now viewed as foreign.

★   ★   ★

In the course of a single year, 1989, the situation went out of control. Riots were occurring on all sides, with the dominant nationality attacking minority groups, but never attacking Russians or the Soviet state apparatus. Anger was directed against next-door neighbours: the Caucasians and the Crimean Tatars in Novy-Uzen in Kazakhstan; the Meskhetian Turks in Ferghana; the Armenians in Baku. These riots extended to Tajikistan in February 1990 (against the party apparatus). Moscow then undertook one final change of leadership in the parties in the Muslim republics, putting in place the teams which would then go through to independence: Nazarbayev (born in 1940 and former prime minister of Kazakhstan) became first secretary in June 1989; the Uzbek Karimov replaced Nishanov, who was summoned to Moscow as president of the Chamber of Nationalities; in Azerbaijan, Mutalibov was appointed first secretary. Almost all were to be elected as their countries' presidents in addition to their positions as party first secretaries, a situation made possible by the new law on elections for presidents of soviet republics in 1990. This gave them the necessary legitimacy to proclaim independence. Kyrgyzstan was the exception. Here, in October 1990, Akayev became president in place of first secretary Masaliyev.

DECLARATIONS OF INDEPENDENCE AND STRUGGLES FOR POWER

Independence was proclaimed on 30 August 1991 in Azerbaijan, 31 August in Kyrgyzstan, 1 September in Uzbekistan, and 9 September in Tajikistan. The others followed later: 27 October for Turkmenistan and 16 December for Kazakhstan, which was rather alarmed by the disappearance of the USSR and the risk of seeing a Slavic bloc emerge which would inevitably draw in the Russian-speaking north of the country. On the initiative of their first secretaries and presidents the communist parties dissolved more or less rapidly and transformed themselves into presidential parties in Kazakhstan, in Uzbekistan (the Democratic Party of the People) and in Turkmenistan (Democratic Party, 1992). The communist parties were marginalised in Kyrgyzstan, Tajikistan and Azerbaijan, with their apparatchiks then joining other political groupings, usually regionally based (for instance the Popular Front for Kulabis in Tajikistan).

The presidents had their positions confirmed at the elections in Autumn 1991, and they then set about consolidating their power. The November elections in Uzbekistan and Tajikistan were freer than elsewhere. Mohamed Saleh took more than 12 percent of the vote standing against President Karimov, and Dawlat Khodanazarov in Tajikistan took 30 percent against President Nabiyev. The Kazakh Nazarbayev, the Kyrgyz Akayev and the Turkmen Nyazov all registered Soviet-style voting figures (more than 90 percent). In only two countries did the opposition succeed briefly in taking power in 1992, before then losing it in 1993: Tajikistan (a coalition of Islamists, democrats and nationalists) and Azerbaijan (the Popular Front).

There were three poles to the opposition movements: the democrats, concerned above all to establish parliamentary democracy; the nationalists, whose main aim was to assert the rights of the titular nationalities; and the Islamists. Collaborations often took place between these three poles. In Uzbekistan the Birlik ('unity') party run by the Pulatov brothers entered into an alliance with the Islamists of Ferghana, while in Tajikistan the Democratic Party allied with the Rastakhiz party. The Erk Party of Uzbekistan (Mohamed Saleh) and the Popular Front of Azerbaijan (Abulfaz Elchibey), on the other hand, were rather secular and pan-Turkist. In fact the border-line between true democrats and nationalists was vague: Shadman Yusuf, leader of the Democratic Party of Tajikistan, revealed himself in 1992 as more nationalist and anti-Russian than the president of the nationalist Rastakhiz party. The true democrats tended to be isolated intellectuals and members of no party, but since their base was only within the urban (and often highly Russified) intelligentsia, they were soon marginalised. The opposition parties were principally nationalist (Birlik, Rastakhiz and the Azeri Popular Front). But other than by the use of manipulation and repression they were unable (except in Azerbaijan) to build a truly popular base. In Tajikistan they only had a role as a result of their alliance with the Islamists, to whom they left the monopoly of armed struggle, since they lacked the means.

The Islamists only broke through at the national level in Tajikistan; else-where they represented regional factions (for instance the Adalat party in Namangan in Ferghana).

The success of the former communist parties is explained partly by the fact that they represented the main body of rural society, that of the notables, the presidents of *kolkhoz* and heads of local 'apparats'. But they were also better than the nationalists in expressing ethno-nationalist demands on the basis of what they had obtained from Soviet administrational realignments. They accepted the borders that had been laid down by the USSR, and this reassured the population. Thus they supported a strategic status quo which the nation-alists were seen to be threatening. Rastakhiz and the Tajik Democratic Party pursued a pan-Tajik line which was critical of Uzbekistan; Erk and the Azeri Popular Front called for closer realtions with Turkey. The maximalism of these movements, even it was often merely rhetorical, was unsettling.

Leaving aside Nagorno-Karabakh, the peoples of the area were not greatly attracted by notions of 'Greater ... istan'. Nationalism was built within the framework of the existing republics, and not on the basis of ideological rationalisations produced by intellectuals extrapolating from concepts of ethnicity. As we have already seen, nationalism was a *habitus* and not a constituted ideology.

The two exceptions, Tajikistan and Azerbaijan, where the opposition took power in 1992, are explained by major internal crises: regionalist tensions in the former case, and war with the Armenians in the latter. But the fact of the opposition winning power is also explained by the uncoupling of the party from the security apparatus, which were controlled by different factions.

Uzbekistan

The transition to independence was marked by conflicts between factions, but these conflicts came to an end with President Islam Karimov's 1992 triumph over his opponents.

Before independence the troubles in Ferghana (pogroms against the Meskhetian Turks in May–June 1989) resulted in Nishanov, who represented the Tashkent-Ferghana faction, being set aside. He took an honorific post as head of state in June 1989, and was then 'promoted' to Moscow, and lost all influence in Uzbekistan. Karimov became first secretary and allied with Shukrullah Mirsaidov, who became prime minister in June 1989 (he was born in Khojent, but belonged to the Tashkent faction). In March 1990, Karimov replaced Nishanov as head of state and Mirsaidov became vice-president. The Twentieth Congress held in June 1990 resulted in a far-reaching renewal of political personnel (the Central Committee had 78 percent new members), and this can be seen as a revenge for Andropov's purges. Karimov had positive things to say about Rashidov during the congress. In August 1991, Mirsaidov supported the Moscow *putsch*, while Karimov, being absent, was not able to express an opinion.

Karimov took advantage of the situation in order to set the country on a fast track to independence, which was proclaimed on 1 September 1991. This was the beginning of a period (a few months) of relative liberalism. Karimov was elected president of the republic in December 1991 with 86 percent of the vote, against an opposition that was active but limited to the intelligentsia: Mohamed Saleh, leader of the 'Turkist' and secular Erk party, took more than 12 percent of the vote. The Birlik party, which was nationalist and often close to the Islamists, was very active, and Islamist movements were active in Ferghana, where the Islamic Renaissance Party (IRP) had a base under the leadership of Abdullah Utayev.

What the central authorities must have found more alarming was the fact that the mufti of Tashkent (Mohamed Yusuf, or Mamayusupov) was developing an independent line. Keeping his distance from the IRP and the

Islamists of Ferghana, he was dealing directly with major Islamic organisations, such as the Muslim World League. He was developing religious education, and was working on making the clergy independent of the political authorities. He found himself in direct conflict with the Committee of religious affairs, a sub-section of the Council of Ministers.

In the face of these many-faceted oppositions, Karimov methodically set about establishing a presidential regime and marginalising his opponents. At the start of 1992, the position of vice-president was emptied of its content. Mirsaidov resigned, and was kept under surveillance by the security services. In the summer of 1992, Rashidov was rehabilitated. The democratic opposition was whipped into line from mid-1992 onwards. The opposition members of parliament were either forced from office or forced to toe the line. A warrant was put out for the Pulatov brothers. One of them was arrested in Kyrgyzstan and extradited. The Erk party was banned in late 1993 and Saleh took refuge in Turkey, which produced a chill in relations between the two countries. The leaders of the Islamist rebellion at Namangan were brought to heel in May 1992, and the leader of the IRP, Abdullah Utayev, was arrested in December 1992. In 1993, the mufti was recalled and replaced by some-body less colourful, while the Directorate of Religious Affairs resumed control of the muftiyyah (former mufti Babakhanov was part of this directorate).

This wave of repression led to a crisis with the United States, whose policy towards Central Asia in the period 1992–4 was limited to a defence of human rights and support for Moscow. However, with his power now assured, Karimov relaxed the pressure on his opponents, not least because they had lost all influence anyway. Presidential pardons were given to several political prisoners in November 1994. Abulmanav Pulatov left for the United States. Mirsaidov resumed political activity (and created a second Adalat party). The multiplication of government parties gave an appearance of democracy: in addition to the party of the president (the Democratic Party of the People of Uzbekistan) there was Vatan Tarakati ('the progress of the nation'), a third party with the name Adalat, and the Milli Tiklanish ('national restoration') party.

The constitution adopted in December 1992 installed a presidential regime. Between 1992 and 1995, all the provincial *hâkims* (governors) were replaced, with the exception of the president of parliament in Karakalpakia, Ubiniyaz Ashirbekov, a close ally of the president. Karimov was in complete control. The parliamentary elections of December 1994 and January 1995 set up an Oli Majlis (upper chamber), the composition of which was 88 percent ethnic Uzbeks and 35 percent members belonging to the local administrative apparatus (district and provincial *hâkims*). There was no real opposition. On 26 March 1995, a referendum extended Karimov's tenure to the year 2000, with a remarkable 99 percent of the vote.

In the meantime, the United States shelved the issue of human rights, and in late 1994 suddenly upgraded relations with Uzbekistan. At the same time, foreign investment began to flow. At the start, there were difficulties on the economic front: having been abruptly cut out of the 'rouble zone', Uzbekistan introduced its own currency, the sum coupon, in November 1993, and the sum itself in 1994. Inflation continued, but the country became self-sufficient in food and energy resources as of 1995.

Despite the economic difficulties and tensions in Ferghana, the regime that emerged with independence is in control of the country and appears to be stable.

Kazakhstan

The replacement of Dinmuhamed Kunayev by Gennadi Kolbin as first secretary of the party in December 1986 led to bloody rioting in Alma Ata, which was the trigger for the dissolution of the USSR. Nursultan Nazarbayev, born in 1940, was appointed first secretary in 1989, elected president in April 1990, and then re-elected unopposed on 1 December 1991. By a referendum held on 30 April 1995, his mandate was extended to the year 2000.

The parliamentary elections of March 1994 were criticized by the Organisation for Security and Co-operation in Europe, but the president had parliament dissolved anyway. New elections were held in December 1995, in which ethnic Kazakhs won two thirds of the seats. In October 1994 a Kazakh prime minister, Akejan Kazhageldin, replaced the Russian Tereshchenko.

As in Uzbekistan, a powerful presidential regime was installed. But Kazakhstan has one fundamental characteristic distinguishing it from other Muslim republics: the dominant nationality does not have the absolute majority, and a large Russian-speaking population inhabits the whole north (or rather northeast) of the country, in territorial continuity with the Russian Federation. The figures for 1991 are 42 percent ethnic Kazakhs and 37 percent Russians. The number of Kazakhs as a percentage has increased as a result of Russian emigration (at least 500,000 Russians are reckoned to have left the republic between 1989 and 1995), but this phenomenon seems to have been limited to the towns of the south, thereby accentuating the north-south split.

This characteristic of the Kazakh situation explains why Kazakhstan was the last of the countries to declare its independence, which it eventually did in December 1991. President Nazarbayev's nightmare was the potential constitution of a Slavic block (Russia, Ukraine and Belarus), which was announced in November 1991 and which would inevitably have been a pole of attraction for the Russian-speaking population. Nazarbayev was therefore in at the start of the setting up of the CIS, the basic principle of which was established at Almaty on 20–21 December 1991. Subsequently, he did what he could to consolidate any factors that might preserve some form of integration between Russia and Kazakhstan. He also made concessions to the

Russian-speaking population: the constitution adopted in August 1995, which reinforced the president's powers, made Russian an official language, although not the 'state language', and replaced the expression 'Kazakh nation' with 'the people of Kazakhstan'. But Nazarbayev also rejected any abandonment of sovereignty, and pursued a policy of Kazakhisation of jobs and of the political arena. The refusal to allow dual citizenship was continued, because that would have led automatically to a quasi-secession of the north. The capital was to be transferred from Almaty to Akmolla, in the centre of the country.

The national currency, the tenge, was introduced in November 1993, after a breakdown in negotiations with the Russian central bank.

However, the authoritarian presidential regime run by Nazarbayev did not have the same meaning as in Uzbekistan or Turkmenistan. Kazakh society is more complex and less monolithic than that in other countries of Transoxiania. Its ethnic diversity, the size of the country, the scale of Russification, the existence of a private sector and a high degree of urbanisation make it far harder to achieve political and policing control than in Turkmenistan. This diversity is reflected in the political and cultural domain. Thus one finds an Islamist party (Alash Orda) operating alongside Russian associations such as Lad ('harmony') and particularly virulent Cossack associations. The role of non-government organisations is stronger here than elsewhere, as illustrated by the Nevada-Semi-Palatinsk ecological movement created by the poet Oljaz Suleimainov, who subsquently became president of the Popular Congress of Kazakhstan.

Turkmenistan

In Turkmenistan, independence, proclaimed on 27 October, apparently created no major upsets. Saparmurad Niyazov, first secretary of the Communist Party since 1985, then president of the republic's Supreme Soviet in 1990 (with 98.3 percent of the vote), was elected president of the newly independent republic in October 1991. He was then re-elected in June 1992 in the course of a Soviet-style election in which he had no opponent and won 99.5 percent of the vote. The Communist Party was dissolved, but immediately gave birth to the Democratic Party of Turkmenistan, which became the president's party (Autumn 1991). All opposition was vigorously suppressed from the start. The small democratic party Agiz Birlik disappeared, a victim both of a degree of repression and a lack of a popular base.

The constitution which was adopted in May 1992 instituted a presidential system, reinforced by a systematic cult of personality. President Nyazov was to be known as Turkmanbashi ('the chief of the Turkmens'), on the model of Atatürk ('the father of the Turks'). His name was systematically given to the main streets of towns, to the airport of the capital, Ashkhabad, and to the only port on the Caspian, Krasnovodsk. The front pages of all the newspapers carried at least three photographs of the president, whose complete works were printed in 500,000 copies. Parliamentary elections took place in December 1994. Only one of the 50 seats was contested by more than one candidate. In 1995, a referendum exended the president's mandate until the year 2000.

However there was visible discontent among the population, due largely to the gap between the president's promises (that he would turn Turkmenistan into the Kuwait of Central Asia, thanks to revenues from natural gas) and a reality which was one of increasing poverty made worse by empty rhetoric (water, electricity and gas are theoretically free, but there are frequent shortages). Demonstrations took place in Ashkhabad in July 1995.

The difficult economic situation, aggravated by the November 1993 introduction of a new currency (the manat), could only be improved by a programme of investing the income from the country's natural gas. However, the unchecked presidential system appears to have had a deleterious effect on the economy: a programme of prestige buildings (the presidential palace and the Gökteppe mosque), a paralysed administration incapable of initiative, the cancellation or signature of contracts that depended on (unpredictable) personal relations with the president (with whom the American Unocal oil company exercised large amounts of influence for a time, but were succeeded by the Israeli firm Merhav), and finally non-reinvestment of these incomes in productive sectors. In short, what was happening was the privatisation of the country to the advantage of Turkmanbashi.

Kyrgyzstan

President Askar Akayev, who was elected unopposed on 15 October 1991, was not a former first secretary of the Communist Party but a member of the Academy of Sciences. At the start, he took a democratic and liberal position, refusing to opt for a strong presidential system. This meant that the country saw a flowering of political parties unlike anything happening elsewhere in Central Asia (the Communist Party, Erkin Kyrgyzstan, the Republican Party, Erk, the Democratic Movement, Ata-Meken etc). The president announced a total privatisation of the economy and of real estate, which no other country of the CIS had done up until that point. However, this desire to turn Kyrgyzstan into the 'Switzerland of Central Asia' gave the country an international reputation which was not matched by its real weight. The country was effectively totally lacking in economic resources.

But this promising scenario soon broke down. Power at the centre was weak, and the president's fine words about democracy became more a token of powerlessness than a programme of reform. The parliament elected during the Soviet era, which consisted of apparatchiks rather hostile to Akayev's reforming intentions, for a long time refused to allow itself to be dissolved after the adoption in May 1993 of a constitution which paved the way for new elections. In August 1994, the president had the parliamentary journal *Svobodnye Gori* closed, thereby alienating the intelligentsia who had initially supported him. Far from clarifying the situation, the elections of February 1995 confirmed the weight of the regional authorities and the tribal structures. The new members of parliament represented principally local interests. This parliament was dominated by the south, which was excluded from power and from the financial manna generated by the privatisations. President Akayev, whose regional power base was the north, then dropped his democratic stance and took a far more authoritarian line. There were trials of the press in July 1995. The director of Erkin Kyrgyzstan, Topchubek Turgunaliyev, was arrested in January 1996.

But power at the centre was relatively weak. In spring 1995, Akayev attempted to get his mandate extended by means of a referendum, but unlike his counterparts in Central Asia he failed. In the presidential elections of 24 December 1995, Akayev was re-elected (with 72 percent of the vote), beating two former Communist Party dignitaries, Absamat Masaliyev (24 percent) and Medetkhan Sherimkulov (2 percent). Masaliyev campaigned under the colours of the ex-Communist Party.

In May 1993, a new currency, the sum, was introduced. The country remained very dependent on Moscow. The Kyrgyz population stood at slightly more than 50 percent of the 4.5 million inhabitants (compared with 21 percent Russians and 12 percent Uzbeks). Russian influence remained strong in the state apparatus, even though 72 percent of members of parliament were Kyrgyz. All the *hâkims* are Kyrgyz.

Azerbaijan

Political life in Azerbaijan has to be seen in the light of the war over Nagorno-Karabakh. When Aliyev lost the last post that he had in Moscow in 1987 (vice-president of the Council of Ministers), Azeris were quick to blame Gorbachev's Armenian advisors, such as Aganbekian (particularly since the petition demanding the attachment of Nagorno-Karabakh to Armenia was made public just after his removal). In February 1988, the Armenians of Nagorno-Karabakh demonstrated for unification with Yerevan. The following month, Azeri refugees from these regions launched a pogrom against the Armenians at Sumgait. A cycle of reciprocal violence was initiated. But Aliyev, like Rashidov, comes across as a victim of Moscow, or rather of a collusion between Russians and Armenians, which brought back old memories for the Azeris (for instance the Baku Commune of 1918). The entry of Soviet troops into Baku in January 1990 sealed the divorce between Azeri opinion and Moscow.

Ayaz Mutalibov, an ex-ambassador and a Moscow man who was prime minister at the time, became first secretary of the Communist Party in January 1990. Aliyev stepped down in disgrace as president of the soviet of

Nakhichevan. In the elections for the Supreme Soviet in October 1990, the opposition took 10 percent of the seats. In August, Mutalibov approved the Moscow *putsch* and immediately afterwards proclaimed independence (on 31 August). In September 1991, he was elected president, but the war in Nagorno-Karabakh pushed the communists and opposition forces into an unaccustomed degree of agreement: a National Council consisting of 25 pro-government members and 25 pro-opposition members was set up in October.

The defeat at Khojali in the face of the Armenians led to the fall of the Mutalibov regime in 1992. He attempted a *coup d'état* in May, but it failed and he then took refuge in Moscow, thereby inaugurating a series of failed *putsches* which were to set the pace of political life in Azerbaijan. In May, the Popular Front took power. In June, the nationalist Abulfaz Elchibey was elected president. He ran an ultra-nationalist policy based on hostility to Moscow and established close relations with Turkey, which sent advisors to Azerbaijan. But repeated defeats at the hands of the Armenians, who were supported by Russia, plus popular disaffection and Russian manoeuvring, led to Elchibey being overthrown in a coup led by the warlord Suret Husseinov. Azerbaijan then saw the return to power of the 70-year-old Haidar Aliyev, who was elected president in November 1993. Within the former USSR such a come-back was exceptional (Shevardnadze, the only former Communist Party Politburo member to have run a republic like Aliyev, belonged to a younger generation). It was all the more remarkable since Aliyev was to take a thoroughly nationalist line in facing down Moscow (refusing Russian military bases and frontier guards). There were several *putsch* attempts against him, first by defence minister Rahim Gaziyev in 1994 (supported by Mutalibov and Moscow), and then on 17 March 1995, by deputy minister of the interior Rushan Javadov, who died during the attempt (which, incidentally, was supported by the Turks). In 1996 the Russians effected a *rapprochement* with Aliyev, and briefly arrested Gaziyev and Mutalibov.

Despite a chaotic political life and regular *putsches*, Azerbaijan enjoyed a degree of political diversity. The elections of 12 November 1995 saw the emergence of three major parties: Yeni Azerbaijan, the president's party; the Popular Front; and Ittibar Mahmedov's Party of National Independence (a business party).

Finally, Azerbaijan has had to deal with unrest among its minorities: the Lezghins, in the region close to Daghestan where they number several hundred thousand, are demanding a republic of their own (the Samur movement); the Party of the Talesh People (which later became the Party for Equality of the Peoples of Azerbaijan) operates within the law; in early 1993 there was an failed attempt to create a Republic of Talesh-Mughan (this was proclaimed by Colonel Alakram Gumbatov). Finally, there is also a Kurdish Equality Party, arising from the presence of several tens of thousands of Kurds in the country.

Azerbaijan depends on income from the exploitation of hydrocarbons to balance its economy.

TAJIKISTAN AS AN EXCEPTION: CIVIL WAR AS A SYMPTOM OF IDENTITY CRISIS

In February 1990, rioting broke out in Dushanbe following a rumour that the government had requisitioned apartments to house Armenian refugees.[6] The demonstrators were basically protesting against shortages of housing and the fact that the Leninabad faction exercised a monopoly of political power. The first secretary of the Communist Party, Kahhar Mahkamov, remained in position in a climate that was becoming increasingly tense. Like his fellow first secretaries in the rest of Central Asia, he was elected president in November 1990 while still remaining first secretary. He supported the Moscow *putsch*, but was then obliged to resign on 7 September, under pressure from the streets. Qadruddin Aslanov (from the south) was appointed acting president by the assembly, and he dissolved the Communist Party and proclaimed independence. On 23 September, former first secretary Nabiyev took power with the support of the conservatives, declared a state of emergency and re-established the Communist Party. But this made little sense, since the party had more or less disappeared in the face of emerging regional clan interests. On 2 October, Nabiyev again dissolved the Communist Party, cancelled the state of emergency and organised presidential elections which turned out to be relatively open. The opposition forces supported the candidature of Dawlat Khodanazarov, president of the (Soviet) Union of Film Directors and a Pamiri intellectual, who took approximately 30 percent of the vote in the elections on 27 November.

At this point, Safarali Kenjayev entered the scene. He was a complex personality: of Yaghnobi origin and born in Hissar (an area to the west of Dushanbe and majority Uzbek), where he still maintained support. He was raised by the father of Qazi Turajanzade, following a Persian tradition of 'twinning' a child from a good family with a child from less favoured circumstances. He then pursued a career as a judge in the province of Leninabad, whose regional identity he adopted. He became president of the National Assembly in December, as a compromise candidate (since he was of the north without originating in the north, tendentially democratic, and close to the *qazi*'s family). He suddenly chose the Leninabadi camp, and targeted the Pamiri minister of the interior, Naujavanov, who had been in the post since 1987. As we saw, Pamiris were promoted within the security organisations (MVD and KGB) on the occasion of the war in Afghanistan.

This attack (the reasons for which were obscure) soon led to a mobilisation among the Pamiris of Dushanbe (organised into the La'l-i Badakhshan ('ruby of Badakhshan') party, who feared that they were again going to be removed from power, 55 years after the purges of 1937. On 26 March 1992, they began a demonstration in front of the republic's presidential palace in Martyrs' (Shahidan) Square. In April, they were joined by the Gharmis, this time under the banner of the Islamic Renaissance Party (IRP, led by Mohamed Sharif Himmatzade), as well as by all the opposition parties. All were officially demanding Kenjayev's resignation, but the real issue was the rising power of the excluded regionalist groups (Gharmis and Pamiris) against the Communist establishment. The Leninabadis then received back-up from the Kulabis. We have already seen how, in the province of Kurgan-Teppe, population transfers among both Gharmis and Kulabis had consolidated antagonisms and had led to conflict over land. These localist conflicts were exported to the capital. They came up from the *kolkhoz* in buses and tractors to support their various factions. It was enough to look at the out-of-town numberplates and the names on the placards to see that this was a localist mobilisation. Shahidan Square brought together Gharmis from Karategin and Kurgan-Teppe, people from Ramit and Kafirnehan, Darwazis, Pamiris and people from Zarafshan (who came individually). To Liberty Square, on the other hand, came people from Kulab, Leninabad, Hissar, Shahrinau, Tursunzade, Lenin and Varzab. The *qazi*, a Gharmi, took a position against Kenjayev, virtually his blood brother. All the ministries and security organisations were split according to the regional origins of their functionaries. Repression as a way of resolving the situation was impossible. On 23 April, Kenjayev resigned. Nabiyev attempted to establish a National Guard, but the KGB and MVD were under Pamiri influence, while the (Russian) 201st Division was under the command of Ashurov, a Gharmi. The defeated Kulabis left Dushanbe on 5 May 1995.

A coalition government was then set up. Officially Nabiyev was still president, but he lost all power. Effective government was in the hands of a coalition of Pamiris (the deputy president and prime minister Akbarshah Iskanderov) and Gharmis. The *qazi* remained off the official stage, but played a considerable role, while the hardline wing of the IRP and the Young Pamiris of Dushanbe set up armed militias. The new head of the TV network, Mirbaba Mirrahim, cut down on Russian-language programmes and broadcast large chunks of Iranian television.

However, while the situation was becoming calmer in Dushanbe the war of the *kolkhoz* was breaking out in the south (see above). The Gharmis, initially victorious, expelled the Kulabis from Vakhsh in June–July, and blockaded Kulab in July. The Kulabis organised militarily, within a Popular Front under the leadership of Sangak Safarov. They procured weapons from Russian garrisons (either bought or given) and launched their counter-attack in September 1992, with the support of Russian troops (the Russian 191st Battalion based in Kurgan-Teppe), except in Dushanbe, where the Russians remained neutral.

This was a savage war: massacres, rape, torture, looting and summary executions. The lower Vakhsh valley was the scene of Serb-style ethnic cleansing. The houses of Gharmis and Pamiris were systematicaly destroyed and the civilian populations fled towards the border with Afghanistan. After a pause of a month, the Amu Darya was crossed at the end of December in very difficult conditions by tens of thousands of Gharmi refugees, taking them into Afghanistan, where they were rapidly taken into the care of the UNHCR.

Nabiyev was forced to resign by an armed group in September 1992, and took refuge in Khojent. An initial attack on Dushanbe by supporters of Kenjayev on 23 October failed. A meeting of parliament in Khojent in November 1992 tried to find a compromise. The Kulabi Imamali Rahmanov was appointed president of the parliamentary Praesidium, but as a last-minute compromise this achieved nothing. Dushanbe fell on 8 December 1992, and Kafirnehan, the last bastion of the Islamic–democratic coalition, fell on 27 December.

The Islamic opposition then withdrew to regroup in Afghanistan, from where they launched increasingly powerful armed attacks, albeit limited to the zones where they had a presence (the upper Gharm valley and Tahvildara), under their commanders Rizwan, Kalandar and Mirza. In order to widen the base of the IRP, they created the Islamic Movement of Tajikistan, led by Mullah Nuri and with the support of Qazi Turajanzade. This movement was completely Islamic and Gharmi. However, in the negotiations sponsored by the United Nations the opposition presented a single delegation, presided over by Otakhan Latifi, a former Soviet journalist and secular democrat from Zarafshan (as were most of the democratic intellectuals). The delegation, called UTO (United Tajik Opposition) brought together the IRP, the Rastakhiz movement, the Democratic Party (from which Shadman Yusuf, who had rallied to the government in 1995, was excluded) and the Pamiris, represented by Khaleq Nazarov, formerly minister for foreign affairs in the coalition government of 1992.

The Pamiris succeeded in preserving their autonomy both de jure and de facto in Gorno-Badakhshan, having reached a compromise with the government: they recognised the suzerainty of Dushanbe, and accepted the presence of government (actually Russian) frontier guards. Their territory became a prime location for the transit of drugs coming from Afghanistan to Osh in Kyrgyzstan, and the Aga Khan Foundation provided food support.

The Dushanbe government was in the hands of Kulabis, who consolidated their power by means of the armed militias emerging from the Popular Front. A constitution (November 1994) and parliamentary elections (February 1995) gave them control of the state apparatus, to the detriment not only of the opposition, but also of the Leninabadis, who had to content themselves with the (powerless) post of prime minister and the ministry of foreign affairs (Tajikistan had fewer than a dozen overseas embassies, and these were generally the province of disgraced leaders). The Kulabis methodically set about plundering offical positions and sources of wealth for the benefit of their faction, and had no interest whatever in running the state. This predatory attitude destroyed the economy and led to their fellow regionalist factions going into opposition. The Leninabadis first tried opting for autonomy, with the support of Tashkent, on the basis of their economic dynamism, but the Kulabis took direct control of the province in December 1993. Various attempts to create a north-based pole were aborted in the face of the refusal of the Russians (who opened a consulate in Khojent in August 1994) to support them. An armed revolt in January 1996, led by the province's military commander, General Mamajanov, failed, apparently after intervention by the Russian FSB (ex–KGB). In May 1996, popular rioting broke out in the north against Kulabi excesses. The ex-prime ministers of the north (Abdullajanov, Samadov and Karimov), who had been pushed from power one after the other in less than three years, eventually joined forces and created a National Renaissance Party in August 1996 to defend the interests of the province of Leninabad, and this time they had the green light from the Russians.

In January 1996, a military uprising actually within the militias of the Popular Front seriously threatened the government. Its leaders, Ibod Boimatov (formerly mayor of Tursunzade, the capital of Hissar, a region to the west of Dushanbe which was majority Uzbek) and Mahmud Khodaberdayev (commander of the 1st Brigade at Kurgan-Teppe), both ethnic Uzbek from Tajikistan, demanded the government's resignation. They were discreetly supported by Tashkent, which was annoyed at Russian intervention in an area that it saw as its own natural protectorate.

The Dushanbe government was forced to give way. In February 1996, the most hardline members of the Kulabi clan (in particular the minister of the interior, Yakub Salimov, and the deputy prime minister in charge of security, Obeydulayev) were removed. But there was no political solution in sight. Tashkent openly pressed for the Kulabi team to be replaced by people from the north, and created an opening for the Islamic opposition, which was officially received by President Karimov in May 1995. But the opposition movements (Islamists, Leninabadis and Uzbeks from the south) were not ready to unite. Moscow and Tashkent eyed each other watchfully, and played off their respective protegés. The Russian troops, who were making a good living out of the country and its various forms of trafficking, were in no hurry to end what for them had been a lucrative conflict. Tajikistan became a Russian protectorate, with the likelihood that it would fall within the Uzbek orbit once the Russians decided to depart northwards. However, in December 1996 the Russians, alarmed at the rise of the Taliban in Afghanistan and the military escalation in Tajikistan, supported the signing of an agreement between Rahmanov and the Islamic opposition, which came into effect in June 1997. A coalition government was established between the ruling Kulabi faction and the UTO, with the latter as a junior partner.

In such a situation, regionalism had good opportunity to prosper, as it had in Afghanistan. In the same way that regionalism in the area had been crystallised by Stalin's policies, so it was now being strengthened by Russia's neo-colonial pretensions.

8

Islam

Muslims in Central Asia are Hanafi Sunnis, as they are in Afghanistan and throughout the Indian subcontinent. Shiites are relatively few in number, and consist of two completely different groups. The urban 'Twelver' (in other words recognising twelve imams) Shiites are of Iranian origin but often turcophone, at least in Samarkand. They are the descendants of traders who came from Persia, and they total a few thousand, living in Samarkand and Bukhara, where they are part of the urban élite. The other group are the descendants of the Persian slaves who were very numerous at the end of the nineteenth century and were generally assimilated: in Turkmenistan they speak Turkmen and are Sunni, even though they are always defined as 'Persians' because they have no tribal genealogy. The second group consists of the Ismailis of Pamir, who recognise seven imams and have heterodox beliefs in Islamic terms. The Aga Khan is their spiritual leader. The Ismailis are not particularly observant and are very secular. They are seen as heretics by both Sunnis and Shiites. They number between 300,000 and 400,000 in Tajikistan, and belong to a broader grouping which is located in the Pamir mountains and is also to be found on the Afghan, Pakistani and Chinese slopes of those mountains. In my opinion, the Shiite Tajiks who feature in censuses in China are neither Tajik nor Shiite, but Ismailis speaking Pamiri languages.[1]

One can speak of two variants of Islam, corresponding to an opposition not so much between Turks and Persians, but between tribal zones (Kazakhs, Turkmens and Kyrgyz) and areas of longstanding urban civilisation that were Islamicised after the Arab conquest (Tajiks and Uzbeks from Transoxiania). The Islam of Transoxiania is a product of the *madrasas* (religious schools) of Samarkand and Bukhara. It is often a fundamentalist Islam, but is supported on the rich Persian Sunni literature developed in northern India during the Moghul era. The dominant figures are the *ulemas*, or doctors of law. In tribal zones, on the other hand, Islam was late in being imposed (sometimes as late as the eighteenth century), and came via the intermediary of Sufi brother-hoods such as the Yasawiyya. It incorporates elements deriving from the shamanistic traditions of Turkic nomads.

One should not overstate the opposition between these two forms of Islam. The Islam of the *ulemas* is strongly influenced by Sufism, while the tribal Sufis do not challenge the orthodoxy of the *ulemas*. The difference is not so much in doctrine, but in the role of the *literati*, the clerics, educated in the towns but implanted and influential within areas of old sedentarisation such as Ferghana. The influence of the Uzbek-Tajik *ulemas* over Central Asia as a whole can still be seen today: the three muftis of Kazakhstan, Kyrgyzstan and Turkmenistan are either Uzbeks or come from sedentary areas that are very Uzbekised. The first, Ratbeg Nissan Bey, comes from Chimkent, an Uzbek town for which he is the member of parliament; the second, Hajji Abdurrahman Kimsan Bay, was born in 1940 in Jangiabad in Uzbekistan; the third, Nasrullah Ibn Abdullah, is from Tashauz, a town in Turkmenistan with an Uzbek population. If one adds the fact that the mufti of Tashkent is also Uzbek, and that the mufti of Tajikistan (in 1994) speaks Uzbek fluently, it becomes obvious that Uzbekistan now carries the torch of Islamic revivalism that was previously borne by the Tajik *ulemas*.

The religious revivalism which emerged onto the scene in 1989 after a period of development underground is not a foreign import. It is the public appearance of a culture and a religious practice that never entirely dis-appeared. This revivalism was moulded in earlier cultural spaces. It is very fundamentalist in Ferghana and in the south of Tajikistan, and elsewhere is much more linked to a simple return of traditionalism.

The political radicalisation of Islam is not an import either. The militant networks existed under the Soviet empire. Here one has to consider the question of the role of Sufism. Alexandre Bennigsen sees Sufism as the clan-destine structure which enabled militant Islam to maintain itself.[2] After the event, this role of Sufism in the sustaining of Islam appears self-evident. But Sufism, as we shall see, is not an organisational system. There are no clandestine *pirs*. In fact, everyone is Sufi, from pro-regime mullahs (Babakhanov under the Soviets, and Hajji Mukhtar Abdullah under Karimov) to the opposition (Qazi Turajanzade). This omnipresence of Sufism rather relativises its political role.

The conservative Islam of the *ulemas*, Sufism and political radicalism: as in Afghanistan, these three poles are not mutually antagonistic in Central Asia.[3] One may belong to just one of the categories, or one may combine all three, as does the Tajik Qazi Akbar Turanjazade, the son of a respected Qaderi *murid* educated at the Islamic university in Amman, Jordan, who was for-merly official Soviet *qazi* in the republic, and also the leading figure in the Islamic Movement of Tajikistan, an opposition group involved in armed struggle.

TRADITIONAL ISLAM IN CENTRAL ASIA

The Hanafi Sunni Islam taught in the *madrasas* of Samarkand and Bukhara derives from a far wider cultural area. When Iran made the transition to Shiism in the sixteenth century, the Persian Sunni tradition continued to flourish in a huge area reaching from Bukhara to Delhi and Bombay. In this area, Persian was the language of teaching and writing. All the religious treatises published in this space, which corresponded to the geographical space of the Moghul, Uzbek and Pashtun empires and emirates, were in Persian. Didactic works were often subsequently translated into local languages (Chaghatay, Uzbek, Pashtun and Urdu), particularly from the nineteenth century onwards, but the basic foundations are identical. Books, letters and debates circulated throughout this area. It was not from Mecca, and even less from Mashhad or Qum, that the *ulemas* of Central Asia obtained their books, but from Lahore, Bombay and Delhi.

This Islamic civilisation obviously developed in all branches of theology: the *hadith* (the sayings of the Prophet), *usul al-fiqh* (the foundations of law), *tafsir* (commentary on the Quran) etc. But it was also supported on a whole body of Persian culture: pursuing religious studies also involved studying philosophy, poetry, astronomy, and even the interpretation of dreams. Sa'adi and Hafez, Bedel and Jami were regarded as the sources for a learning of fine language. At the theological level, debate focussed on the role of Sufism and philosophy. The orthodoxy was clarified by Shah Wali–Ullah of Delhi (1703–62), who preached strict respect for the *sharia* but allowed for a spiritualist Sufism, stripped of practices involving the worship of saints and belief in a real union with God. The orthodox Sunni culture of Central Asia and the Indian sub-continent cannot be understood without its Sufi dimension. It also develops a critique of Shiism, which accentuates the split with Iran. At the end of the nineteenth century, the great Indian university at Deoband was a beacon for this orthodoxy, backed by a very rich culture.[4] Connections between *ulemas* and Sufi *pirs* were very commonplace. The Naqshbandiyya brotherhood, founded in Bukhara in the fourteenth century, spread to India and Afghanistan. Many *ulemas* of Central Asia went to study in India, and as we shall see this tradition sometimes continued clandestinely during the Soviet era.

In concrete terms, this Islamic culture was transmitted via 'guide books' whose originals were in Persian, and which seem to have been compiled in the eighteenth and early nineteenth centuries. They were very common throughout Central Asia, in lithographed versions from Bukhara, from the Indian subcontinent, and even from Kazan. With the campaign against Islam between 1924 and 1927, the repression of the *ulemas*, the closure of the great *madrasas* and the ban on travel, the parallel *mullahs* in Central Asia were cut off from outside influences until the early 1980s. But in their small private libraries they preserved these works from the last century, and the books provided the basis of a knowledge that was maintained and transmitted over a period of 70 years.

Throughout the Uzbek and Tajik areas, there is a homogeneity in these libraries. Interestingly, the works in Persian are the same as those which one finds among Afghan and Pakistani mullahs and in the Northwest Province.[5] On the other hand, works written in Turkic languages, generally in Tatar, originate in Kazan.

The most widespread book is undoubtedly the *Chahâr kitâb* or 'four books', a compendium of knowledge for the good Muslim, and the *Haftyek*, which is used in memorising the required minima of Islam in Arabic.[6] These books contain chapters on the basic principles of Islam and elements of literature, mysticism, cosmogony and sometimes also folk wisdom in the style of Sa'adi. Thus what was being transmitted was not only a knowledge of the basic dogma and rites of Islam, but also the *adab*, the 'guide to proper ways of living', in other words a culture and an ethic embodied in a religious vision of the universe. The style of these books is designed to aid memorisation, with alternating rhythmic prose (*nazm*) and poetry. They serve as manuals both for village mullahs and for fathers seeking to pass on Islamic culture to their children. One should not underestimate the impact of this traditional culture among young people, particularly in the countryside, in Tajikistan and Ferghana. In particular, Persian speakers have privileged access to this literature, even though it was not transcribed into Cyrillic.

In the small Tajik enclave of Sukh in Kyrgyzstan we had an opportunity to see the library of the town's mullah, which he had inherited from his father. He was able to read books in Persian, and his library included: the *Chahâr kitâb*, the *Mokhtasar* (a compendium of law) by Sadiq Khwaje Khojenti; the *Tafsir* (commentary on the Quran) by Yaqub Charkhi (the Naqshbandi *pir* whose tomb is today to be found in Dushanbe); the Hedayat ('guide') by Timur Khwâja Margelani – all of which were printed in Khojent with the exception of a *Zaruriyât-i dini* ('indispensable elements of religion') printed in Lahore. The mullah also had two copies of *Ilm hâl* ('the science of solutions') in Arabic, written by Ibrahimov and printed in Kazan in 1915, as well as a *Ta'alim ol salât* ('the teaching of prayer'), also in Arabic, by Abul Haj Samarqandi and printed by the Karimovich press in Kazan in 1915. The only book which he was not able to decypher was a work by Kursawi, *Jama'a al ramuz* ('the collection of secrets'), a lithographed volume from the University of Kazan (1909) written in Tatar in the Arabic script.

Thus he had no readable books by the Jadids. The works of Kursawi and Marjani were in Tatar and used the Arabic alphabet, which makes them hermetic even for an Uzbek mullah. Russian translations never reached the countryside. Islam, as it has been kept alive in Transoxiania, is thus quite unaware of the reform movements of the past century. The effect of the tsarist and Soviet censorship of the Jadid movement was to favour conservative currents of throught. The only Jadid whose writings were circulated in Tajik and the Cyrillic alphabet was Ahmed Makhtum Qalla (Dânish) (1827–97), but he was not a theologian. He was used for his criticism of the 'feudalism' of the emirates. The effect of all this was that Islam, as it survived, tended to a more traditional form of the religion, somewhat open to mysticism and philosophy. The return of reformism, in the form of a more modernised Islam, was to take place by way of the official clergy, who were the only ones in contact with the contemporary Muslim world, and through various clandestine networks whose precise history still has to be written.

THE SUFI BROTHERHOODS
A Sufism That is Omnipresent and Takes Many Forms

Central Asia was the birthplace of at least two major Sufi orders. The most important is the Naqshbandiyya order, founded in Bukhara by Bahauddin Naqshband (1317–89), in a Persian-speaking environment; the other is the Yasawiyya order, founded by Ahmed Yasawi (d. 1166), whose mausoleum is to be found in the town of Yasi, renamed Turkestan (today in Kazakhstan, but with a majority Uzbek population). The Yasawiyya, whose practices included old shamanic rites deriving from the nomadic tribes, developed principally in the Turkic world. It was to give rise to the Bektashi of the Ottoman empire and the Khalwati of Azerbaijan. Other brotherhoods took root in Central Asia: the Qaderis and, to a lesser extent, the Cheshtiyya.

The dividing lines between brotherhoods are ill-defined. Genealogies and practices are both likely to overlap. The Naqshbandis generally practise the silent *zikr* (repetition of the name of God) and the Qaderis the vocal *zikr*, but sometimes it is the other way round. Today there are signs of a timid return to the zikr. For instance, in Namangan in 1996 there was a circle of 200–300 people taking part in a Naqshbandi vocal *zikr*. The basic principle of a brotherhood is the allegiance of a disciple, or *murid*, to a *pir* and his successors, in exchange for initiation. Membership is sometimes community-based (a family, clan or entire solidarity group). One should not see these brotherhoods as a system of centralised networks around a charismatic figure. In fact, the brotherhoods may disperse and duplicate while still keeping the name and the memory of the original brotherhood. The founding *pir* appoints a *khalifa* as his deputy and successor. In order to extend the brotherhood, he sends *khalifas* into mission areas; these *khalifas*, in the name of the brotherhood, go on to found a hereditary line of transmission (*selsele*). After several generations the successors of the *khalifa* may in turn proclaim themselves *pirs*, and send off other *khalifas* as missionaries. At any given moment these new branches may give rise to a new brotherhood, or they may keep the name of the original brotherhood while having their main reference in a local *selsele*. This technique of 'layering' (a branch taking root at a distance away from the original trunk) explains both the dispersion of the brotherhoods and also the fact that they have no centre, except in the imagination of certain writers.

Sometimes the spiritual descendants and the hereditary descendants become separated. The members of a Sufi family who have no specific religious education may continue to be revered. They acquire a *barakat*, or hereditary mystic aura. But anybody combining a double legitimacy (as both *ulema* and Sufi) has considerable prestige. One should not imagine that Sufism in Central Asia is antagonistic with the scholarly Islam of the *ulemas*, as is the case in the Maghreb. Sufism, and certainly Naqshbandism and Qaderism are the vectors of an orthodox Islam, whose fundamentalism is only tempered by their mysticism and their rooting in ancient Persian culture.

Another characteristic of the brotherhoods of Central Asia, particularly the Naqshbandiyya and the Qaderiyya, is that they recruit undifferentiatedly in both turcophone and Persian-speaking populations. An Uzbek *murid* may have a Tajik *pir*, and vice versa. Furthermore, networks may be created between spaces that are at a distance from each other. For example, the Tajik Naqshbandis of Kasansoy, in Uzbek Ferghana, have their *pir* in Turkestan – Ishan Mullah Abdul Wahid, whose local *khalifa*, Mullah Jura Akhund, died in 1988 after a life untroubled by the Soviet authorities. In the same way, during the final period of the Soviet Union Damollah Mohamed-e Sharif Hissari, the Naqshbandi *pir* of the town of Hissar in Tajikistan (d. 1990, the father of Fatullah Khan Sharifzade, the Tajik *qazi* from 1993 to 1996), had been able to establish a very broadly-based network of disciples in Uzbek Ferghana (Kokand and Namangan).

In the countryside, the families of a *pir* or a *khalifa* generally live around a *zyarat*, the tomb of a 'holy man', which is a source of pilgrimage, the guarding of which brings income and prestige to the family in charge. However, not all *zyarats* are associated with a family in situ, and not all Sufi families necessarily have a *zyarat*. The major Sufi families are recognisable by their names, which feature the elements 'pir' and 'ishan', or the suffix '-zada' preceded by 'jan' or 'sharif'.

This rural implantation of the brotherhoods, generally deriving from families who came bringing the good word from afar, explains a particular characteristic of Sufism, which is exaggerated in the tribal regions: the correspondence between Sufi families or clans and segmentation into solidarity groups. This correspondence works at the local level, even though the Sufi family in question may have disciples who are geographically far away. This characteristic of Sufism is common to many tribal regions: it duplicates and simultaneously transcends tribal segmentation. A clan or a group follows a *pir* who, by definition, comes from elsewhere and is not a member of the tribe. The *pir* is thus in a position to arbitrate in conflicts between segments, but his own group may transform into an endogamous caste, or may set up a tribal segment which is simply more prestigious than the others, but functions according to the same logic (such as the Ishân-Khwâja among the Lakays). The group thus loses its religious specificity.

In tribal regions (among Kazakhs, Turkmens and Lakays) one thus finds 'religious' clans who claim Arab origins (they are often called *khwaja*, and among the Turkmens *àvlat*, in other words, *awlad*)[7]. They provide mullahs while at the same time being an integral part of the tribal structure. They speak the language of the local ethnic groups.

This identification between a 'holy man' and a solidarity group has an unusual twist in the *kolkhoz*. *Kolkhoz* which are lucky enough to have the *zyarat* of a noted saint on their lands gain prestige from the fact, and keep the tomb carefully maintained. The Lenin *kolkhoz* in Dushanbe contains the *zyarat* of Yaqub Charkhi, Tajikistan's most famous Naqshbandi. The minaret, recently rebuilt, stands 100 metres from an imposing statue of Lenin, which was still standing in 1995. Nobody seems to find the coexistence of the tribe's totem and its saint contradictory.

In 1994, the Kulabis, who have been seen as neo-communists, celebrated with great pomp the four-hundred-and-eightieth anniversary of Mir Sayyid Ali Hamadani, the great Sufi *pir* whose tomb is in the town of Kulab.

Sufism and Politics

Sufi affiliations do not necessarily correspond to political affiliations. They create personal links, which may contribute to political mobilisation or may, on the other hand, maintain links between opposing groups, but in Central Asia they do not have a direct political expression.

A recent example illustrates both the importance and the limits of Sufism in politics. The spiritual chief of the Tajik opposition, Qazi Akbar Turajanzade (b. 1947) is a Qaderi. His father, Ishan Turajan, is the *murid* of a famous *pir* from Kurgan-Teppe, Hazrat Ishan Khalliljan. But the Qazi's successor, who was appointed mufti of the republic by the Kulabi government, is also a Sufi, this time a Naqshbandi: Fatullah Khan Sharifzade (assassinated in January 1996) was the son of a Naqshbandi *pir*, Damullah Mohamed Sharif Hissari, who was highly respected (including by the *qazi*). Sufi solidarity here is not expressed in the political affiliation, but in the mutual respect which the families have for each other. Mohamed Sharif was appointed *sar khâtib* (incumbent of the mosque) of Hissar district by Turajanzade in 1988. When Sharifzade was assassinated, Qazi Turajanzade denounced the crime. By the same token, the *qazi*'s father has lived in Dushanbe undisturbed throughout the civil war. The real basis of political mobilisation is, as ever, regionalist. What counts is the fact that the *qazi* is a Gharmi and Sharifzade a Hissari (a district which joined the Kulabis before then embarking on an uprising in January 1996, the month in which the new *qazi* was murdered; there is arguably a connection between the two events).

Another famous Naqshbandi *pir* in Tajikistan was Ishan Abdurrahman Jan of Ab-i Gharm, who died in July 1991. The newspaper of the Islamic Renaissance Party issued an obituary for him at the time, as did Safarali Kenjayev, parliamentary president and an adversary of the *qazi*. His son, Hajji Abdulquddus, was close to the *qazi*. Ab-i Garm is in the Gharm Valley.

The great Sufi families provide the main religious personnel in both camps: the official muftis who replaced the contestatory muftis in both Uzbekistan and Tajikistan were both Naqshbandis.

149

After independence, some of the Turkish brotherhoods made attempts to establish links with the branches present in Central Asia, and even to gain a direct implantation there. The Naqshbandiyya of Istanbul, under the leadership of Esat Cosan, has been particularly active in Bukhara.

Official Islam

The repression of Islam was very severe at the time of the *hujum* (from 1927 onwards). But in 1943, as we have seen, Stalin set up a system of four muftiyyas with territorial coverage, of which only one, that of Baku, corresponded to a precise republic. These muftiyyas did not have a national anchor point, even though the mufti of Ufa was always a Tatar and the mufti of Tashkent an Uzbek.

Two offensives against Islam were to follow, one under Gorbachev in 1986 (this foundered under the weight of the general liberalisation). It was Khrushchev who dealt the heaviest blow: 25 percent of official mosques were forced to close between 1958 and 1964,[8] and the effect was particularly felt in Tajikistan (16 out of 34) and Uzbekistan (23 out of 90). The four official mosques in Turkmenistan stayed open, and of the 26 Kazakh and 34 Kyrgyz mosques only one in each republic closed. These figures are indicative of the weight of Islam in Tajikistan and Uzbekistan compared with the other three republics. But when the storm passed, other official mosques were to re-open, or would be tolerated. Dushanbe had eight official mosques in 1990.

The muftiyya system escaped the offensive because Khrushchev needed a Muslim showcase for his charm offensive in the Third World. The education of all religious personnel in the USSR was at that time provided by a secondary school, the Mir-e Arab school in Bukhara (reopened in 1948) and the Imam Bukhari University Institute in Tashkent. The muftiyya of Tashkent (defined as the 'Spiritual Directorate for Central Asia and Kazakhstan') was held from 1943 until 1989 by a Naqshbandi dynasty: Ishan Babakhan ibn Abdul Majid Khan, from 1943 to 1957, followed by his son, Ziautdin Babakhanov, from 1957 until 1982, and finally his grandson, Shamsuddin Khan. The mufti of Tashkent had authority over the leading *qazis* of the other four republics.

Soviet theology students were kept away from international currents of thought up until the Brezhnev period, but in the late 1960s they began to be sent abroad to complete their education. They went, of course, to 'friendly' countries, but they were also sent to famous institutions. The aim was not to turn out 'red mullahs', but on the contrary theologians and scholars who would enjoy recognition from their peers in the Muslim world. Nobody was sent to revolutionary Iran, where the only real synthesis between Marxism and Islam was taking place – the only real Muslim 'liberation theology'. They were sent to Libya (for example, Mohamed Yusuf, mufti of Tashkent in 1989) and to Syria, but also to Egypt and Jordan (the *qazi* of Tajikistan, Turajanzade). This insistence on classic Sunnism and this suspicion of Iran explains why the present Shiite *sheikh ul-islam* of Azerbaijan, Shukur Pashazade (in post since 1980) is the only one of the leading *ulemas* of the latter Soviet period never to have studied abroad. He does not speak Persian, whereas all his Sunni colleagues speak fluent Arabic, and he refuses to locate himself within the system of allegiance to a grand ayatollah.[9]

One unintended consequence of this policy of openness towards the Sunni Arab countries was that the young students of religion who were sent there came back deeply influenced by the thinking of the Muslim Brotherhood. These young *ulemas* displayed their political loyalty towards the USSR, but at the same time they were elaborating an uncompromising brand of Islam. However, they were not to be found among the anti-Soviet dissident movements. They were cautious, and played a long-term game of compromise with the authorities and a re-Islamisation of society. They were also suspicious of any nationalism which might undermine the muftiyyas and the idea of a common Muslim entity for all the Russias.

They made themselves available for major international conferences as Moscow required, but with less than impressive results. The Islamic conference in Tashkent in September 1980 was a failure, on account of the invasion of Afghanistan, but the one in Baku in October 1986 was more of a success. However, their presence there made it possible for them to appear as interlocutors in the eyes of the major Islamic organisations.

This official clergy was never cut off from the parallel clergy. Both came from the same environment: that of the provincial Sufi religious families. The official mullahs always had their initial education at the hands of the parallel mullahs. Mamayusupov, born in Andijan in 1953 and the son of the mullah of the mosque at Bulagbesh, studied in Libya and was appointed mufti in March 1989; he would have known Rahmatullah Alloma (Allâma), the most famous of the clandestine religious leaders during the Soviet era (who died at the age of 31 in 1981). The channels of communication have always been open, not least as a result of family and local links. The official mullahs who did not become muftis were sent to run the official mosque of their district of origin, where they re-established their old informal contacts with the parallel mullahs. The policy of the official mullahs was not to suppress the parallel clergy but to control it. This would plainly entail waiting for a change of policy in Moscow with regard to Islam, but not necessarily the dissolution of the USSR.

Parallel Islam

The fact that this parallel Islam existed was because of the repression, but also because this repression was ineffective, at least in the countryside. The village mosques had all been closed. To fight against religion, a 'Society of Atheists' had been created. The frontal attack on Islam pushed many *ulemas* to seek refuge in the countryside – men such as the father of Abdulghaffar Khodaydad, the head of the Islamist militias in Dushanbe in the summer of 1992, who had fled Samarkand to seek refuge in Vakhsh in the 1920s.

However, the anti-religious campaign remained superficial. At the start it was very sporadic. The local mullahs tell of difficulties in the 1930s (particularly between 1932 and 1937), then during the Khrushchev period, and finally a brief period of repression under Gorbachev (more or less related to the Afghanistan intervention and a general criticism of the way the south was going in 1986–7). This was followed by a sudden wave of tolerance, beginning in 1988. The important thing was that the local mullahs were able simply to melt into the landscape of the *kolkhoz*. They were signed on as tractor drivers and mechanics, or simply as peasants. Since they had not done their studies in the big *madrasas*, and had their knowledge from their fathers and grandfathers who had been mullahs before them, these village mullahs (*mollah-bacha* in Tajik) were hard to find for the KGB of the towns. The mullah of Sukh, to whose library I refer above, was a carpenter in the *kolkhoz*. The parallel mullahs were protected by their solidarity groups, who employed them to officiate at rites such as for burials and weddings. Children came to them discreetly, outside of official school time, to learn the basic catechism. These mullahs had a few dozen religious books that had been handed down from their fathers and grandfathers, including the Chahâr-kitâb. Their knowledge of Arabic and Persian in the Arabic script was minimal, but they were able to pass on an oral knowledge, and especially the practices of Islam.

Appearances were preserved during the Soviet period: the mullah had no particular style of dress, apart from a turban if he was old. All the mosques were converted into warehouses, and if there was a *zyarat*, the *kolkhoz* simply had to declare it as a 'museum' and provide a guardian, and pilgrimage could continue discreetly as before, with the revenue going to the *kolkhoz*. The main concern of the cadres was to 'avoid bother'. If a problem was not raised, then it did not exist. The repression was also limited by the structure of the KGB itself: either it was local and complicit in what was going on, or it was town-based and unaware.

Here one should challenge the idea of 'clandestinity'. Although the village mosques were effectively closed, the practice of religion continued unabated. Male children were all circumcised, there were separate cemeteries for Christians and Muslims, and Muslim funeral rites were observed by all. What was less respected was the requirement for hallâl food (although pigs were not reared), the practice of prayers five times daily and the ban on alcohol. But there was a drop in the number of meals served in canteens during Ramadan. No party secretary would ever have been buried without the presence of a mullah who, after all, was only a kolkhozian with a white beard. In the countryside, working meetings of cadres would take place in an office with table and chairs, under a portrait of Lenin; they would then be followed by a banquet in the open air, where the assembled party would sit on cushions and where a brief *fatiha* would be recited, with hands together and raised, before eating (and drinking). Parents and grandparents would often undertake a minimum teaching of the foundations of Islam: the Chahâr kitâb was not only the preserve of mullahs. At the time of the sudden tolerance after 1988, I was surprised to see how familiar the apparatchiks were with the daily rites of Islam, even if none of them prayed. In his memoirs, Safarali Kenjayev, the *qazi*'s opponent, repeatedly cites his Muslim credentials and quotes the Quran.[10]

Once this period of tolerance was established (in late 1988 and early 1989), with no particular fanfare, the parallel mullahs left their jobs in the *kolkhoz* (albeit keeping their plots of land), put on turbans and long robes and installed themselves in the *mahalla* mosques which were either reopening or were being built. These mosques, with their rectangular groundplan, would have a gallery on two sides, with wooden pillars generally sculpted free of charge by artisans who had maintained the old traditions. All the inscriptions are in the Arabic alphabet, sometimes not very well copied. Saudi money began to flow from 1989 onwards, and the big mosques were renewed and enlarged. At this point, small quarrels began over precedence and rivalries, over who would have the recognition of the muftiyya, who would be recognised as the imâm-khâteb of the village or, indeed, who would have access to the manna from Saudi Arabia. There followed political alignments and loyalties which had little that was ideological about them and which would often counterpose the pro-muftis with the 'independents', who would be pro-government when the mufti was anti, and vice-versa.

The final anti-Islamic campaign, in 1985–7, was launched to counter the penetration of 'Wahhabism' among the parallel mullahs. But, as in the British tradition on the Indian sub-continent, this term was used as a catch-all for all radical reformers opposed to the colonial power. It functioned as a pejorative label which up until 1991 had nothing to do with Wahhabism in the strict sense – in other words with the puritan religious doctrine preached in Saudi Arabia. However, the use of this new term did correspond with a certain reality: the appearance among the parallel mullahs of young intellectuals with a modern education who became the advocates of a more radical and political Islam, on the model of the Muslim Brotherhood or the Afghan Muhajedin and, later, of the Taliban.

The reasons for the sudden disappearance of any trace of anti-religious repression at the end of 1988 remain obscure. On the one hand, the Russian withdrawal from Afghanistan lessened the notion of the Islamic threat; on the other, Soviet ideologues had begun to re-evaluate the role of Islam;[11] and finally the rise of nationalism and outbreaks of rioting provided other priorities. In any event, in 1988 the weakening of the central power of Moscow gave a greater degree of latitude to local apparatchiks, who had nothing against Islam and were even keen to see a re-establishment of tradition and 'good manners'.

THE ISLAMIST RADICALISATION

On 8 March 1987, the Afghan Muhajedin launched an operation on Tajik territory in Panj, facing Imam Saheb, the base and birthplace of Gulbuddin Hekmatyar. Another operation took place on 8 and 9 April 1987, on Moskovski. In March 1987, a few dozen kilometres further to the north, there was a demonstration in favour of the Afghan Muhajedin. One of its leaders was arrested, tried and sentenced. This was Abdullah Saidov, a surveying engineer who today is known as Sayyid Abdullah Nuri, the head of the Islamic Movement of Tajikistan. His father, Nureddin Saidov, was the director of a *sovkhoz*, and his elder brother was secretary of the local branch of the Communist Party. He was described as a 'Wahhabi' by the Communist press. But Nuri's profile is typical of the development of a modern Islamist militant:[12] born in 1947 and educated within the government's system of secular education, trained in geodesics, he came from the middle classes (in this instance rural). But he also came from a traditional family, and had followed a parallel religious education in an environment that was deeply impregnated with Sufism.

Nuri's story says a lot about the links between traditional parallel Islam and the radicalisation of the 1980s. His teacher in matters of Islam was Qari Mohamed Rustamov Hindustani (who was born in Kokand in 1892 and died in Dushanbe in 1989). As his name suggests, he was educated in India, at Deoband to be precise, before the Second World War. When he returned to the USSR, he was arrested and spent 15 years in Siberia. Once freed, he opened a clandestine *madrasa* in Dushanbe, which was closed by the KGB in 1973. But pupils and teachers alike came out of it safely, thanks to family connections and corruption. Among the students were the future founders of the Tajik branch of the Islamic Renaissance Party, including Nuri and Himmatzade, but also a key Islamist figure in Uzbek Ferghana, Allâma Rahmatullah. Within this network there circulated not only the classic books from the library of a parallel mullah, but also Islamist works brought in from abroad (Muslim Brothers such as Sayyid Qotb, or the works of Mawdudi). The Soviet invasion of Afghanistan in 1979 contributed to a radicalisation of this network.[13] Nuri's declarations and statements identify him clearly as an Islamist close to the Muslim Brotherhood, and discreetly critical of the cautiousness of the official *ulemas* and traditional mullahs. He stresses the impossibility of separating religion from politics, defends an idea of Islamic economy against capitalism and communism alike, and supports the Algerian FIS.[14]

A similar radicalisation affected all the Muslim areas in the USSR. In June 1990, the Islamic Renaissance (*nehzat*) Party (IRP) was set up in Astrakhan, on the initiative of Muslims from the Russian FSR, along with Daghestanis and Tatars. This party published journals in various languages of the USSR, including *Hedayat* in Persian and *Al Wahdat* in Russian. According to its statutes (in the Tajik version) the party's aim was 'to unify Muslims over the entire Soviet territory'.[15] The party's headquarters were in Moscow. It presented itself explicitly as a 'socio-political organisation' (*ijtemâ'i wa siyâs-si*). Its programme denounced ethnic and national conflicts. It was firm in the view that it respected the constitution and rejected terrorism. It did not contest the then form of the USSR. At the same time, its position had a lot in common with militant fundamentalism: an emphasis on preaching and conversion (in particular among Slavs), a denunciation of the official clergy, a demand for Islamic schools, a call for Islamic social justice based on the *zakat* (Islamic tax) and the *sadaqat* (alms-giving). Its basic references were traditionalist Sunni, with a touch of anti-Shiism. It also supported the Algerian FIS.[16]

The organisational vocabulary of the IRP was either that to be found in all the Islamic organisations of the contemporary Muslim world, or that of the communist tradition. The party congress (*anjoman*), made up of representatives (*vâkil*) of base cells (*majlis-i omumi-yi tashkilat-i ibtidâ'i*), elects a 15-member Council of Ulemas, which proposes to congress the candidature of the *amir* who, on the recommendation of the Council, appoints a coordinating committee (*koordinatsya*). In 1990, the *amir* was Ahmed Qadi Akhtaev (an Avar from Daghestan), with his deputy, Valiahmad Sadur (a Tatar from Moscow, and Indonesia specialist). The party made a lot of space for intellectuals who, without being *ulemas*, could 'respond to today's problems on the basis of the Quran and the Sunna'. As elsewhere in the Muslim world, these 'Islamist intellectuals' played a major role, given the absence of high-level *ulemas*.[17]

The IRP made a breakthrough in Tajikistan, under the name of the Hizb-i Nehzat-i Islami, presided over by M. Himmatzade, with Dawlat Osman as his deputy. Mullah Nuri was the third leading figure in the party. In Uzbekistan, under the name Islam Uyghonish Partyasi, the party was led by Abdullah Utayev, originally from Ferghana (he was arrested in December 1992, and subsequently disappeared).

The IRP hit two major problems in its attempts to establish a position: nationalism and the official clergy. Since it was explicitly created on a Soviet basis, the IRP identified with the programmes of the Tatar Jadids from the early part of the century, including the idea of unifying the Muslim community throughout the empire. The only additional feature was a notion of missionary activity among the Slavs, which was fed by the moral crisis of Russian society. Islamist activists now saw themselves as being at the head of a universalist movement for a renewal of lifestyles and no longer as the defenders of a dominated community.

But in this the IRP was running counter to the real evolution of the society: the fact that nationalisms were taking root and growing. It was caught unprepared by the declarations of independence in 1991, and very soon divided along ethnic and national lines. The 'Soviet' IRP repudiated its Tajik branch in autumn 1991, for its alliance with the nationalists and its frontal attack on the Soviet system. The central IRP wanted to maintain what remained of Soviet Union, and supported President Nabiyev. But the Moscow IRP was also split, between Tatars and Caucasians: the former wanted to impose Tatar as the preaching language in Moscow mosques, while the latter wanted to keep Russian. In fact, the IRP was imploding on all sides, along ethnic lines of cleavage. However, the Uzbek and Tajik branches succeeded in maintaining good relations.

As for the official clergy, this was divided into two tendencies: those who wanted to ride the wave of Islamism, and those who wanted to stick with the new national authorities. In Uzbekistan, the mufti, Mamayusupov (who signed himself Mohamed Yusuf in Arabic), was also close to the Muslim Brotherhood line; he was not looking for an Islamic party to emerge onto the political scene, but at the same time he maintained a distance from the independence government. In Tajikistan, Qazi Turajanzade was close to the IRP, although not a member. However, the events of 1992 were to lead to a collaboration between the *qazi* and the IRP: 1994 saw the announcement of the creation of an Islamic Movement of Tajikistan, of which Nuri was the president and Turajanzade the number two.

More disconcerting for the Islamists was the conjuncture between Islamic radicalisation and the expressions of localism. We have seen how in Tajikistan the IRP had a presence almost solely among the Gharmis (leaving aside the two Kulabi mullahs, one of whom, Abdullah Abdurrahman, had been the head of the Islamic army based in Afghanistan in 1995). This does not necessarily mean that the Gharmis were more religious than their Kulabi adversaries: we have seen the role played by the Kulabis in the *basmachi* war. The Kulabis also experienced a religious revivalism: during his report to the Twentieth Congress of the Tajik Communist Party in January 1986, first secretary Mahkamov denounced the shortcomings of atheist policy, and explicitly attacked the two provinces of Kulab and Kurgan-Teppe. Political affiliations were reactive: given that the Gharmi élite was in the IRP, the Kulabis had no choice but to withdraw, apart from a few mullahs of particularly firm convictions.

In Ferghana, Adalat, an Islamist movement, held some areas of the town of Namangan in the spring of 1992, before disappearing. This movement appeared to have been the expression of 'groups of bad lads' or *futuwwat*, linked to a particular *mahalla*, who were members of a sporting association (generally kung fu) and who met in a mosque, on the model of the *zurkhana* of Tehran and the *payluch* of Kandahar in Afghanistan. This was thus the expression of local solidarities, in opposition to the state. The leader of the Namangan movement (January–March 1992) was Taqirjan Yoldashev. The famous Uzbek singer Dadakhan Hassan created an Islamic movement in Ferghana in 1992. The fundamentalist mullahs of Tashkent were for the most part originally from Ferghana. In August 1995, word came of the arrest of Sheikh Abdul Vali, imam of the large parallel mosque in Andijan. Here one can see how the Islamist implantation in Uzbekistan corresponded broadly to a regionalist identity – that of Ferghana, which was not well represented in the central government. In 1997, an off-shoot of the Adalat and IRP, the Hizb-ul Tahrir (Liberation Party), headed by Yuldashev and Namangani, launched armed actions from Afghanistan.

In the other countries of Central Asia, the Islamist influence was even less substantial. In Kazakhstan, the IRP had virtually no impact, and the Islamist movement was embodied in the small Alash Orda party (this, curiously, took the name of the great party of the revolutionary era, which was very little Islamic and very much nationalist). Alash Orda led a campaign against President Nazarbeyev and against the mufti, Ratbeg Nissanbayev. In Kyrgyzstan, although Osh was a leading location of Islam, the ethnic conflicts between Uzbeks and Kyrgyz seem to have prevailed over any trans-ethnic expression of Islam. In Turkmenistan there was no sign of Islamist movements. In Azerbaijan, an Islam Partyasi ('Islamic party') appeared in around 1992. Rather influenced by Iran, it was particularly active in the camps of Azeri refugees who had been chased out of Nagorno-Karabakh, and was to be banned in 1996.

The defeat of the Islamist movement in Tajikistan had two paradoxical consequences: on the one hand, Islamism no longer appeared as an ideological alternative to sovietism, nationalism and localism. But on the other, it also became normalised: by allying with the democrats and nationalists, the IRP appeared all the more legitimate as an actor in Tajik political life, inasmuch as it represented a regionalist group that had been systematically kept out of power since the founding of Tajikistan. The fact that the real leaders of the opposition coalition were the *qazi* and Mullah Nuri reinforced this presence of the Islamist movement on the national political scene. The 1997 agreements on a coalition government gave a definitive legitimacy to the Islamist movement, which dropped most of its Islamist ideology in favour of references to the nation and democracy. In Tajikistan, as elsewhere in the Middle East, Islamism has turned into islamo-nationalism.

★　　　　★　　　　★

Does this mean that the impact of Islam was limited? In Central Asia, we find the same phenomenon that we noted throughout the Muslim world: political Islam, with a state project, turns to a new form of nationalism, but gives way, on the strictly religious field, to a conservative neo-fundamentalism which seeks to reform society and lifestyles, but does not necessarily cross the political threshold.[18] This tendency is reinforced by the role played by Saudi financing and educational institutions and by associations of preachers coming from abroad (such as the Jamat ut-Tabligh from the Indian subcontinent). What is at issue now is not only politics but also culture: attacks on marriages where people drink and play music; the promotion of a strict practice of Islamic ritual without reference to a national culture; and a critique of Sufism and traditional religious practices. Wahhabism takes the place of Hanafi Sunnism in sectors of society that are suffering an identity crisis.[19]

157

THE NEW MUFTIYYAS AND DIVISION
OF THE COMMUNITY

The national relocation of Islam led to the setting up of new muftiyyas, this time corresponding very precisely to national boundaries.

From 1993 onwards these muftiyyas were very closely controlled, following the model operating in Turkey, by a Directorate of Spiritual Affairs (the *dyanet* in Turkey), attached directly to the Council of Ministers or the presidency of the given republic. In Uzbekistan, Mohamed Yusuf was considered too independent, and in April 1993 he was replaced by Hajji Mukhtar Abdullah, a Naqshbandi from Bukhara, who had not been educated abroad. He subsequently went into exile. In Tajikistan, Fatullah Khan Sharifzade, the son of a Naqshbandi *pir* from Hissar and an ex-kolkhozian, was appointed mufti on 12 February 1993 by an assembly of *ulemas* in the presence of Dustiyev, the regime's strong man. He was assassinated on 21 January 1996, and in June 1996 was replaced by Hajji Amanullah Ne'matzadeh, aged 52, since 1988 imam of the oldest mosque in Dushanbe and a former railway employee. Here one might note that governments preferred to recruit among relatively uneducated parallel ex-mullahs rather than among the élite who had been educated in the Arab countries during the Soviet era.

In Kyrgyzstan, Hajji Abdurrahman Kimsan Bay was appointed mufti in August 1993 by the first conference of Muslims of Kyrgyzstan. He succeeded the former *qazi* of the Soviet era, Sadikian Kamalov, a pro-democrat. Kimsan Bay, who was born in Jangiabad, Uzbekistan, in 1940, is an Uzbek. In Kazakhstan, the Kazakh muftiyya was re-established, and old nationalist demand, as from January 1990. The new mufti, Ratbeg Nissan Bay (or Nissanbayev, or Nissan-bay oglu) was the former official *qazi*. He was also member of parliament for Chimkent and owed his position to Nazarbayev. He was opposed by the Alash Orda.

In Turkmenistan, Nasrullah Ibn Abdullah, who was official *qazi* during the Soviet period (under the name of Nasrullah Ibadulayev), became mufti and, from April 1994, president of the Comittee for Religious Affairs. His deputy was Andrei Sapunov, head of the Orthodox church. Ibadulayev is an Uzbek from Tashauz, educated at Al Azhar in Egypt.

This fragmentation is also to be found in Russia. The mufti of Ufa, Talghat Tajuddin, in post since 1982, was opposed as mufti for the whole of Russia by the mufti of Moscow, Ravil Gaynuddin. Two independent muftis also stood for the post, Gabdulla Galiulin for Tatarstan, and Mohamed Nigmatulin for Bashkortostan.

There exists therefore no supranational manifestation of Islam over the whole territory of the ex-USSR. The new national clergies in the Muslim republics are controlled by the state. Islam does not represent an independent supra-national political force.

All the new states associated themselves with Islam. Only the constitutions of Turkmenistan and Kazakhstan proclaim explicitly that the state is secular (*dünyavi*), but both countries belong to the Organisation of the Islamic Conference, as do all the others. The other constitutions do not mention Islam. But all the states recognise the presence of Islam and take steps to mobilise a certain Muslim legitimacy, while at the same time controlling the clergy and putting down radical Islam. The presidents of these countries take part in the major Muslim ceremonies, and readily use religious expressions. By the same token, the mufti of each republic is present on all major public occasions. Sufism is rehabilited by university academics as both movement and doctrine.[20] Uzbekistan laid on a major commemoration of Bahauddin Naqshband in Bukhara, and used the fact that both the Yasawiyya and the Naqshbandiyya originated in Central Asia as a way of opposing a 'national' Islam to fundamentalist and Wahhabite influences which were rather anti-Sufi and which were described as foreign and contrary to authentic Islam.

★   ★   ★

The post-independence mosques are organised within a dual structure, deriving from the division between the official clergy and the parallel clergy. First, the incumbent of the 'official' mosques (*masjed-i jame'* in Persian) in the major cities hold the title of *imâm-khâteb*, approved if not directly appointed by the republic's mufti or his provincial representative. These mosques are generally financed externally (the municipality, Arab countries, the state, hâkims, collections). Then there are the small mosques, known in Tajik as the *panj-vaghti* ('where one does the five prayers') and in Uzbek *besh-vaghti*, which usually represent the *mahallas* and solidarity groups. They are run by former parallel mullahs who have rarely done much by way of study. These *mollah-bacha* are members of the local community, or are taken on by them. The state does not try to control these small mosques.

The muftis, on the other hand, have taken steps to supervise the parallel clergy, by appointing *imâm-khâtebs* on the model of the official administrative hierarchy (provincial, district-level, and major-city level). There has often been virulent conflict over questions of who controls the *masjed-i jame'*. This attempt at control has rather alienated the small village mullahs and self-proclaimed imams, who have often mobilised localist and political support in order to preserve their independence. The result of this has been that the clergy in turn has been split along regionalist lines, playing into the hands of the local powers and the state, which has not hesitated, when necessary, to support former parallel mullahs against the official Soviet clergy when it contests state policy (in Uzbekistan and Tajikistan). In Azerbaijan the unshiftable *sheikh ul-Islam* Shukur Pashazade survived through all the regimes: having allied himself with the Directorate of Religious Affairs in the council of ministers (under Mustafa Ibrahimov), he brought the Islamic university into line (its rector, Sabir Gassanli, resigned in July 1996), while a new law made the opening of mosques dependent on registration with the muftiyya.

There also exists a third structure, which involves the setting up of 'Islamist' mosques by the back door: a radical mullah instals himself in a given mosque, but through his teaching he reaches a wider section of the population than just the local *mahalla* or village, often very much to the detriment of other local mullahs. The congregation then becomes ideologically motivated. These mosques, which were closed in Turkmenistan and Tajikistan, are tolerated in other republics, but in Uzbekistan they have become the object of police checks and arrests among their leadership.

Finally, there are networks of Islamic institutions established from abroad. These are basically Turkish organisations. The official network, the Dyanet (directorate of religious affairs), works in co-operation with government directorates of religious affairs and undertakes to help in setting up an ortho-dox and functionarised clergy, through the construction of *imam-hatep* high schools (in the Turkish pronunciation), on the Turkish model, combining an Islamic *education* with a modern education. The other networks are extensions of Turkish religious brotherhoods of which the most effective is the Nurcu, although there are also the Fethullachi, a new-style brotherhood focusing on education.[21] They have opened modern schools and religious institutes. The Fethullachi have a journal entitled *Zaman*, which is translated into all the local Turkic languages. Their influence has been strong in Kazakhstan and Azerbaijan, but they have been received with reservations in Uzbekistan.

Iran has no religious influence, since it lacks Shiite intermediaries and as in Afghanistan has not proved capable of a breakthrough in Sunni environments. The Islamic influence is thus carried via pro-Western countries such as Turkey and Saudi Arabia, which limits the repression to which they might otherwise be subjected.

9

From Independence to Emerging Nationalism

THE INVENTION OF THE NATION-STATE

The problem of the newly independent states of Central Asia is at once simple and insoluble. As we have seen, they were born during the Soviet period. But their independence was created in opposition to that period. One cannot imagine Kyrgyzstan making Stalin the father of its nation. Furthermore, they are not able to refer back to the period preceding Sovietisation or Russian colonisation in the way that can be done among the Georgians or in the Baltic countries, because what existed in that period, the emirates and the tribal confederations, does not fit with the ethnic-national legitimacy which they are building today. Only Azerbaijan has been able to refer back to an earlier model of nation-state – the republic of 1918, whose flag it has adopted. But all the others are in a position of having to invent new flags. Similarly, the debates on the concept of the 'Muslim nation' among the Jadids in the early part of the century are no longer relevant for states whose main concern is to affirm their specificity and to reject all new supra-national entities. Thus the identity that is being created is somehow timeless, with no historical reference points other than mythical founding figures taken from Soviet historiography. These countries are taking the conceptual matrix of Sovietism, in a 'secularised' form (in other words stripped of its eschatological dimension – the fusion of peoples), as a way of anchoring the present in a timeless and ahistorical past. The new independences are being constructed on a foreclosure of history.

★   ★   ★

The first aim of the independent states has been to give themselves the symbolic panoply of all independent states: a flag, a national anthem and a coat of arms. The process of nationalising the state framework inherited from the

161

Soviet era was at first nominal: institutions and streets were given new names. But since they lacked a coherent body of historical references, this manufacture of symbols initially looked more like a patching together of bits and pieces, rather than a return to historical roots. The designs of their flags are heavily symbolic and tend to feature land and sky: Kazakh and Kyrgyz suns, Uzbek and Turkmen stars, Kazakh and Uzbek skies. The Tajik flag adopts the Iranian national colours in reverse. Uzbekistan, Turkmenistan and Tajikistan have large amounts of green, a colour not used by the Kazakhs and Kyrgyz, who are less concerned to establish their Islamic credentials.

The new dates of national holidays combine elements deriving from the Soviet period, Islam, the Persian tradition and recent nationalism: in Tajikistan, these holidays are 21–22 March (Newruz), 1 May and 9 May (Victory Day), 22 June and 9 September (Independence Day). To these are added the movable Muslim feasts (the end of Ramadan, the Feast of the Sacrifice), plus the old Zoroastrian festivals (Mehrgan and Sada). In Uzbekistan, we find Newruz, Independence Day (1 September), together with the Muslim holidays and 8 March and 8 December. The eclecticism says a lot about the vague nature of the chosen reference points. They have a catalogue from which to pick and choose. Medals and titles are also invented: the Tajik newspaper *Payam-i Dushambe* of 24 August 1993 announced the creation of a title, Unvân, or 'hero of Tajikistan', and the orders of Sharaf ('honour') and 'Spitamen'. Uzbekistan created the title of 'Hero of Uzbekistan', of which the first recipient, needless to say, was the country's president. Turkmenistan inevitably created the Order of Turkmanbashi, with a portrait of the president surrounded by diamonds. The iconography and layout of newspapers, the style and ritual of speeches, the repetitive enumeration of titles, all follow Soviet forms, but their content is now national.

In all the countries, the previously existing administrative terminology is replaced by words from the Arab–Persian political tradition, or from earlier Turkish terminology: thus hâkim ('governor') replaces the *obkom* and *ispalkom* ('president of a soviet'); *shura* (Tajikistan), *kengash* (Uzbekistan and Turkmenistan) and *kenesh* (Kyrgyzstan) replace soviet, and *vilayat* ('province') replaces *oblast*. Parliament in Turkmenistan becomes the Khalq Maslahati (Council of the People) (here *maslahat* refers back to a traditional council of clan elders), while in Uzbekistan parliament is the Oli Majlis and in Tajikistan the Shura-ye Oli (both meaning 'supreme assembly'). This terminology never takes on the new terms introduced by the Turks and Iranians in the 1920s in their attempt to de-Arabise the language (*il* and *ostân* for 'province', instead of *vilayat*, which was common to the whole cultural region).

Some place names are changed, but names relating to recomposed identities created under the Soviets are preserved. For example, in Tajikistan the town of Leninabad reverts to its former name, Khojent, but the province keeps the name Leninabad (the suffix of which – -*abâd* – thus refers to a town which no longer exists), because the localist identity of the Leninabadis is very

162

much a Soviet creation, and does not correspond to a pre-existing province. Tselinograd reverts to Akmolla in Kazakhstan, and Krasnovodsk in Turkmenistan becomes Turkmanbashi; Kirovabad reverts to Ganja in Ajerbaijan. In Tajikistan, Orjonokidze-abad reverts to Kafirnehan, and Frunze in Kyrgyzstan becomes Bishkek. The names of those responsible for Russian conquest are the first to be removed.

Street names also change: Marx and Lenin disappear, to be replaced by Rudaki (Tajikistan), Turkmanbashi (in Turkmenistan), and Independence and Rashidov in Uzbekistan, although Tashkent keeps its Pushkin and Chekhov Streets. The *kolkhoz*, as we saw above, have their own way of doing things: they are given the names of their founders, or of national heroes, except in the case of *kolkhoz* that were created *ex nihilo*, where the Soviet name has become emblematic.

But behind the fresh coats of paint, the presence of the USSR can still be read more or less wherever you look, in the names of places, street-name signs that nobody has bothered to remove, the slogans which dominate public buildings, calling for peace and friendship between peoples, the monuments to the dead, the statues of Lenin etc. It is, of course, a washed-out USSR, rusting away, with nobody bothering to repaint it. Sometimes the Soviet past is marked by a simple emptiness: the empty plinths of statues, and places which formerly held portraits of Marx and Lenin, which have not been replaced by others. The signs and the iconography of everyday life are still Soviet: old Intourist photos display the kaleidoscope of folk culture of the other socialist republics (without the 'former'); old calendars kept to decorate an empty wall; there is the roll of honour of workers or employees at the entrances to workplaces; notices giving production targets on the walls of *kolkhoz*; and also hammers and sickles and stars as decorative motifs on door trims, corbels, pediments and lintels, which are now the acanthus and oak leaves of an unrivalled neo-classicism.

Collective Memory and Individual Memory

In the operation of naming things at the local level, the logic which operates is often different from that of the new nationalisms which one sees setting to work. It has to be related to the 'psychology' of adults and older people, suddenly called upon to view their pasts with new eyes. The logic of the new states is to invent a clear nationalist legitimacy, but one which does not break too abruptly with the Soviet period which gave birth to the new republics and is thus part and parcel of their legitimation. The logic from below, on the other hand, is to preserve memories of people, and the rituals of social life, and to guarantee a continued identity for groups that were often founded as a result of the regrouping imposed by collectivisation, whether or not these reflect traditional identities that existed prior to the Soviet period (clans, tribes etc). Leaving aside the historical and ideological references associated with statues of Lenin and place names such as 'Proletar' or 'Red October', these names refer to a past that has been lived, a set of people's memories that is not a parenthesis. At the individual level, the 'construction of socialism' and the 'great patriotic war' do not represent history with a capital H, but events which, in large part, are the real basis of people's social identity.

These memories, which during the Soviet period articulated individual lived experience, state ritual and history (via teaching in schools, commemorations, etc), suddenly find themselves deprived of a context: the 'great patriotic war' which so cruelly marked a whole generation loses its meanings within the new histories, unlike collectivisation, which is the basis of new social regroupings. This need not to abandon their citizens' pasts has led the newly independent countries to surreal celebrations and commemorations: Uzbek television dedicated a long evening's broadcasting to the events of 9 May 1945, complete with a reunion of old soldiers, but at no point did you see the flag beneath which they had fought: it was as if there had been a war between Uzbekistan and 'fascism'.

In the same way as individual people, the new countries need to be able to reappropriate the Soviet period, but within different registers: individual memory is today detached from collective memory.[1] What is one to do with medals that were won in a war that no longer has meaning? What does one do with awards that were once the pride of model Soviet workers? The trips to Moscow, the commemorative badges and lapel pins, the diplomas with their hammers and sickles, the whole *cursus honorum* which meant that one was 'someone'? Soviet society concealed the deep duality between the nomenklatura and ordinary people by a whole system of distinctions and honours: medals for old soldiers and model workers, days dedicated to different professional categories etc. Everybody had an opportunity, at one time or other, to be, if not famous, at least honoured. What appeared to the outside observer a posed ritual (formal photographs on the front pages of newspapers showing model workers who for a moment have escaped their anonymity; rolls of honour at the entrances to factories etc) was experienced and lived as a social recognition. One is still struck by the number of people who wear insignia in their lapels. These insignia place them within an order which is not so much social as commemorative: I did such-and-such... I am so-and-so... There were very few material advantages attached, there was no power. At best they might get a place of honour at some banquet or commemoration, and their photograph in the newspaper, and a degree of social recognition which culminated in their funeral – the announcement enumerating the list of their titles, a *curriculum vitae* written on paper, or stone, or perhaps even bronze. Now, though, all these things which previously marked a person's existence as being positive are no longer meaningful: the fact of having been an old soldier from the war between the Russians and the Germans, a Hero of Socialist Labour, a handshake with some Soviet leader, a member of a delegation en route to

Moscow, the winner of some prize or other. The teleology of everyday life has disappeared.

One can say that a Soviet *habitus* still exists. It is particularly noticeable in the image of the state, as an apparatus beyond criticism and a transcendental power, but one which is now transferred to the person of the president (in Uzbekistan, but particularly in Turkmenistan), whose principal quality is to ensure the well-being of his people (in concrete terms this means maintaining a system of subsidies for basic products which are distributed via the institutions in which the people work). The president is supposed to be another of those 'good princes' who ensure the rule of justice, maintain civic peace, and feed the people. The fact that the plaque on the new statue of Tamerlane in the centre of Tashkent speaks of the prince's 'justice' says a lot about the reinvention of models from the past.

THE SEARCH FOR A PAST

All new nations re-evaluate or construct their pasts. But what is striking in Central Asia, in the new namings of streets and towns and in the promotion of national heroes, is the absence of almost four centuries of history, broadly speaking from the start of the sixteenth century to the purges of 1937. The Shaybanids, the nineteenth-century emirates, the Jadid reformers and the early Bolsheviks are little or not mentioned. In Tashkent, there is a Tamerlane Square, an Independence Street, an Akhundbabayev Avenue (the only Uzbek leader to have survived the 1937 purges), dozens of Rashidov *kolkhoz*, even a Karl Liebknecht Street, but no Fayzullah-Khojaev Square. Even the celebrated Uzbek Jadid poet Hamza (d. 1929) has disappeared from the new hagiography.

The rewriting of history takes as its starting point Soviet periodisations and concepts and changes only the values attached to them. It has two main focuses: the valorisation, against Moscow, of post-1937 apparatchiks who are erected into champions of the national identity; and the search for a mythical past existing prior to the modern historical period. In Uzbekistan, they pay homage to Rashidov and Tamerlane, two figures familiar in Soviet propaganda, but the Jadids and the Shaybanids are neglected, as they were under the Soviets.

The real founding past is in fact the Soviet era. Thus the Soviet perspective is preserved, but at the same time the role of the Russians is systematically re-evaluated negatively. The Russians are described as colonisers, but the history being used is that which they themselves wrote of the peoples that they colonised, changing only certain aspects. The underlying idea is that the present nations were actually already established (but had not yet appeared) during the 1930s, despite Russian and Soviet pressures. The argument is that the national movement was present during the Soviet era, but existed despite Moscow. During 1991 and 1992, a series of books appeared which rehabilitated the struggle against tsarism, the Kazakh revolts of 1916, and the *basmachis*, and Madamin Beg in particular.[2] The Turkmens turn the site of Gök-Teppe, where the Tekke tribe was successively victorious and defeated (1879–81), into a place for foreign delegations to visit. Communist leaders who were vilified under Andropov and *perestroika* are rehabilitated: Rashidov in Uzbekistan; Kunayev in Kazakhstan (in February 1994, Karl Marx Street in Almati was renamed Dinmohamed-Kunayev Street). Ghafurov remains the father of Tajikistan, and is honoured by all parties. Even the minor local Uzbek notable Adilov, who was attacked by the Russian press in 1988, was briefly rehabilitated.[3]

As always, behind the national dimension of the debate on rehabilitation you also find an underlying presence of regionalist splits. In the fierce debates taking place in Tajikistan in 1990–2, rehabilitations were carried out on the basis of the regional origins of those purged in the period 1933–7. It was a question not of defending their political project but of defending group honour. A Pamiri author wrote a small book to defend Shahtimur and all the purged Pamiris,[4] but nobody thought to celebrate the memory of Abdullah Muhiddinov, the president of the first Tajikistan *sovnarkom* between 1924 and 1929 and the prime mover in freeing Tajikistan from Uzbek tutelage (he was to disappear in 1933). He was from Bukhara, and there is no Bukhariot faction on the Tajik political scene. As a rule, fellow travellers and the early local communists did not belong to the regionalist factions that took power after the 1937 purges, which partly explains the silence about them. Debarment is also explained by the origins of the élites, as if some original sin had to be expiated. To rehabilitate all those sentenced during the Stalinist era would be to throw suspicion on the origins of the new political élite.

Reservations about the Jadids can be explained by the fact that they did not identify with nationalism in the modern sense of the term. For them the term *milli* or *melli* ('national') did not refer to modern nation-states but to the whole community of Muslims in Russia. Unlike the new national project, it was inseparable from pan-Islamism and pan-Turkism. The Jadids also offered a reform model, against autocracy, which could be read as an implicit criticism of the authoritarian presidential regimes which characterised the new governments. (However, Karimov did sing the praises of Fitrat in a speech in December 1991.)

It was no accident that only Azerbaijan rehabilitated the Jadids (Rassulzade features on the country's new banknotes), because they eventually converted to the national ideal, having proclaimed independence in 1918.

An American author notes that 'curiously, Uzbek historians have rarely blamed Soviet scholars explicitly for the damage done to their historiography'.[5] There is nothing surprising here. Uzbek historians today adopt precisely the Soviet matrix, and simply alter its negative assessments of certain historical figures, such as Tamerlane. The aim is the same: to obliterate the Turkestani identity in favour of an Uzbek ethnic identity, but with the added ingredient of Uzbekistan's desire to pose as a legitimate rallying-point in Central Asia.

It was inevitable that the basic concepts of the Soviet model of the creation of nations would be adopted, because they facilitate the identification between 'nationalism' and given ethnic groups which underpins the legitimacy of the new states. The historians of the new Republics adopted wholesale the conception of ethnogenesis of the founding peoples of the republic, and only stripped it of its final stage, which was the future fusion of nationalities into *homo sovieticus*. The vision of history underpinning the new states is certainly not Marxist, but it is very Soviet.

The most delicate operation in this way of seeing things is how to show that the present territory has always been inhabited by the dominant nationality. This is generally done by annexing the different populations that have peopled the national territory. The Turkmens do this in the same way that the Kemalist historians of Turkey did, by 'Turkmenising' all the peoples that, in various phases, lived in the territory of present Turkmenistan, including those speaking Iranian languages.[6] An Azeri university academic declares confidently that the Turks as a people appeared around 2000 BC, around Lake Urumieh in Iranian Azerbaijan.[7] Nationalist Tajik intellectuals see the Sogdians of the first millennium as the authentic Tajiks. The Tajik historian N. Ne'matov provides an overview of the history of his country which turns it into nothing less than the heir of all the Iranian-language populations of Central Asia. In outlining his nationalist position, he makes brief mention of the Soviet period – not negatively – because how could Tajikistan be explained without the USSR?[8] In Kazakhstan much attention is now being given to the first Kazakh khanate, in the fifteenth century, the supposed five-hundred-and-fortieth anniversary of which was celebrated in 1995. Kazakhstan also annexes for the purposes of its bank notes Al Farabi (870–950), the Muslim philosopher who was born in the south of present-day Kazakhstan but who presumably spoke Persian, particularly because in that era there were no Kazakhs in that region. The Kazakh Jadids of the last century are viewed ambiguously, because they were also instruments of Russification, as was Chokan Valikhanov.[9]

This desire to match a people to a land perhaps explains a further historical 'oversight' in Uzbek historiography: the period of the Shaybanids. At first sight, their omission is incomprehensible: after all, the Shaybanids founded the first truly Uzbek dynasty in 1500, within the present geographical confines of Uzbekistan. But there is an explanation for this hesitancy: the Shaybanids arrived only in 1500, which would imply that something other than Uzbekistan must have existed before that period. In order to root the nation in history, historians prefer to 'Uzbekise' Tamerlane and Babur, the two famous sovereigns who ruled over all or part of Central Asia from the fourteenth to the sixteenth centuries, even though neither of them was actually an 'Uzbek'. Tamerlane was a Turcophone of Mongol descent (from the Barlas tribe), as was Babur. Both spoke Chaghatay, which was indeed the ancestor of present-day Uzbek, but which differed from the Qipchak dialects spoken by Uzbeks in that time. In the sixteenth century, having been chased out of Central Asia – precisely by the Uzbeks of Shaybani Khan – Babur wrote: 'For almost 140 years the capital of Samarkand belonged to our family. From where came the Ôzbek foreigner and enemy who made himself master of it?'[10] As ancestors go, they could perhaps have found someone more congenial.

The independent republic of Uzbekistan prefers to adopt the Chaghatay heritage, Uzbekising it in the same way that the Soviets did. As regards the role of Ali Shir Nava'i as the founding poet of 'modern Uzbek literature', they simply went along with the Soviet analysis. It was Soviet Russian orientalists who turned him into an 'Uzbek' writer, because previously he had been considered a bilingual author writing in Turki and Persian. A. Fitrat had even written an article in 1925 on Ali Shir Nava'i's Persian-language poetry. The Turkmens and Azeris also lay claim to him.[11] Fitrat defended the (correct) idea of a culture proper to Central Asia. This brought him the criticism of being a 'nationalist' (in the pan-Islamist sense of the word). After his appropriation by Soviet Uzbekistan, Nava'i was to be served up in a variety of guises: the five-hundredth anniversary of his birth was celebrated in 1926 and in 1941 (by both the lunar and the solar calendar). During the war in Afghanistan, he was mobilised again, to symbolise the cultural links between Afghanistan (he was born in Herat) and Soviet Central Asia.

But the real founding father was Tamerlane, whose statue replaced that of Karl Marx in the centre of Tashkent. The refusal of Soviet historiography to accept the idea of a 'Turkestani' identity left two possibilities: to ignore the Chaghatay episode and Tamerlane; or to make Tamerlane an Uzbek and to turn Chaghatay into 'Old Uzbek'.[12] They opted for the second solution post-1936, although Tamerlane continued to be viewed as a negative figure.[13] Already in 1968, Ibrahim Mumimov, president of the Academy of Sciences, was attempting a rehabilitation of Tamerlane, but this was immediately condemned by Moscow.[14] In short, modern Uzbekistan changes the values but not the basic data that it inherited from the Soviet era – in other words the 'Uzbekness' of Tamerlane. The choice of Tamerlane also serves another function, here diverging from the Soviet heritage: it seeks to turn present-day Uzbekistan into the heir of the greatest empire that Central Asia had ever seen, with a vocation as a regional power.[15] Thus it is to assume a purely Central Asian identity, at a big distance from the Ottoman empire, which Tamerlane crushed in 1402. It is thus also to assume the Turkic-Persian heritage characteristic of Timurid civilisation, but in order to Uzbekise it.

LANGUAGE AS A CRITERION OF NATIONHOOD

In the republics of Central Asia, we are now seeing a rapid movement of de-Russification, pursued mainly for political and sociological reasons. The question of language is particularly sensitive, because it distinguishes partici-pating citizens from passive citizens. All the republics had already installed their languages as national languages well before the declarations of independence (July 1989 in Tajikistan, September 1989 in Kazakhstan). Similarly to the situation in Algeria after independence, the struggle against the language of the 'coloniser' was everywhere being carried out by people who actually spoke it better than their national languages. But there were definite signs of a return to the national language, even in places where ten years previously people had been making efforts to speak only Russian with their children. The movement was most marked among the Kazakhs, since Russian was so dominant there. The Turkmens, on the other hand, had remained largely Turkmen-speaking. And among Uzbeks, observation of the political scene reveals a constant progression of Uzbek, from the day of independence to a point of maturity in 1996. Among the Tajiks, Persian has always been a prestige language among the secular intelligentsia, religious milieux and part of the rural population.

After independence, all the states except Tajikistan passed strict laws designed to promote their 'national languages', which was always the languages of the dominant ethnic group. In Kyrgyzstan, Article 8 of the law of September 1989 requires that all officials be able to speak Kyrgyz with their subordinates, which in theory excludes the majority of Europeans from positions of responsibility. Similar laws are to be found in Uzbekistan and Turkmenistan, and they are actively applied. Only Kazakhstan and Tajikistan (joined in 1996 by Kyrgyzstan) maintain Russian, not as an official language but as a language of communication between 'nationalities', below the level of the official language. Language laws are stricter in Central Asia than in the Baltic countries: functionaries who are unable to comply are demoted and sometimes removed from their posts altogether. In the Baltic countries, a Russian professor of Latin in the university is entitled to teach his course in Russian, but he has problems getting himself registered as a citizen. In Uzbekistan the reverse is true: the Russian professor of Latin at the University of Tashkent was replaced by an Uzbek in 1993, but he had no problem getting a passport and voting rights. The Russian language practically disappeared from walls and posters in Turkmenistan. The new bank notes are all single-language, while Uzbek visas are in Uzbek and English. When a second language is required nowadays, it is English.

Language policy is particularly applied in areas involving struggles for social promotion, not so much between Russians and 'Muslims', but between indigenous Russified and educated élites coming from the countryside. Before independence, whatever ethnic group one belonged to, in order to make a career one would have had to have come through one of the so-called 'Russian schools'. The level of education was higher, and Russian was the language of government and of social prestige. Less promising pupils went to the local-language schools. However, such pupils, who were often driven by the demographic pressure of the Central Asian countryside, welcome the strict application of language policy because it is a way of breaking into jobs that had previously been reserved for Russian-speakers. Rather than resisting this movement, the Russified élite which is in power today decided to get one jump ahead. It pressed for the national language to be the country's sole language, partly in order to defuse the potential threat posed by these young people coming from the countryside, who could be attracted by Islamism, but also because, once the Soviet myth had disappeared, the national reference was the only basis of legitimation.

In three of the countries (Uzbekistan, Turkmenistan and Azerbaijan) this promotion of the national language also involves a change in the alphabet. In most of the countries, commissions have been set up to oversee language reform, dealing with two main issues, 'de-Russification' and 'nationalisation'. In other words, there is an abandonment of any attempt to bring the Turkic languages closer together or to homogenise them. Here one needs to examine in different terms the language situation in Tajikistan and Azerbaijan on the one hand, and in the Turcophone countries of Central Asia on the other.

Turkish and Persian or Azeri and Tajik?

In Tajikistan the issue was that of a return to Persian; the other countries are concerned to distance themselves as far as possible from the Turkish model, while at the same time pursuing similar kinds of reform. Azerbaijan is something of a case unto itself: just as there is no Tajik 'language', so there is no Azeri language, any more than there is a 'Québécois' language. But there is a manner of speaking, a relationship with forms of language preceding those currently spoken in the metropolis, and a linguistic practice which has become rather autonomous from the language spoken in the country from which it took its name.

In Tajikistan, an International Foundation for the Tajik-Persian Language has been pursuing its labours since *perestroika*, and regardless of the return to power of the conservatives. The reform which it envisages is to return to Persian, and to promote the Arabic-Persian alphabet (in the written form this alphabet cancels out differences of pronunciation between Tajik and Persian, differences which had been highlighted in the transition to Cyrillic). A journal (*Saman*) has been published in both alphabets (Cyrillic and Persian), with Russian words being replaced by Iranian words. Despite the ideological hostility of the present Dushanbe government to Iran, an Iranian bookshop has opened in the centre of the city, and is well-stocked. An Iranisation of vocabulary is taking place spontaneously, under the influence of an Iranian cultural model which provides more of a living language, and which has radio stations, newspapers, universities etc. One should also note that in Dushanbe, as a result of the war, there are no school books available for children; only the Iranian bookshop is in a position to provide books, which are without ideological colouring but are in Persian. Thus Russian words are spontaneously being replaced by words from Iranian Persian, and not by words from the old Persian that was in use at the start of the century, and which is still in use in Afghanistan. The Russian word *samoliot* ('aircraft'), when it is replaced, is replaced by the Iranian neologism h*âvapeyma*, and not by the old Arabo-Persian word *tayyara*, which is used among Afghan Persian speakers, and was also used by the *basmachis* of 1924.

This movement enjoys a consensus which goes beyond regionalist splits between intellectuals, even though the civil war of 1992 cemented differences in linguistic practices. Apparatchiks tend to speak either dialect or Russian, while mullahs and intellectuals speak a very classical Persian, keeping their traditional pronunciation, which is correctly reckoned to be closer to the classical. The apparatchiks' reticence as regards a model which is Persian (and thus more Islamic and oriented towards Iran) explains why the constitution adopted in September 1994 proclaimed not Persian but Tajiki to be the official language. This may have been a political gesture to Russian-speakers and Uzbeks, but it was also a result of nationalist reservations.

One finds a similar ambiguity in Azerbaijan: it is accepted that Azeri is a Turkish language, but there is an unwillingness to align with the Turkish spoken in Turkey, either in pronunciation or in vocabulary, even though, with the scale, presence and accessibility of Turkish media, Turkish words are slipping into everyday life and are understood by everyone. The difference between the two vocabularies is not in the Russian influence, which is decreasing, but in the Persian foundations, which were held in common with Ottoman Turkish but were partly purged from the Turkish spoken in Turkey by Atatürk's reforms. In Baku today, people still say *sefarat* and not *büyük elçiligli* for 'Embassy', and *anjoman* instead of *dernek* for 'association'. The fact that the constitution also states that the official language is Azeri and not Turkish can also be seen as a gesture of national affirmation in the face of a new big brother reckoned to be too invasive. In the same way, in their adoption of the Latin alphabet the Azeris have made an effort to introduce small differences, such as the reversed 'e' in 'Azerbaijan', where Turkish would use a normal 'e'. Needless to say, the slight but real difference in pronunciation plays no phonological role and could pass unnoticed. However, another element also comes into play: Azeri is far more Persianised than the Turkish spoken in Turkey, because it was not affected by the reforms of 1926. This makes it possible to maintain links with Azeris from the south (Iran) whose language is even more Persianised. The choice of a definition of national language has a lot to do with strategic choices: Greater Turkey or Greater Azerbaijan. Now more than ever, linguistics becomes political.

The Heightening of Differences Between Turkic Languages

Within the totality of the Turcophone countries of Central Asia, language reform operated at two levels: it replaced Russian loan words, and changed the alphabet (except, in the latter instance, in Kazakhstan and Kyrgyzstan).

At both levels the reforms have systematically avoided anything that might bring the Turkic languages closer to each other, let alone closer to the Turkish spoken in Turkey. The word 'Turkish' is not to be found anywhere in Central Asia. Thus linguistic policy operates on the same principle as the reforms introduced by Stalin: the exacerbation of linguistic divergences between republics by means of changes of alphabet and the use of loan words. This is an additional proof that today's nationalisms are effectively an extension of the Soviet system rather than a break with it, as we have already seen in their handling of history.

In order to replace Russian words (which generally relate to objects or concepts that could be defined as 'modern'), they draw on old Arabic-Persian sources rather than adapting the neologisms which Turkey massively created during the 1920s: airport (*aeroport* in Russian) becomes briefly *tayyaragah* in Uzbekistan ('place of the aircraft', an Arabic word with a Persian suffix) and not *hava limani*, the Turkish choice in the 1920s, 'flight' became *parwaz*, an Iranian word. Even in Kazakhstan and Kyrgyzstan, they use *hâkim* and *vilayat* from the Arabic-Persian even though the language is far less 'Persianised' than Uzbek. But the *öz türkçe*, the 'pure Turkish' so dear to Atatürk, is not on the menu. The choice is thus resolutely Central Asian and not pan-Turkist. Unlike Tajikistan, which is attempting to Persianise itself, the Turcophone republics are seeking to emphasise differences and to inscribe their languages within their own reconstituted histories. Nobody appears keen to reintroduce the pan-Turkic dimension, rather to the disappointment of Turks from Turkey.

In autumn 1993, Turkmenistan and Uzbekistan decided to go over to the Latin alphabet (the law of 2 September 1993 in Uzbekistan). Turkmenistan set it in motion from the top down: the Latin alphabet was to be used on bank notes and government billboards even before it was taught in schools (Soviet voluntarism was still alive and well). The Uzbeks, more prudently, began by publishing and teaching their new Latin alphabet before changing official alphabet usage.[16] Here, three things should be noted: neither of the two used the Latin alphabet employed in the 1930s, and neither co-ordinated with the other with a view to unifying transcription choices. Both airily ignored the proposal for a joint Turkic alphabet put forward by a commission of specialists at the University of Marmara (Turkey) in 1993.

In rendering certain phonemes that are typically Uzbek ('gh', 'ng', but also 'tsh', 'y', long 'u' and short 'u'), the Uzbek Latin alphabet does not revert to the choices adopted in the short-lived Latin alphabet that ran from 1930 to 1940. This means that in less than a century Uzbekistan has known five alphabets (Arabic, modified Arabic, Latin – which was itself modified – Cyrillic and new Latin).[17] It also ignores vowel harmony, which is common to the entire Turkic world, and is practised by large numbers of Uzbek speakers. The Uzbek and Turkmen alphabets have different transcriptions for phonemes which are identical and which could have been transcribed in the same way. For instance, the Uzbek and Turkmen sh and kh, which are pronounced in the same way in both countries, are transcribed as '$' and 'H' in Turkmenistan, and 'Ş' and 'X' in Uzbekistan, corresponding to the Turkish 'Ş' and 'H'. The Uzbek government modified its Latin alphabet in 1996, but along the same lines: 'sh' is now transcribed as 'sh', with two letters, and 'dj' is transcribed as 'j'. The Turkmens use 'Ұ' for the undotted Turkish 'ı' (it has been suggested that the presence of the '$' and the 'Ұ' is explained by the fact that the dollar and yen signs are present on all computers, unlike the 'Ş' and the undotted 'ı', which is certainly the case on the computer owned by the author of the present volume).

This determination to create differences where they did not exist previously, or where they could have been avoided, is very reminiscent of Stalinist language policy: in imposing the Cyrillic alphabet in place of the Latin – which itself had previously replaced the Arabic-Persian alphabet for all the languages of Central Asia – Stalinism had deliberately exacerbated the differences between languages. Nationalisms are being constructed not just against Moscow but also against neighbouring countries and against all potential regional groupings.

Curiously, certain Russianisms continue to be preserved within official turns of phrase, such as the cumbersome 'airport of the name of Turkmanbashi' (Turkmenbashi Adyndaki), or the 'university of the name of Firdawsi' (Dâneshgâh be-nâm-i Ferdows) in Tajik (from the Russian *imeni*). A cumbersome style is still the mark of the apparatchiks.

NATIONALISM AND ETHNICITY

The creation of national entities takes as its starting point ethnic legitimacy as it was defined by Soviet theory. The republics continue to exist according to their political birth certificate of 1924. They counterpose this ethnic nationalism to all universalist ideologies, such as pan-Turkism, pan-Islamism and pan-Turanianism (the latter refers to the uniting of all the countries of Central Asia within a single political entity, separate from Turkey). The problem is that not all citizens are members of the dominant ethnic group, and not all members of the dominant ethnic group live in the country. So while maintaining the principle of ethnic legitimacy, the new states have a two-fold project: on the one hand, to keep their 'non-native' citizens when they are 'European' and to assimilate the others; and on the other to be very cautious in approaching the question of ethnic minorities living abroad, in order to maintain a status quo on frontiers.

The system inherited from the USSR tends to create a distinction between 'citizenship' (*grajhdanstvo* in Russian, *sharhvandi* in Tajik and *fuqaralik* in Uzbek), which is defined in purely political terms, and 'nationality' (*natsionalnost* in Russian, and *mellat* in Persian and Uzbek), which correspond to one's national/ethnic affiliation (in which the ultimate criterion is language). Before independence in these countries, there was no contradiction, inasmuch as 'nationality' referred to the republic or autonomous territory, whereas citizenship was in relation to the USSR. The counterposition between 'ethnic nationality' and 'citizenship' was transcended by the existence of a supranational identity. The disappearance of the USSR exploded the notion of the supra-ethnic state and left a collection of nationalities in search of a state of their own. The situation was particularly serious because the Soviet system had contributed to fixing, or to creating, ethnic belonging: thus the forms for the ten-year censuses carried the obligatory heading 'nationality', and it was not even possible to declare yourself 'Soviet' (as you could claim to be 'Yugoslav' in Yugoslavia). The only permitted way round this was to declare oneself as 'Russian', which would not have been a transcendence of ethnicity but an affirmation of the superiority of a given linguistic group. This ethnic identity (even if it was based on cultural factors, particularly language, rather than racial ones, which distinguishes it from approaches based on the South African or even American model) is deeply anchored in the consciousness of the people. A Russian of Central Asia sees himself above all as Russian, and will see the acquisition of an Uzbek passport simply as an administrative action, which he may also regard as demeaning, not as a change of identity. Among Muslims, exteriority between groups is not so strong, but a Kyrgyz living in Tajikistan will describe himself first as 'Kyrgyz', and an Uzbek from Tajikistan, when questioned about his identity, will reply 'Uzbek': each would offer ethnic identity before citizenship.

This problem of the bridge between 'nationality' and citizenship is not being confronted directly by the new countries of Central Asia, but it becomes an issue in their political and administrative practices. There are two possible, albeit rather extreme, solutions: either accept the multi-ethnic nature of the new republics (in other words returning to the Soviet frame of reference), in which an 'Uzbekistani' would not necessarily be Uzbek (and vice versa); or reserve full citizenship for the dominant nationality, or at least to people who spoke its language (given that language is the ultimate criterion of ethnicity within the Soviet context). None of the republics of Central Asia have opted clearly for one choice or the other. On the one hand, by pursuing the promotion of their national languages, countries are encouraging an identification of nationality with the dominant ethnic group. All the countries except Kazakhstan and Azerbaijan have rejected terms such as 'Uzbekistani' or 'Turkmenistani' for distinguishing the citizen from the member of the dominant ethnic group. Every citizen of Uzbekistan is thus an 'Uzbek'. But on the other hand, at the official level, all ex-Soviets living in a given territory have the right to citizenship within it, unless they explicitly renounce it. Kazakhstan did introduce a distinction within its 1993 constitution: any citizen, whether Russian or Kazakh, is a 'Kazakhstani'. But within popular consciousness, and also within actual administrative practice, what dominates is the ethnic conception of identity. The question of language (which automatically raises questions of ethnic/national identity, since everyone knows that Russians living outside Russia almost never learn the local languages) does not appear as a condition of citizenship, but only as a condition of participation in the state apparatus. This contradiction is to be found in the inconsistencies of official terminology. In 1996, an Uzbek passport had two pages covering the identity of its holder, the left page in Uzbek and Russian, the right page in Uzbek and English. The first page will bear two different entries: *millat/natsionalnost* ('ethnic group') and *fuqaralik/grazhdentsvo* ('citizenship'). An ethnic Uzbek has respectively 'Uzbek' and 'Uzbek'; a Korean living in Uzbekistan has 'Koreali' and 'Uzbek'. But the other page carries *fukaralik*/nationality (in English) followed by 'Uzbekistan', the name of the country.

This absence of an explicit choice between citizenship and nationality means that there is a growing contradiction between the juridical framework of the new constitutions, which privilege the concept of citizenship, and the real practices of the countries concerned, which emphasise ethnicity. The constitutions of the republics of Central Asia state that all inhabitants of the republic in question are to be considered citizens, independently of their 'nationality' (in the ethnic sense). Almost all of them (with the exception of Turkmenistan and Tajikistan) have rejected the demand made by Moscow in October 1993, that Russians should be given dual citizenship, but they are all intent on avoiding exoduses of their European populations, which suggests that the aim is not to get rid of the Russians. Here we have a very different situation to that in the Baltic countries. Russians living in Central Asia find it no more difficult than a Muslim to get a passport indicating that they are citizens of Uzbekistan or Kazakhstan. However, the concept of a citizen who is not also a member of the given ethnic community is not easy to impose in everyday life.

The unstated policy of these countries is everywhere to strengthen the identification between nationality and the dominant ethnic group, as is shown in the insistence on using the suffix -stan ('the country of the...') attached to the name of the dominant racial group: so today we have Kyrgyzstan and Turkmenistan as opposed to Kyrgyzia or Turkmenia. Kazakhstan, Kyrgyzstan and Turkmenistan have all initiated annual conferences addressed to their 'fellow countrymen abroad' and to the diaspora (in Turkmen in the text). These 'fellow countrymen' are defined exclusively in ethnic–linguistic terms. Such gatherings are held, for example, on the occasion of Nation Day, which in Tajikistan takes place every September (even after the return to power of the former communists). In Tajikistan the official Payvand ('link') association is responsible for organising this annual conference bringing together 'Tajiks' living abroad (here there is an ambiguity as to whether what is being addressed is 'Tajikness' or the Persian world in general). In July 1990, at Ashkhabad, a Society for Turkmenistan was set up to handle relations with fellow countrymen abroad, to be followed by the Vatan ('motherland') Association. In May 1991, a first conference of overseas Turkmens in Ashkhabad set up a Humanitarian Association of Turkmens of the World which, between 25 and 27 October 1993, organised an international conference bringing together Turkmens from Turkey, Iraq, Iran and even Sweden (these turned out to be Turkmens from Iran who had fled the Islamic Revolution). Kazakhstan accords Kazakh nationality to all ethnic Kazakhs from abroad, but not to Russians from Moscow. Every year, there is a *kurultay* or 'grand assembly' of Kazakhs of the world. In Azerbaijan this contact function is fulfilled by the Yurddash ('compatriot') party and by the Cultural Centre for Azeris of the World (run by Zohrab Tahiri). This promotion of the dominant ethnic group, even if it is not anywhere laid down by law, has the obvious result of creating a split between 'nationality' and citizenship which, in the long term will lead to citizenship being refused to a sizeable part of the population, or to their assimilation being required. However, in the minds of the leaderships it is clear that assimilation is envisaged only for other 'Muslims' and not for 'Europeans', who would thus be condemned either to leaving, or, more likely, to a status of Ottoman-style *millet*, in other words as protected minorities with their own schools, churches, and customs, and perhaps enjoying certain privileges to make up for their exclusion from the political arena. This would not be the kind of *millet* of the Ottoman era at its height, but rather that of the nineteenth century, where the minority was sponsored by a Western great power. Such a situation would presumably satisfy the Russians, who are more concerned for their security and the preservation of their identity than for citizenship status within states which, for them, are not in any sense real.

The concept of an ethnic community wider than the national community does not, however, translate into territorial demands – not least for fear of a domino effect. If these countries began making demands for the territory on which their 'nationals' (in the ethnic sense) lived, then Russia would be entitled to ask for half of Kazakhstan. The fact that nationalities are so intermingled means that the question has been put on ice. So what one sees is a wavering between a deterritorialised conception of citizenship (the Russian demand for dual nationality goes in this direction) which could fit with the notion of *millet* referred to above, and a purely juridical concept of nationality, this time in the Western sense. It is significant that Uzbekistan is the country which has the largest numbers of members of its ethnic group living outside its borders (among its five neighbours), but at the same time it refuses to grant citizenship to these ethnic Uzbeks. Major Uzbek populations, sometimes locally in a majority, are to be found in Chimkent and Jambul in Kazakhstan, Osh in Kyrgyzstan, Khojent and Hissar in Tajikistan, Kunduz and Mazar-i Sharif in Afghanistan, and Charju and Tashauz in Turkmenistan. However, Uzbekistan has remained very cautious in handling the ethnic issue: during the Tajik civil war of 1992 ethnic Uzbek refugees from Tajikistan who had fled to Uzbekistan found that they were refused status as either citizens or residents. Tashkent did not shift on this, even at the time of the massacres in Osh in 1990. Uzbekistan certainly has a policy of extending its influence among Uzbeks abroad (General Dostum in Afghanistan, and Khodaberdayev in Tajikistan), but it has no great ethnic project: the 'Greater

Uzbekistan' of which people speak is strategic rather than ethnic. Up until now, and contrary to the position of the Russians who are pursuing demands for dual nationality, there is no movement among the Muslim groups living outside the republic of their 'nationality', for example among the Tajiks of Uzbekistan, to claim a citizenship of their eponymous republics. This is not a situation comparable to that of the Hungarian minorities in Romania and Slovakia. The logic of solidarity groups and deeply-engrained localism means that, at least for the moment, ethnic minorities are rooted within the political fabric of the countries in which they live.

In the cases where there actually are ethnic conflicts, they operate at a strictly local level and have not thus far been taken on board by the newly-emerging states. Conflicts over land (or resources) always develop at the local level. If they happen to bring two ethnic groups into conflict, these are then seen as expressing local interests, and not the national interests of the country that bears their name. The riots in Osh (a majority-Uzbek town in Kyrgyzstan) broke out because the law on land privatisation, which was particularly radical in Kyrgyzstan, favoured Kyrgyz to the detriment of Uzbeks.

In fact, the Uzbek-Tajik case is the only instance in which two separate Muslim populations find themselves so entangled. Everywhere else, the territorialisation imposed by Stalinist territorial realignments created its own reality. Apart from Kazakhstan, all the national ethnic groups have an absolute majority in their republics. With the departure of the Russians, the weight of the national ethnic group is duly increased. The pogroms at the end of the *perestroika* period chased out recently-arrived Muslim groups such as the Tatars and the Meskhetians. Thus one has a process of ethnic affirmation by nationalists, a marginalisation of the European population, and the assimilation of minority Muslim groupings, with a persistence of tensions at the countries' borders. Within this overall *schema*, two cases deserve extra attention: Kazakhstan, and relations between Uzbeks and Tajiks.

In Kazakhstan, the Russian population will never accept marginalisation, because it is a large community, very long established, often rural, and continuous with Russia in territorial terms. There is nothing to suggest that a 'Kazakhstani' identity is likely to develop among the Russians. On the contrary, hostility between Europeans and Kazakhs seemed to be on the increase, which is not the case in the other republics where Russians are not under threat merely for the fact of being Russian. Thus the idea and the very existence of a Kazakh state seems likely to be brought into question sooner or later, given the strong prevalence of the ethnic-nationalist identity over other possible models of the nation-state.

The other atypical instance is that of the Uzbeks and Tajiks. The two cultures are very close, intermarriage between them is frequent, and their populations are strongly intermixed and often bilingual. Many people would find it hard to say whether they were Tajiks or Uzbeks. It is not uncommon to find families in which a brother says that he is Uzbek and a sister says she is Tajik – and vice versa. This 'natural' assimilation works to the advantage of Uzbek as a dominant language in Central Asia. The Tajiks, having in 1924 lost control of their two historical cultural centres, Samarkand and Bukhara, have difficulty convincing themselves that Tajikistan is a nation-state rather than a collage of autonomous provinces. They feel themselves to be in a minority and under threat. Thus it is no accident that Tajik intellectuals have developed a hardline nationalism, at odds with their actual powerlessness, which has driven them to ally with the Islamists. In a parallel development, the Uzbek government, while repressing the irredentism of the Tajiks of Samarkand (this appeared briefly between 1990 and 1992), has maintained a Tajik-language system of education in the Tajik majority districts of Uzbekistan, as well as a national Tajik-language newspaper (*Âvâz-i Tâjik*, 'the voice of the Tajik'). After 1992, the considerable weakening of the republic of Tajikistan removed any threat of Tajik irredentism over Samarkand and Bukhara, and distanced the Tajiks of Uzbekistan from notions of pan-Tajikism, which had been discredited by the traumatic experience of the civil war. In fact today it is only Tajikistan's status as a Russian protectorate that prevents it falling into the Uzbek orbit. But the close links of the new coalition government in Dushambe (1997) with the Afghan Tajik commander Ahmed Shah Masud has renewed the Uzbek concern about pan-Tajikism.

Thus in Central Asia there is no necessary correspondence between the strategies of individual countries and ethnic conflicts, since these express themselves at a local level and not within a strategic logic of conflicts between competing national interests. The integration of the Muslim minorities is well under way everywhere, whereas the Russians are marginalised, except in Kazakhstan, where sooner or later the ethnic question will become an issue.

Central Asia is not Yugoslavia. The ethnic question is well under control among the region's nation-states.

THE PROMOTION OF A NEW NATIONAL ÉLITE

National élites have taken up almost all the political and administrative offices in all the countries, including Tajikistan, despite the Russian control. The 'national' ethnic group is over-represented in political positions in relation to its weight in the local population as a whole. All the *hâkims* are locals in all the republics except Kazakhstan. In Uzbekistan, the Council of Ministers had only three Russians in 1993, and they were all in subordinate posts (a fourth vice-prime minister, Voznenko; Piliugin as first deputy minister for defence; and Mikhailov, the minister for local industry). In Turkmenistan, in June 1996 only one minister was Russian (Otchertsov, in economy and finance). In Tajikistan and Kyrgyzstan Russians were present in the military and security apparatus, but absent from the parliaments and political parties (in 1996 Tajikistan's minister of the interior, Blinov, was Russian). To the extent that the political scene is dominated by 'localism', the Russians are excluded, since they have no regionalist base.

The issue of the promotion of a national élite was more critical in Kazakhstan, because it was done at the expense of the country's large Russian-speaking population. In order to consolidate Kazakh domination, the government had been moving towards changes in the administrative map even before independence: in August 1990, two *oblasts* were added to the 18 already in existence: Mangistau and Turgai, majority Kazakh-speaking, were carved out of two *oblasts* which had been majority Russian-speaking (Guriyev and Tselinograd). In the elections of March 1994, 105 out of the 176 members of parliament were Kazakhs, and 49 Russian. In the elections for the Majlis in December 1995, 44 out of 67 deputies were Kazakhs, with the rest comprising 19 Russians, two Ukrainians, one German and one Korean. It is noteworthy that only five nationalities were represented, compared with 12 in the previous parliament. In the senate, which was elected at the same time, we find 32 Kazakhs, 13 Russians, one Ukrainian and one Uighur. The shrinkage of the span of ethnic representation is obvious. Kazakhs monopolise two thirds of the seats, even though they make up only 45 percent of the population. Ethnic homogenisation (by a reduction in the number of recognised Muslim ethnic groups) and over-representation of Kazakhs compared with 'Europeans' go hand in hand. In the upper reaches of the state, after 1994 the Russians only had one first deputy prime minister, Vitalia Mette, coming after President Nazarbayev, prime minister Kazhageldin and another first deputy prime minister, Isingarin. The administration was also entirely 'Kazakhised': in 1995 only four of the 13 hâkim were Europeans (of whom one had a German name).

In Uzbekistan, 86 percent of the members of the Olli Majlis elected in December 1994 were ethnic Uzbeks (compared with 77 percent in 1990), which is higher than the percentage of Uzbeks in the population as a whole (75 percent).

At the level of education, local students are systematically favoured as a result of the application of language laws. Even though at university level teaching in many subjects is done in Russian, the entry examination may involve a test in the local language (Uzbekistan and Turkmenistan). In any event, Russian-speaking students cannot call on a network of people with influence who might help them short-circuit the exams. One Russian-language university branch remains open in Kazakhstan and Kyrgyzstan, but admission to government jobs is limited by the law on language, and by the de facto hegemony of local people in the key positions. In Tajikistan and Turkmenistan, the Russians have lost the demographic weight that might have enabled them to maintain an effective Russian-language university branch. Furthermore, the increasing poverty of the Russian-speaking population (more marked than among the Muslims, because they are almost all on salaries or pensions and have no support networks in the countryside) precludes the use of backhanders that might make things a little easier.

179

The new intellectual élite which is being created recruits among the children of the former Soviet nomenklatura which is today in power. Their place of education tends increasingly to be the foreign and private schools that have set up in the republics, the most gifted going to Western universities. A network of Turkish schools is also gradually developing; in general they are private schools, supported by religious brotherhoods based in Istanbul (Fethullachi). In these schools, the second language is English, and they often serve as a launch-pad for education in Western countries. Within ten or 20 years Russian will no longer be the preferred foreign language of the élites; it will give way to English.

This emergence of new élites is taking place more slowly in the military arena. As we have seen, the Soviet army had few senior officers of Muslim origin. Numbers of these chose not to return to their countries of origin. Thus it is going to take years for real national armies to be established. There is a split between those countries aiming for total military independence within 15 years, and those intending to preserve some form of military integration with Russia, within the CIS. In the former case (three countries: Uzbekistan, Turkmenistan and Azerbaijan) officers are sent to train in Turkey and the United States. In the meantime, Russian officers serve under contract in the Turkmen and Uzbek armies, but there are no longer Russian bases in those two countries (in 1995 the Uzbek head of general staff and deputy minister of defence was, however, still a Russian, Piliugin). The Azeris refuse to accept any Russian officer and any Russian military presence in their country, as a result of the support given by Russia to the Armenians. Kazakhstan and Kyrgyzstan have accepted military integration within the framework of the CIS: the Russian army has bases in Kazakhstan. The Tajikistan regime depends for its survival on a Russian expeditionary force of about 20,000 men. In early 1996, the chief of staff of the Tajik army was a Russian, Cherbatov; but the real fighting units are local militias.

In all cases, the vast majority of the rank and file are Muslim recruits and conscripts (in Uzbekistan in 1993, 85 percent of conscripts were Uzbeks, although Uzbeks were only 75 percent of the population). The various governments are more concerned with reducing Russian influence than with setting up sizeable armies. The Uzbek army had fewer than 70,000 men in 1996. The pacifism of the independent states in relation to their neighbours, as noted above, goes hand in hand with a concern not to develop too strong an army, partly for economic reasons, but also presumably in order to avoid the creation of a counter-power within the state. In no case do we see the development of a military élite such as one finds in Turkey and the countries of the Middle East. The army is not the foundation of state and nation. Military personnel trained in the Soviet tradition of subordination to the civil power are gradually making the transition to the technicist and professional model of the USA. In the power networks that we have studied, we found not one military figure. In Uzbekistan, the minister of defence until 1997, General Rustam

Ahmedov, comes from Ferghana, and thus does not belong to the dominant group. In fact, in the countries that are at war (Azerbaijan and Tajikistan) the main bulk of operations is carried out by militias or by troops recruited on a regionalist basis, who are often 'privatised' by their chiefs (for example, the Tajik 1st Brigade, under the orders of Khodaberdayev, which in January 1996 rose up in revolt, after having fought the 11th Brigade for control of Kurgan-Teppe).

In all cases except Kyrgyzstan, the KGB (often renamed KNB, the Committee of National Security) is exclusively in the hands of the locals.

Finally, there is a small religious élite in the republics, educated in the Islamic institutes linked to the muftiyya and in the few religious high schools (*imam khateb*) set up by the Turkish religious administration (Diyanet), within the framework of its inter-state co-operation programme. But many mullahs are trained in the institutes sponsored by the Muslim World League, in the Gulf states, outside state control.

THE SEARCH FOR A NATIONAL IDEOLOGY AND CULTURE

The demise of the USSR left a large ideological hole. As we have seen, the various nationalisms did not develop via ideological constructions. There is no nationalist literature. Nationalism is a code, a *habitus*, a cluster of references that are more folkloric than anything else. However, there is a 'national sentiment', or sense of belonging to a culture of one's own, even if it has been systematically impoverished and diminished by the Soviet machine.

Of course, it is not absolutely necessary that this hole be filled. The issue could perfectly well be avoided, as in Kazakhstan, by enabling the establishment of an economic liberalism and a culture of individual self-advancement. Presumably, various ideological constructions might then come in to occupy part of the country's intellectual space: ethnic nationalism or Islam. Moreover, there has been a breakthrough by Protestant religious sects in all the countries of Central Asia, including among Muslims, induced by a climate of disorientation. American non-governmental organisations are offering Jesus as a bonus with English-language and computer courses.

However, the politicians are making efforts to restore, if not a national ideology, at least traditional values, with a more or less Islamic colouring, but referring back to so-called older national cultures. This insistence on ethics (*adab*), or simply on manners (*akhlâq*), is not new. In the countries of Central Asia, the normative discourse of Sovietism was impregnated with a traditional morality, probably closer to Sa'adi than to the Quran, but certainly a far cry from socialist ideology. It spoke of sin (*gunah*), virtue, honour, virility etc.[18]

An interesting synthesis between an 'idealist' discourse deriving from the Soviet period and a re-reading of the religious tradition was advanced by a leader of one of the last communist parties existing as such in Central Asia. Shabdalov, the general secretary of the Tajik Communist Party, wondered aloud how the disappearance of the Soviet Union could have come about.[19] It was, in his opinion, because people had forgotten 'ideological work', which in the 1980s had been entrusted to the third secretary in each district, in other words downgraded in importance. The Islamists, says Shabdalov, are well aware of the importance of values. This weakening of ideological education has led to a 'corruption of morals'. The Persian terms that Shabdalov uses here (*fasâd-i akhlâqi*) are precisely the tems used in the Islamic vocabulary, particularly in Iran. Thus it is morality, and not the economic system, which becomes the basis of all political order. Shabdalov continues by singing the praises of moralities that have 'survived for a thousand years'. Here the reference is not necessarily to Islam, but to the ethics of the Persian poets such as Sa'adi, whose writings and fables are still valued for their morality, and are inscribed within an ethical framework. What is needed, says Shabdalov, is for members of the party to wake up to the 'fundamental moral principles of the Party which, in many respects, are shared with the ethical vision of our ancestors'.

This way of rehabilitating an ethical discourse based on Persian and Muslim traditions can be found in the press throughout Central Asia. In Tajikistan, for example, you find uplifting quotations from the classical authors, the *Pandnama* ('books of advices'), being quoted (often in permanent running heads). You also find texts that are more Islamic in inspiration, but equally with a bearing on ethics and the proper way of life. For example, on 30 October 1993 the *Tiraz-i jihan* newspaper (the organ of the executive committee of the Council of Deputies of the People in the town of Khojent) contained the heading 'Dars-i adab' ('a lesson in good manners'), with an article entitled 'Dar adab-i salamkardan' ('on the proper manner of greetings') taken from a classical Islamic work by Hussein Va'iz-i Kashifi, the Futuwatnama-yi Soltani. Thus even people with a nostalgia for the old USSR are likely to be involved in a search for new meanings deriving from former times.

At the same time, this quest for authenticity has a deleterious effect on women's status, as we have already noted each time indigenisation takes a step forward. In the period between 1990 and 1994, the percentage of women members of parliament in the Uzbek parliament fell from 9 to 6 percent. The practice among notables of having concubines is becoming common, and almost official.

Leaving aside questions of morals, there is clearly an official return to traditional values. In 1993, President Karimov wrote a book entitled *Uzbekistan: National Independence, Economy, Policy and Ideology* (*mafkura*). In the same year, a law was passed on the urban *mahallas* which rehabilitated this traditional structure in an explicit attempt to return to ancestral values. The law confers significant power to the *aqsaqal* ('white beards') or 'elders'. For example, their signature is required on marriage applications submitted by young couples, and this gives them considerable powers of social censorship, since the elders are always more religious than the young people. We find a similar development, but this time informal, in Kyrgyzstan: *mahalla* councils (*kenesh*) elect the heads of the *mahalla* (*maalybashi*).[20] Karimov has established a presidential contest for the 'best daughter-in law', whose most valued quality is of course to obey her mother-in-law. The state gives official backing to a return to traditional values, both in its means of self-organisation and in its values.

The rehabilitation of traditional society also applies in the realm of the arts, particularly classical traditional music (*maqam*), which helps to fill out television programmes which would otherwise be rather empty. First-class musicians are now getting an airing. An artistic space is being created which breaks with the folklorisation of the Soviet era.

SOCIO-ECONOMIC DEVELOPMENTS: PRIVATISATION VERSUS TRADITIONAL SOCIETY

All the republics are embarked on the road to privatisation, but at different speeds. Two tendencies are developing, both of which lead in the direction of the market economy. The first of these is a gradualist approach to reform, which maintains the basic powers of the state and the nomenklatura intact (Uzbekistan, Turkmenistan and Tajikistan). Here, convertibility of the currency has not been achieved, and the state maintains control of foreign trade, exchange rates and industry. The second is liberalisation and privatisation (Kazakhstan and Kyrgyzstan). Currency convertibility is now a reality in Kazakhstan, and both countries allow freedom of investment and repatriation of currency. Here limits are imposed by the low level of foreign investment and the poor functioning of the banking system.

The republics of Central Asia would have preferred to have had a longer transition period, remaining for a while within the rouble zone. But they were more or less ejected from it by the Russian national bank, and were obliged to create their own currencies (the tenge in Kazakhstan, the manat in Turkmenistan and Azerbaijan, the sum in Uzbekistan and Kyrgyzstan, and the Tajik rouble in Tajikistan). At the same time, the IMF and the World Bank have been applying pressure for liberalisation and the total privatisation of land, trade and industry.

If the republics of Central Asia are less burdened than Russia and the Ukraine with obsolescence and low productivity in their industrial sectors, this is a result of their low level of industrialisation. In Kazakhstan, the most developed of the southern countries, in 1991 agriculture supplied 37 percent of GDP, compared with industry's 31 percent. The situation was very difficult after independence, but seems to have improved since 1995, except in Tajikistan. In 1995, inflation in Kazakhstan was running at 60 percent per annum, compared with 3000 percent in 1993; in Uzbekistan, the figure went from 1280 percent in 1994 to 110 percent in 1995. In Kyrgyzstan, it went from 80 percent in 1994 to around 31 percent in 1995. Foreign investment is arriving in countries that look promising (Uzbekistan, Turkmenistan, Kazakhstan and Azerbaijan), but is avoiding Tajikistan and Kyrgyzstan.

The problems posed by privatisation are basically two-fold. It breaks down the traditional *kolkhoz* structures and thereby creates a notable risk of social destabilisation: these structures hitherto provided a way for the population to absorb the sudden poverty resulting from the collapse of the USSR, via solidarity networks. The second problem is that privatisation is often illusory: it works to the advantage of solidarity groups that hold power at either local or national level. Privatisation may simply involve the transfer of state property to the solidarity groups. Even when it is supposedly total, as in Kyrgyzstan, under the auspices of the US Price Waterhouse company, it is not transparent: it is clear that the privatisation of land is taking place to the advantage not of individuals but of lineage segments,[21] or even *kolkhoz* notables.

In Kazakhstan and Tajikistan it is the Communist Party élites and the mafia which profit from liberalisation. The Tajik Khizmat company, run by ex-minister Sayfuddin Turayev (from Ura-Teppe in Leninabad province) came into existence simply by the privatisation of the ministry of industry, consumption and services to the profit of the minister in question. The department of bread and grain was also privatised, by the Abdullajanov family. Sometimes the state form is preserved, but the income from an operation or a foreign-trade department is paid directly to a particular group or family. The state is thus effectively leased to networks of power. In Tajikistan, a deputy minister is in a position to re-sell for convertible currency cotton that he bought from the *kolkhoz* in roubles, and bank his profits in a foreign account. As in the case of privatisation, state control can be equally illusory. Here the maintenance of a statist structure does not necessarily mean control by the state, but the use of that structure in order better to satisfy private interests.

Another aspect slowing privatisation of land derives from the relationship between the *kolkhoz* system and social stability. The weight of clientelistic relationships, the rooting of apparatchiks within the countryside, the size of the underproductive rural population (and the hope that they will not descend on the towns), and finally the fear that poverty-stricken populations are going to flock to the Islamist banner mean that the authorities may be hesitant about putting IMF reforms into practice. Uzbekistan is a case in point.

However, once openness begins to be a reality one notes a perverse effect which is bound eventually to have major political consequences: a decoupling of the new states apparatchiks, who are urbanised and rely on networks of income in convertible currency, and their rural base, which up until now has been the key to political factionalism. Even when corruption is limited, the state tends to underpay the *kolkhoz* for their cotton, since this is a major source of foreign exchange. There thus tends to be a split between the former apparatchiks, with the rural notables opposing both the suffocating presence of an omnipresent state, and absolute privatisation, which will spell the end of the *kolkhoz* system.

The *Kolkhoz*: Between Privatisation and Tribal Cooperatives

Whatever the brand of reform under way, the *kolkhoz* continues to be the expression of a rural solidarity group, and becomes an actor in the economic arena, reinforcing the status of its president as an economic agent. The *kolkhoz* is, to a certain extend, an independent economic actor: it fixes its prices (except in the case of agro-industrial raw materials such as cotton, of which a given quota – 60 percent in Uzbekistan – has to be supplied to the state at below market price), negotiates directly the selling, and particularly buying, of the goods needed (fuel, fertiliser), engages in barter, and decides on investment (for example, upgrading the local industry by building a canning plant). *Kolkhoz* autonomy is not, at least for the moment, contested by an urban bureaucracy, precisely because the power of the apparatchiks is anchored in the countryside. But this autonomy is limited by compulsory deliveries of industrial crops, difficulties of access to credit, banking facilities and foreign currency.

The relations which the *kolkhoz* president has within the state apparatus, or within the network of other *kolkhoz* presidents, enables him to find the necessary inputs for *kolkhoz* life, which independent peasants would be incapable of acquiring on the free market, since such a market does not exist at this level. Here the inputs in question are especially fertilisers, pesticides, fuel and components for agricultural machinery. The *kolkhoz* president engages in barter operations with his factory-manager peers, but he also tries to obtain aid from the relevant ministries, by playing on personal connections. In Central Asia, although there is a high degree of corruption, the state apparatus survives because it interlocks with influence networks: there exists no mafia independent of the state or the regionalist groupings, except in Kazakhstan.

The power of the apparatchiks presupposes the maintenance of the *kolkhoz* structure as it stands. Peasants do not want to see the *kolkhoz* dismantled. They need its communal structure partly in order to provide their share of inputs, but also because it is their means of access to politicians, a means of relating to the state apparatus, a way of protecting themselves against the state and the ambitions of other symmetrical groups (clans, factions, neighbouring districts etc), regardless of the ideological banners under which these rivalries express themselves.

Land reform is thus not a key question. The situation develops year by year, and the position on land ownership is far from clear. There have been cases of real privatisation, but they appear to be limited in extent. Some broad generalisations can be made for Central Asia as a whole: production takes place within the framework of the *kolkhoz*, which functions as a 'solidarity group'; but the peasant considers his invidivual plot to be his personal property. For other landed property, there are two possibilities: either farm work and production remain collective, which seems to be the case in agro-industrial regions (cotton); in this case the peasant is a waged agricultural worker, but with a particular relationship with the *kolkhoz*, because the fact of being a wage-earner makes him a member of a solidarity group. Or the *kolkhoz* hands over its land for individual exploitation by peasants, in a relationship reminiscent of tenant farming and sharecropping: the peasant rents the land and the tractor, is supplied with seed and fertiliser, and benefits from *kolkhoz* services, in exchange for a portion of his crop (in the Pakhtakar *kolkhoz* in Kabadian, Kurgan-Teppe district, Tajikistan, the percentage was 50–50 in May 1992): this is known as the *ijara* ('leasing') system. Trade in kind rather than sale to the *kolkhoz* is explained by the crisis of the monetary system. On the other hand only the *kolkhoz* has access to agro-industrial markets (while these are not necessarily state-run, they operate via the intermediary of protagonists who are either institutional or have connections to networks at ministry, *kolkhoz*, state-company level etc).

Here, three questions arise. What do the peasants think of this new system? How do apparatchiks now find themselves in a position to extract personal income? And does this system favour the emergence of an entre-preneurial spirit, or does it freeze the *kolkhoz* into a situation of routine and low productivity?

From the point of view of the peasants, who generally approve of the redesigned *kolkhoz* system, the issue is not land appropriation, but whether they have the use of land under a system of stable guaranteed rights. One finds this position in regard to the collective *kolkhoz* land, but also when a peasant decides to open up a piece of land that has not so far been cultivated, in order to appropriate its produce without necessarily seeking formal ownership of that land. For the peasant, the maintenance of a kolkhozian right over land is the sign of his personal belonging to a solidarity group, the *kolkhoz*, which provides him with a systematic framework for economic exchanges, but also with social and political protection.

The peasants' reticence about challenging the formally collective nature of property does not derive from a collectivist mentality forged under the years of Sovietism; on the contrary, as soon as they are able, peasants shift to working the land by means of the extended family. Nor does this reticence have strictly financial motives: the wage paid by the *kolkhoz* generally represents only 10 percent of a kolkhozian's income. But the preservation of the collective fiction is what makes it possible for the *kolkhoz* to have an existence as a solidarity group. Thus the peasant benefits from the political weight of the *kolkhoz*, from its connections to the state appa-ratus and a wider network of factories and other *kolkhoz*, not within the framework of a state planning which has long since disappeared, but within a network of political power and trade. For a start, the peasant considers it necessary to belong to a solidarity group; as we have seen, this is his conception of access to politics. Second, only the *kolkhoz* is in a position to supply not only access to the inputs necessary for production, but also social services (transport, education). Third, a privatisation of land would result in whole swathes of excess population being driven into the towns, whereas the *kolkhoz* makes it possible to keep this workforce on the land and thus preserves the cohesion of solidarity groupings. Finally, the peasants have a concept of property that is closer to that of customary right, as in the *sharia*, than to the possessive individualism so dear to the West. It is of course possible that this practice of customary usage is a leftover of pre-Soviet times, but more probably it is a result of efforts made by certain mullahs or notables to rethink and legitimate the *kolkhoz* within a 'Muslim' framework, without changing its basic structures. Whatever the reason, such a reading makes it possible to understand the transition, in other words how the *kolkhoz* system has managed to become independent of the ideological framework that gave birth to it, and at the same time remain a perennial part of the landscape, regardless of the ongoing changes. We met religious peasants in Uzbekistan, for example, who used the term *ihyâ*, the *sharia* concept of bringing vacant land into use (when an individual sets about farming previously non-irrigated land, this gives him a form of property right), to explain how it was that they had taken over areas of non-irrigated land, which they had then irrigated themselves; the *kolkhoz* official, on the other hand, referred to the same operation as a concession. Thus private initiative can be reconciled with the preservation of the *kolkhoz*'s ethos, because a single given operation can be capable of two readings. The fact that peasants do not enjoy formal ownership of land does not worry them unduly. The stability of a right of usage derives from a continuity in the farming of a given piece of land by a given family and the recognition of that continuity by a solidarity group (for example via the right to hereditary transmission). All of this is guaranteed not by laws but implicitly, by custom, which itself relies on the stability of these new solidarity groups and on the retraditionalisation of interpersonal relations with *kolkhoz* managers.

Thus it is possible to arrive at four readings of an identical transmittable and permanent right of land usage within an extended family framework: as a concession granted by the *kolkhoz* (this is the manager's point of view); a transmittable right of usage to a piece of land that has been farmed by a family, often coupled with waged work on land devoted to agro-industrial production (this is generally the reading among peasants); the application of *sharia ihyâ* (this is the viewpoint of peasants who begin farming on land not being cultivated by the *kolkhoz*); or, finally, although it is never described as such, tenant farming and sharecropping.

The word *dehqan*, which is so common in Central Asia as to be used also in Russian (transcribed as *dehkhan*), means 'poor peasant', but also sharecropper.

Traditionally sharecroppers are linked to landowners by a relationship which goes beyond the economic aspect, and which translates as a form of clientism within the framework of a solidarity grouping. The managers of today's *kolkhoz* are tending to rediscover this kind of socio-economic relation with the new peasants – in other words the former kolkhozian brigade workers. At the economic level, the *kolkhoz* supplies seeds, water, fertiliser and machinery; the peasant works on land of which he is not the owner. His contribution is often paid in kind, a typical sharecropping relationship. Sometimes the relationship is closer to tenant farming, with the peasant paying money to hire land and tractors from the *kolkhoz*. However, as we have seen, the fact that monetary circulation is poor favours the sharecropping relationship.

Total privatisation is a non-starter, but even when it does take place it may be illusory. It may simply provide an opportunity for *kolkhoz* presidents and apparatchiks to sign over into their own names a proportion of collective land, or to divert a percentage of the inputs (petrol, seed) to their own privatised farms. If we view the *kolkhoz* as new tribes, then privatisation can be seen on a par with what happened in the Ottoman empire, when the establishment of a land register (*tapu*) made it possible for tribal chiefs to claim collective land as their own property, thereby transforming members of their own tribe into sharecroppers. A study of land privatisation conducted in Uzbekistan shows that most of the few private *fermir* (derived from the English 'farmer') do not in fact own their land. Rather, they have *ijara*-type contracts which keeps them more or less within the structure of the *kolkhoz* (they are known as *ijaradagi fermirlar* – as opposed to the *mustakil fermirlar* who are completely independent but who, in Ferghana district in 1997, made up only 4.5 percent of the 'farmers', who themselves represented only 6.5 percent of the families on the *kolkhoz* [personal research, 1997].

Local authorities have a determining influence on the enactment or blockage of reforms. The process of privatisation of collective farms in Kazakhstan reveals considerable differences between provinces, differences which do not correlate with ethnic composition (the district of Mangistau, with its slight Kazakh majority, did not privatise a single farm in 1994, whereas the district of Western Kazakhstan, with a similar ethnic balance, privatised 103 out of 119).[22] In the district of Sukh (Uzbekistan) which we visited in 1993, the local authority simply refused to hear of privatisation, and seemed to be unaware of the changes in legislation.

The rural exodus, which up until this point had been avoided, seems only to have started after independence,[23] but in the towns it has been balanced by the departure of Europeans. Towns in Central Asia are rapidly becoming indigenised. They are also being 'nationalised' (the Kyrgyz authorities in Osh favour Kyrgyz in the buying of building plots, to the detriment of Uzbeks). The towns are growing via the construction of new *mahallas* which reproduce the rural solidarity groupings. The links between town and country thus remain very strong, except when they intersect with an ethnic division (in Osh this involves urban Uzbeks and rural Kyrgyz).

Apart from the phenomenon of departing Europeans, Central Asia has not generally been subject to major migration movements. However, there are two exceptions: the exodus of hundreds of thousands of Tajiks fleeing the civil war of 1992 (most of whom went to other countries of the CIS) and immigration from China. Kazakhstan has recently seen the arrival of 300,000 Chinese, with several tens of thousands also arriving in Kyrgyzstan. According to rumours, many of them are Han Chinese, in other words ethnic Chinese and not Muslim refugees, a fact which has raised concern among officials over the real intentions of the Chinese authorities.

10

A New Geo-Strategic Context

CONVERGENCES AND DIVERGENCES BETWEEN THE REPUBLICS

The republics of Central Asia share a common strategic environment, but they also have specific individual constraints which means that each has been developing its own strategies, and these are increasingly divergent. There are no perspectives for the establishment of new blocs or new regional alliances. The basis for foreign policy in each of the republics is still multilateralism. Russian influence is in decline, and neither Iran nor Turkey have made significant breakthroughs. The energy factor and the competition between different roads for pipelines are the main strategic stakes.

The first constraint common to all the republics is that they are all land-locked. All of them are seeking direct access to international markets in order to be able to export their raw materials in exchange for hard currency. They are hindered by the fact that up until now the main channels for exportation (oil pipelines and railways) have passed through Russia. The second constraint is the weight of Russia itself, not only because of the land-locked nature of Central Asia, but also as a result of Russian neo-imperialism, which has become apparent since 1993 (a military doctrine which defines the frontiers of the ex-USSR as the strategic frontiers of the Russian Federation; a presence of Russian frontier guards everywhere except in Azerbaijan and Uzbekistan; the scale of the Russian population in Kazakhstan; and the presence of the Russian expeditionary corps in Tajikistan).

In order to emerge from their geographical isolation and to break out of the Russian sphere of influence, the Muslim republics have been looking to Western countries, particularly the United States, both in order to open new routes (the Caucasus, Turkey and even Afghanistan) and to guarantee old ones (the Caucasus and Russia). The republics are not looking to attach themselves to new restrictive regional organisations, whether it be the CIS or the OEC (the Organisation for Economic Co-operation, which brings together the Muslim republics of the ex-USSR and Turkey, Iran and Pakistan). Nobody is looking to set up a system of alliances between the republics. Relations between them are relatively cool: there are few direct links, particularly as regards air transport; embassies have been slow in opening; and political summits are rare and tend to be a matter of form, despite the signature of technical agreements (customs, visas etc). Finally, the republics are suspicious of any attempt to rebuild regional spheres of influence, either under the aegis of Turkey, Iran or Russia, or under one of the republics themselves.

There is a split between those republics seeking maximum separation from Russia (Azerbaijan, Uzbekistan and Turkmenistan) and those which cannot permit themselves the luxury. Thus the question of Russia remains key in the region's strategic development.

The Weight of the Russian Presence: Kazakhstan, Kyrgyzstan and Tajikistan

Kazakhstan is the only country of Central Asia to have had a true nationalist movement before the Soviet period (Alash Orda), but it is also the country that has undergone the highest degree of Russification. Kazakhstan is obsessed with the risk that its northern Russian-majority territories might secede. Solzhenitsyn's statement in 1990, that the future of Russia depended on a re-centring on the Slavic core, and thus on a partition of Kazakhstan, created tremendous resentment in Kazakhstan. In order to avoid the risk of a split, President Nazarbayev resolved to stick with Russia while at the same time pursuing a Kazakhisation of the country's domestic political apparatus. In a word, he wants to hitch the Kazakh wagon to the Russian train, but throw the Russians out of the first class compartment. This policy, although adroit in the medium term, will only hold long-term if the demographic balance changes firmly in favour of the Kazakhs. In 1995, 45 percent of the population was Kazakh and only 35 percent Russian (plus 5 percent Ukrainians). This is the highest figure since the start of the century. But birth rates among Kazakhs are today roughly on a par with those of the Russians. The only possibility for Kazakhs to become a majority will be Russian emigration, but the Russians have no reason to leave the north, although they have been quitting the south. The split between the two peoples is becoming more marked. Already in 1979 only 0.66 percent of Russians living in Kazakhstan were reported as speaking Kazakh, and the growing physical separation between the two populations means that this figure is unlikely to improve.[1]

This Russian constraint explains the delay in the proclamation of the country's independence, as well as Kazakhstan's key role in the setting-up of the CIS (the Almaty Declaration of 20–21 December 1991); the signing of integration agreements with Russia in the areas of customs, armed forces and frontier guards; the recognition of Russian as the language of official communication; the rejection of nuclear weapons (which have been either destroyed or returned to Moscow); the lease of the Baikonur base to Russia etc. Particularly important was Kazakhstan's April 1996 signing of an economic integration agreement with Russia and Belarus, which left the other countries of Central Asia wrong-footed. At the same time, as we have seen, the Kazakhs have not agreed to the granting of dual nationality, and the Kazakhisation of the political and administrative apparatus is proceeding apace. Thus one should not count on a drop in the level of Kazakh nationalism. On the contrary, the integration taking place within the CIS is generating major frustrations among Kazakh youth, and may end up leading to outbreaks of nationalism.

Kazakhstan is attracting inward investment, both American (for example, Chevron) and Japanese. It has complex relations with China: the Chinese have never recognised what they regard as the unfair treaties which gave Semirechie and the lower reaches of the Ili to Russia, and they criticise Kazakhstan for its alleged support for the Uighurs of Sinkiang, but at the same time they are hopeful of building an oil pipeline which will link the Caspian with Beijing, passing via Sinkiang. The Kazakhs are very opposed to Chinese nuclear testing, and it is also worth noting that there are several tens of thousands of Uighur refugees in Kazakhstan. The demographic density of Kazakhstan (six inhabitants per square kilometre) puts it in a position of weakness in relation to both China and Uzbekistan (122 and 45 inhabitants per square kilometre respectively).

The situation in Kazakhstan is thus extremely fragile and at the mercy of sudden worsenings of ethnic tensions. These seem more or less inevitable. In order to defuse them it would be necessary to give the Russians an autonomy within a federal framework, which would almost certainly initiate a process of gradual partition. President Nazarbayev refuses to envisage any form of federalism, and this explains the decision to move the capital northwards from Almaty to Akmolla.

Little Kyrgyzstan has no choice but to stick with its larger Kazakh neighbour, to which it is anyway close in linguistic terms. It thus remains pro-Russian, and is also wary of too great a Chinese presence. However there is no great international interest in the country, since it lacks major natural resources.

For the moment, Tajikistan exists under Russian protectoracy. Moscow's goal in maintaining a military presence in Tajikistan is to keep a foothold in Central Asia until it can pursue a more assertive policy in the whole area. In order to strengthen the basis of the Kulabi-led government, and hence the legitimacy of its own military presence, Moscow has agreed to push for a coalition government between the Kulabis and the Gharmis (June 1997), but is not ready to grant the Islamic opposition and its Iranian godfather a real say in security and military matters.

Despite their dependence, neither Kyrgyzstan nor even Tajikistan are pre-pared to renounce their sovereignty. They joined each other in protesting on the occasion of the symbolic vote of the Russian Duma annulling the dissolution of the USSR in 1996. The need for alliance with Russia does nothing to limit the thorough-going de-Russification which is under way in the republics of Central Asia.

Uzbekistan, Turkmenistan and Azerbaijan

Uzbekistan sees itself as the major regional power, and it has the means to be just that. It has 23 million inhabitants, of whom 75 percent are Uzbeks, which makes it the most populated country to the south of Russia; to these have to be added the large Uzbek minorities in neighbouring countries, amounting to some 2.5 million. This gives the Uzbeks around half the total population of Central Asia. They have means of exercising influence abroad (General Dostum and his likes in Afghanistan, and a number of Uzbek leader-ship figures in Tajikistan). Uzbekistan is self-sufficient in energy, as well as being the world's second-largest producer of cotton, and fourth-largest gold producer. It achieved food self-sufficiency in 1996. Thus it can afford to see itself in the big league. It openly criticises the Kazakhs' tail-ending of Russia and Turkmenistan's isolation. Uzbekistan wants to play an active role in Tajikistan, and in 1994 dissociated itself from Russian policy, backing the Leninabad faction against the Kulabis. It is clear that Uzbekistan is trying to extend its influence over the whole of Transoxiania, and in particular to dominate Tajikistan, although it is not formally challenging existing borders.

Uzbekistan is the most land-locked country in the world: in all directions at least two countries separate it from the open sea. However, relations with its direct neighbours are not good. Relations with Tehran are very chilly. The visit by President Rafsanjani in October 1993 did not go well; in May 1995, President Karimov supported the American embargo against Iran. A visit by Shimon Peres in July 1994 incurred Tehran's wrath. And Tehran's determination to open a cultural centre in Samarkand was viewed with suspicion in Tashkent.

Relations with Turkey are paradoxically also very cold: in 1994 grant-aided Uzbek students in Turkey were recalled following Turkey's granting of political asylum to Mohamed Saleh, the leader of the ERK opposition party. Uzbekistan gives the Turks fewer facilities in the area of religion and education than the other Turcophone republics. In particular, it has no *imam-hatep*-style religious high school. Tashkent resents the fact that some of its opponents are living in Turkey, and find some support in the press and academic circles.

Uzbekistan has succeeded in breaking out of dependence on Moscow. In 1995, trade with non-CIS countries exceeded that with CIS countries (60 percent as against 40 percent). Foreign investment (Western, Japanese and

Korean) reached $5 billion between 1992 and 1996. The South Korean Daewoo company invested $1 billion in a car factory in Ferghana, which was opened in 1997, while the refinery in Bukhara, recently rebuilt by the French company Technip, will help meet the country's fuel needs. In 1996, Tashkent had succeeded in establishing a broad degree of macro–economic and financial stability (debt servicing below 10 percent of export receipts; currency reserves at more than six months' worth of imports; and limited inflation).

Tashkent has been openly playing the American card, and the relationship has been mutual. There has been a succession of high–level American delegations, including US Defence Secretary William Perry. A military co–operation agreement with the United States, within the US's IMET programme, has enabled the country to break free of the Russians. Joint manoeuvres took place in 1996 and 1997. But this military co–operation, although it raised many expectations in Tashkent, will probably remain at a very limited level.

★   ★   ★

Turkmenistan's only guarantee of independence is by selling its natural gas. Exports fell to 33 billion cubic metres in 1995, but according to estimates, with between 12,000 and 21,000 billion cubic metres of reserves, Turkmenistan has the third– or fourth–largest resources in the world. There may be a chance of the country escaping isolation via Iran. A swap agreement, plus the 13 May 1996 opening of the Sarakhs–Mashhad–Tedjen railway to the Iranian port of Bandar Abbas, are fast reaching their limits. A higher degree of external funding is going to be needed. In the face of American hostility to the Iranian connection, Turkmenistan has pinned its hopes on the construction of a gas pipeline through Afghanistan, to be built by the US Unocal company with support from the Saudi company Delta. But Unocal left the project in August 1998.

Turkmenistan has agreed to grant dual nationality to its Russian–speaking citizens, but there is little risk here, since the majority Turkmen community enjoys a strong degree of cohesion. There are only around 300,000 Russians in the country as a whole. Turkmenistan is in the process of becoming a 'gas republic' in which the power of some major international companies and that of a megalomaniac president sit comfortably side-by-side.

★   ★   ★

Azerbaijan is also playing both the oil card and the American card in order to consolidate its independence. Relations with Russia are tense: Azerbaijan is the only Muslim republic of the ex–USSR to have rejected not only Russian military bases but also Russian frontier guards. Relations with Iran are bad, because Iran supports Armenia and is suspicious of an Azeri nationalism which could spill over into Iranian territory. Azerbaijan is also at odds with Iran and Russia over the status of the Caspian Sea (it wants the Caspian to be divided between all the countries surrounding it, whereas the Russians and Iranians want joint control). Relations with Turkey lost their warmth with the fall of the Elchibey government, which enjoyed strong support among Turkish nationalists. At the same time, British and US oil companies control the various consortia which have embarked on developing the oil-fields of the Caspian.

Azerbaijan's major problem is the occupation of a fifth of its territory by Armenians. The Azeris have no faith in an agreement reached under the aegis of the Minsk Group (bringing together the countries of the Organisation for Security and Co-operation in Europe (OSCE), but within which Russia enjoys a determining influence) and would rather see direct American mediation. The Russians, as often, are balancing between two policies in order to retain influence: keeping vivid the local conflicts or playing on economic co-operation through the pipelines they control. The consequence is a lasting stalemate.

THE NEW STATES AND RELATIONS
WITH RUSSIA: DELINKING

The delinking from Russia of the countries in the south of the former USSR is a long-term certainty. It is already a reality in countries that have fully won independence (Uzbekistan, Turkmenistan and Azerbaijan); it is also likely to happen in the three others, probably at the expense of a secession of Northern Kazakhstan. Russia has effectively failed in the transition from a traditional imperial structure to the setting up of a modern strategic sphere of influence, principally because of a lack of economic tools, but also because of its narrowly neo-imperial, territorial and military view of political in-fluence. Russia has no intermediate economic channels (for example, it has no multinationals, apart from the Lukoil company, which fancies itself as another Chevron). And Russia's withdrawal works to the benefit of the United States.

Russia was counting on long-term economic, military and cultural con-straints in order to maintain its influence. However it has failed at all levels.

Economic Delinking

There has been an ongoing debate on relations between Russia and the Soviet Muslim republics: was this a colonial relationship in which Russia bought raw materials (cotton, oil and gas) cheaply in order to transform them into industrial products, and was Russia interested chiefly in cheap Muslim labour; or, on the contrary, was Russia investing massively and endlessly in a south that was structurally underdeveloped? In fact, both points of view apply. Cotton and oil were bought well below market prices, but Moscow also provided energy at prices equally below the market price. Regions such as the province of Gorno-Badakhshan lived entirely by perfusion. The system of interdependence within the Soviet economy was such as to ensure that the economies of individual countries would prove to be unviable in the event of independence. But at the same time the ways in which this system operated means that today's independent republics have been spared the burden of large sectors of unproductive industry.

In any event, the economic reorientation of the Muslim republics is tending to reduce the weight of Russian influence. Russia only has influence in the crisis-ridden sectors of coal mining and metal-processing. In the modern sectors, the breakthroughs are being made by the West and the 'tiger' economies (South Korea etc). If Russia wants to play a role it will have to operate within the logic of the market (with, for example, Lukoil, which, incidentally, is run by an Azeri, Alikperov), and this will require not only a cultural revolution but more importantly a level of investment that is still beyond its reach. In any event, if Lukoil succeeds in making itself independent from the Russian state it will operate within a market logic and not as a strategic extension of the state.

Moscow has lost its influence because it has nothing to offer. Russia offers no assistance in the field of economic development: the terms of export contracts involving transit via Russia are unfavourable to the countries of Central Asia (particularly Kazakhstan and Turkmenistan). Economic pressures on the republics have pushed them towards the West. At the time when three of the southern republics (Uzbekistan, Kazakhstan and Tajikistan) were asking simply to remain within the rouble zone, Moscow set such difficult conditions that they were forced to create their own national currencies in short order. Open blackmail and threats to shut down oil and gas pipelines meant that the republics had to look for other outlets, which they found thanks to the US desire to establish economic control in a region which might become one of the world's main oil exporters.

Russia has been slowly driven out of the markets of the southern republics. In Uzbekistan, the country's trade with non-CIS countries in 1995 exceeded trade with the CIS. In Azerbaijan in the same year, 37.7 percent of foreign trade was with the CIS, and only 13 percent of this was with Russia (compared with 21 percent with Turkey, 12 percent with Iran and 10 percent with Dubai). In the case of Kazakhstan, the country with the closest links to Russia, 52 percent of exports went to Russia in the first quarter of 1995, compared with 67 percent the previous year. Economic logic carries more weight than big-power threats (military pressure and the threat of blockades).

Russia is not in a position to guarantee positive economic co-operation (the sending of experts, aid, loans and investment etc).

The Limits of Strategic Influence

From a strategic point of view, up until 1996 Moscow was able to maintain its presence in territorial and military terms (military bases and frontier guards). Since 1994, the Russians have tried to build into all co-operation agreements with the south a clause specifying agreements on frontier guards and military integration. However, these requirements bear little relation to any real threat: neither Iran nor Afghanistan is likely to invade the republics of Central Asia. The truth of the matter is that the Russian army is part and parcel of the troubles which it claims to be controlling (civil wars and drug trafficking). Russia is able to maintain its presence thanks to local crises (Nagorno-Karabakh and Tajikistan), and therefore does not seek to resolve them. This heightens regional instability, and threatens to drag Russia into a military quagmire which will present problems, particularly given the way in which the war in Chechnya revealed the depth of the crisis in the Russian military. Moreover Moscow is able to maintain its influence with lame-duck countries such as Tajikistan and Kyrgyzstan, but is being slowly driven out of the countries that count (for example, Uzbekistan). Russia's insistence on maintaining military bases and frontier guards seems oddly anachronistic: what is the point of mounting guard over a Tartar desert when the real threat is coming from the rear? This insistence on maintaining a Russian military presence is heightening tensions, and in no sense guarantees Russia a presence in the longer term.

All in all, the Russians can be seen as adding fuel to the fire of local crises. They contrived the failure of all inter-Tajik negotiations between 1994 and 1996,[2] and have tried to destabilise both Azerbaijan and Georgia. Here they have used principally negative pressures (blockades, suspensions of oil deliveries, losing the Volga-Don Canal to Azeri ships in 1992, and supplying arms to the various factions). This is a very traditional and territorial conception of Russian imperialism, but it is at odds with present-day developments (the rise of nationalisms, the role of oil, and the diminishing importance of frontiers).

The Absence of a 'Pro-Russian' Party

Another limit on Russia's influence is the absence of real pro-Russian parties in the independent republics, based either on the old nomenklaturas or on the local Russian-speaking populations. Moscow makes little attempt to intervene directly in the domestic political life of these countries (except of course in Tajikistan). It has never attempted to set up a 'Russian party', and has not been in a position to undermine the cohesion of the ruling national élites. In fact, the current *schema* is similar to that of the Brezhnev era, inasmuch as Moscow is obliged to deal via established ruling élites, without wanting, or being able, to establish a closer and more direct control. Russian neo-imperialism ignores the strong tendencies in Central Asian societies to consolidate their nationalism (linguistic and demographic de-Russification, the progressive reshaping of foreign trade, an identification of the interests of ruling élites with independence, and a practice of social promotion expressed in ethnic terms). However, experience shows that military-strategic power is superficial when it has neither political relays nor a social grounding in the countries where it hopes to gain an implantation, and when the military means at its disposal are falling apart and riddled with corruption.

The Russians have never hesitated to abandon people who had previously been perceived as 'their' men, such as the Azeri Mutalibov, who was arrested in Moscow in April 1996, together with Rahim Gaziyev, who was handed over to Baku. Not only does Moscow lack any 'indigenous' support, but it also has no political channels or go-betweens among the Russian-speaking minorities (which are anyway decreasing in number). Russian emigration from south to north did not begin with independence.[3] As we have seen, Moscow has never sought to promote élites emerging from the Russian-speaking population of the south. The Russians of Central Asia who have kept their Russian citizenship are rather legitimist and not inclined to political upheaval: in the second round of the presidential elections in 1996, Russian voters in Uzbekistan voted 68 percent for Yeltsin and 28 percent for Zyuganov. The only sign of a militant movement is to be found in Kazakhstan (the Lad party and various Cossack movements).

Cultural De-Russification

The decline of the Russian language is irreversible. Russian teachers are leaving, faced with the prospect of receiving neither wages nor promotion; Russian is now no longer favoured in schools (through priority allocation of audio-visual materials); Russian newspapers are expensive and increasingly hard to find; Russian television is less and less present (partly because of political censorship and partly because the Moscow-based broadcasting companies ask for huge fees); travel is increasingly expensive; the élites now learn English; and Moscow is not supplying aid volunteers, teachers, scholarships or books. Public-spending cutbacks and the fear of clandestine immigration, in Russia as elsewhere, is reducing the country's ambitions to be a major power and to having a strong international presence.

TWO MYTHS: PAN-ISLAMISM AND PAN-TURKISM

With the declarations of independence in Central Asia, there was a brief resurgence in speculation about pan-Islamism and pan-Turkism. As regards the latter, one should note that the Ottomans failed to gain a foothold in Central Asia, except in Azerbaijan, where their presence in 1918 acted rather as a stimulus to nationalism. In fact, relations between Turkey and Central

Asia suggest something of an ongoing misunderstanding. The Central Asian élites were pan-Turkist at the start of the twentieth century, at a time when Turkey's development into a modern nation state were taking it away from Asia and towards Europe. In 1992, when Turkey under President Özal redis-covered its eastern vocation, the countries of Central Asia were in the first flush of their independence and had no desire to reconnect with a 'Turkish' identity. It is reported that when President Özal was touring in 1993, a Kyrgyz poet greeted him with the following verse: 'You left [Central Asia] on horse, and with slant eyes/You come back in an aeroplane, and with blue eyes'. You would need to be an Istanbuliot to take this as a compliment.

In the event, after a moment of high-flown fancy, the Turkish govern-ment opted for greater realism. A quasi-ministry of co-operation (TYKA) took charge of co-operation relations at the official level, while the private sector lost no time in seeking out areas in which Turkey could play a role (construction, consultancy, information technology, transport, schooling and higher education). Istanbul became a focal point for the informal economies of all the countries of the ex-USSR. But trade with Russia and the Ukraine was ten times more significant than trade with Central Asia. Turkey was not in a position to act as a sponsor of the 'Turcophone peoples' against Moscow. Major Western companies have no desire to subcontract to the Turks the business of penetrating the markets of Central Asia. So Turkey has lowered its sights, and plays a discreet but long-term role, particularly in areas such as religion and education.

In fact, the pan-Turkist message has always been borne by people on the losing side – the likes of Enver Pasha. It has functioned as a substitute for Kemalism, which never sought to play the pan-Turkist card: the Kemalists favoured the fall of the independent government of Baku in spring 1920 because it was viewed as being pro-British, at a time when Ankara wanted a direct relationship with Soviet Russia, which it saw as an ally. A university-based pan-Turkism did develop subsequently, among many descendants of immigrants of the Caucasus and Central Asia, but outside any connection with the official policies of Kemalist Turkey.

The solemn return of the ashes of Enver Pasha in the summer of 1996 marked a second burial of pan-Turkism.

★　　　★　　　★

Iran was not particularly happy with the collapse of the USSR. Already at the time of the Congress of Versailles, Persia had opposed the independence of Azerbaijan, demanding that the conquered province be returned. Iran, as the last multi-ethnic and ideological empire in the region, fears the emer-gence of nation-states founded on ethnic criteria. Iran's only real allies are the Shiite minorities, which are more or less absent from Central Asia. Iran distrusts the ethnic connection, and offers little support to Sunni Persian-speakers, be they Massoud in Afghanistan or Turajanzade in Tajikistan.

(This, however, does not prevent the Americans, firm believers in ethnicity, from thinking that Iran is active in their support.) There is no development of an Islamic solidarity. On the contrary, Iran is supporting the Armenians (the bridge over the Arax, the building of a road, and financial loans).

Partly as a result of American containment, but also a result of ineptitude, Iran has suffered a loss of influence beyond its borders: in Afghanistan, with the victory of the Taliban in September 1996; in Azerbaijan, with its virtual exclusion from the oil consortium in 1995; and in Tajikistan, with the ousting of the Islamic-democratic government in 1993. The possible building of the trans-Caspian pipeline from Turkmenistan to Turkey through Baku is likely to signal an end to Iranian hopes of functioning as the main bridge between Central Asia and the outside world. Paradoxically, Iran's best relations are with the Armenians. The good relations between Tehran and Moscow will not be of much use if the Russian withdrawal from the zone in the face of the Americans is confirmed. Although Iran's international diplomacy is far more pragmatic than the rhetoric would suggest, Iran is cruelly short of allies and remains blocked by American ostracism. Europe carries little weight in the region, not least because it has no political desire to make a role for itself in the region.

★ ★ ★

The main breakthrough in Central Asia has been made by the Americans, and it basically arises out of oil and gas interests. Chevron and Unocal are political players who talk with individual countries (or rather their presidents) on a one-to-one basis. The oil companies are likely to end up playing an increasingly important role in the region. The endorsment by the American government of the trans-Caspian Baku-Ceyhan pipeline (November 1997) is a clear indication of the US strategic design to bypass both the Russians and the Iranians. But the achivement of this great project depends on the oil market.

The process of creation of these nation-states has been in a sense artificial. But even in the face of major economic and strategic constraints they are flourishing. The new states are far from banana republics. They take their places within an international context which will offer support if they have something to offer, and if they express a desire for that support. If not, then their existence is of no particular interest, as in the case of Tajikistan. But, despite the present trend towards globalization and supra-nationalism, our world is still one of nation-states, even failed ones like Afghanistan. Even in this case, the attributes of statehood have their reality, beyond flags and coloured spots of land on the maps of children's encyclopediæ. Borders do remain, as well as passports, citizenship amd a seat at the UN. And what seems at first glance an artificial patchwork, makes new sense by adapting itself to the evolutive geostrategy of an area in the making.

Notes on the Text

INTRODUCTION

1 Anderson, *Imagined Communities*.
2 Badie, *L'État importé*.
3 Bayart, *L'Historicité de l'état importé*.
4 As the exception that proves the rule, in this book you will find an Uzbek Muhitdinov and a Tajik Muhiddinov. This concession to linguistic specificities makes it possible to distinguish between homonyms, which are particularly frequent in the region.

CHAPTER 1

1 For a critique of the concept of ethnic group see Digard (ed.), *Le Fait ethnique en Iran et en Afghanistan*. On ethnic identities in Central Asia see Roy, 'Ethnies et politique en Asie centrale' in *Des Ethnies aux nations en Asie centrale*; also Centlivres and Centlivres-Demont, *Et si on parlait de l'Afghanistan?*
2 Allworth, *The Modern Uzbeks*, p. 143.
3 Menges, 'People, languages and migrations' in Alworth, *Central Asia*, pp. 72f. There are other possible classifications, but they all maintain an opposition between Oghuz and Qipchak. See Louis Bazin, 'Les peuples turcophones en Eurasie', *Hérodote*, no. 42, 1986.
4 On the 'great game', in other words the rivalry between Russia and the British empires in Central Asia, see Hopkirk, *The Great Game*.
5 Roy, *The Failure of Political Islam*, chapter 10.
6 The treatise against Shiism written by Shah Abdul Aziz Dehlawi, the son of Shah Walliullah, the great reforming theologian of the eighteenth century, *Tohfe-yi isnâ'i 'ashari* ('A present for the Twelvers') is still in print (latest edition published in Persian by Hakikât Kitabevi, Istanbul, 1988, distributed in Peshawar for the benefit of the Afghans).
7 At the time of the partition of the Indian subcontinent, Pakistan decided to adopt Urdu, the language of India's Muslims, as its official language, rather than Punjabi, the language of the majority ethnic group living in what is today Pakistan. The constitution of the Islamic Republic of Iran makes Persian the only official language, but at the same time it permits the use of regional languages, unlike the situation under the Shah, but more importantly it stipulates that the guide does not necessarily have to be an Iranian. Finally, one should note that there are many Azeris among the activists of the Islamic revolution.
8 See Centlivres, *Et si on parlait de l'Afghanistan?*; see also Roy, *Groupes de solidarité*.
9 The terminology used to define identity groups is almost always of Persian origin (albeit originally Arabic terms, they have passed through the filter of Persian), even among groups that have never been under Persian influence. *Tire*,

the Turkmen term used to define a lineage segment, means 'clan' in Persian; among the Chechens and Daghestanis the word '*tohum*' is used (*tokhum* in Persian) meaning 'sowing seed'.

10 Centlivres, *Et si on parlait de l'Afghanistan?*; see also Digard (ed.) *Le fait ethnique en Iran et en Afghanistan.*

11 Rakowska-Harmstone, *Russia and Nationalism in Central Asia*, pp. 172f. In Uzbek, they say '*mahalchilik*', and in Azeri '*yerbazlik*'.

12 I have used the *Russian-Uzbek Dictionary* of the Uzbekistan Academy of Sciences (1983); the *Soviet Tajik Encyclopaedia* (1988 edition); and Kiselevoy's *Russian-Dari Dictionary* (Dari being the Persian of Afghanistan) (1986), which is the more eclectic of the three, since *qawm* is translated by terms from the whole range of Russian classifications: '*rodnya*, lineage segment, klan, clan, *plemya*, tribe, *narodnost* and *narod*'. For translation attempts made in the 1920s, see Baldauf 'The Making of the Uzbek Nation', *Cahiers du monde russe et soviétique*, vol. 32, January–March 1991, p. 92; the multiplicity of translations is the same as in present-day dictionaries.

13 Richard, 'Du nationalisme á l'islamisme: dimension de l'identité ethnique en Iran', in Digard, *Le fait ethnique*, p. 271.

14 The examples in this paragraph come from fieldwork carried out in 1992 and 1993, respectively in southern Tajikistan and the Ferghana Valley.

15 Wixman, *The Peoples of USSR*, under the heading 'Uzbek'.

16 Personal research, April 1992. On the settlements in Kabadyan, see Vincent Fourniau, 'Irrigation et nomadisme pastoral en Asie centrale: la politique d'implantation des Ouzbeqs au XVIé siécle', *Central Asian Survey*, vol. 4 no. 2, 1985.

17 Wixman, Ronald, 'Applied Soviet nationality policy'.

18 Baldauf, 'En Asie centrale', in *Cahierss du monde russe et soviétique*, p. 90.

19 On the term '*Sart*' see Shalinski in Orywal (ed.), p. 292; also Subtelny in Manz (ed.), *Central Asia in Historical Perspective*, p. 49 and Baldauf, 'En Asie centrale…', in *Cahier du monde russe et sovi»tique*, p. 79.

20 Swietochowski, *Russian-Azerbaijan, 1905–1920*, p. 25.

21 On the 'Arabs' in Central Asia as a whole, see Barfield, *The Central Asian Arabs*.

22 The Tajik-speaking *khwaja* in Chadak whom I questioned described themselves as descendants of voluntary converts to Islam; but those interviewed by John Schoeberlein Engel in other districts of Ferghana defined themselves as descendants of the companions of the Prophet, which is more in line with the rest of the Turkish-Persian space (*Central Asia Monitor*, no. 2, 1996, p. 17).

23 Personal field research between 1991 and 1993.

24 One finds this argument in other parts of the Muslim world. It is, for example, used by the *ashraf* of Egypt (*Middle East International Journal*, Autumn, 1994, p. 613).

25 According to John Schoeberlein-Engel, the *khwaja* are indeed descended from a well-defined genealogy which relates them back to the leading religious figures of the early days of Islam (*Central Asia Monitor*, no. 2, 1996, p. 17). In my opinion, not all the groups of *khwaja* are so precise about their origins, but apart from that (endogamy, belonging to different linguistic groupings, the affirmation of religious origins and the Soviet system's hostility towards them) our observations agree.

26 The *khwajas* apparently took Chadak, in the Ferghana Valley, in the seventeenth century (Choukourov, p. 93). The opposition between the two groups is to be found elsewhere in Uzbekistan. Carrére d'Encausse mentions a caste of 'Khwaja

of Juybar', near Bukhara, who had a monopoly of key posts in the emirate's religious administration, and claimed to be descended from the Caliphs (*Réforme et Révolution*, p. 59); here they belonged to a Sufi order (the Yasawi), *ibid.* p. 66.

27 Karmysheva, 'On the History of Population Formation in the Southern Areas of Uzbekistan and Tajikistan', p. 10.
28 See Bouchet, 'Tribus d'autrefois, kolkhoz d'aujourd'hui'.
29 On tribal memory in general, see Barfield, *The Central Asian Arabs*, p. 9.
30 On the example of tribalism in Iran, see Bazin 'Les turcophones d'Iran: aperçus ethno-linguistiques' in *Le Fait ethnique*, p. 50.
31 For a list of the names of Uzbek tribes, see Allworth, *The Modern Uzbeks*, pp. 34 and 260; also Manz (ed.), *Central Asia in Historical Perspective*, p. 49 (Mangit, Ming, Qarlik, Kungrat, Kenegez, Kitay, Qipchak, Qangli, Chaghatay, Katagan, Durman, Lakay); also Vambéry, *Voyages d'un faux derviche dans l'Asie centrale*, p. 303 (here we find the Kiptchaks). Vambéry notes the existence of people living far apart, having no resemblance, and speaking very different dialects, who claim to be members of the same tribe. In Sarazm in Tajikistan (personal observation), the Uzbeks call themselves Shaybani Khan and are divided into Oray, Gurach and Chubat. They say that there are Barlas and Qipchaks in Penjikent and Hazars (Ming) in Urgut. In Kabadyan today (the village of Yangi Yol) people call themselves Shaybani, divided into Durman (coming from Balkh), Kungrat, Urgut, Lakay, Qijat and Karluk. The Uzbek settlement of the region substantially predates the Soviet period.
32 According to Broxup, 'Basmachi', *Central Asian Survey*, vol. 2 no. 1, 1983.

CHAPTER 2

1 See Mendras, *Un État pour la Russie*.
2 See Lazzerini, 'Volga Tatars in Central Asia', in Manz (ed.), *Central Asia in Historical Perspective*.
3 *Voyages d'un faux derviche dans l'Asie centrale*, p. 318.
4 Swietochowski, *Russian-Azerbaijan, 1905–1920*, p. 13.
5 Carrére d'Encausse in Allworth, *Central Asia*, pp. 159–60.

CHAPTER 3

1 Keddourie, *Afghani and Abduh*.
2 On Muslim reformism, see Bennigsen and Lemercier Quelquejay.
3 Bennigsen and Lemercier Quelquejay, *Les Mouvements Nationaux*, p. 40.
4 Swietochowski signals the first transition, in the geographic space that concerns us, of the term '*millet*' from the sense of 'religious community' to that of 'nation' in an article in the Azeri satirical journal *Kashkül* in 1891, where, in reply to the question 'What is your *millet*?', the answer suggested by the author of the article is 'Azerbaijani Turk', instead of the answer given spontaneously by the man in the street, 'Muslim and Turkish' (p. 33).
5 A good brief account of Gasprinski can be found in Ilber Ortayli, 'Reports and Considerations of Ismail bey Gasprinskii in Tercüman on Central Asia', in 'En Asie centrale soviétique', *Cahiers du monde russe et soviétique*, p. 4f.
6 Swietochowski, *Russian-Azerbaijan, 1905–1920*, p. 59.
7 *Ibid.*, p. 75.

8   The main defence movements in favour of the caliphate after the 1914–18 war were to be found in Central Asia, Afghanistan and India.
9   Swietochowski, *Russian-Azerbaijan, 1905–1920*, p. 88.
10   On Gasprinski's admiration for the Japanese model, see Ilber Ortayli, *op. cit.*, p. 44.
11   Carrére d'Encausse, *Réforme et Révolution*, pp. 241–2.
12   Thus we find Zinoviev calling for holy war (*ghazawat*): see Carrére d'Encausse, *Le Marxisme et l'Asie*, p. 55. It also needs to be explained why King Amanullah of Afghanistan was seen as a progressive while the emir of Bukhara (supported by the Afghans) was branded a reactionary.
13   For a bibliography on Sultan Galiev, see Bennigsen and Lemercier-Quelquejay, *Sultan Galiev.*
14   Rohrlich, *The Volga Tatars*, p. 98.
15   *Ibid.*, pp. 65–8; see also Lemercier-Quelquejay, *Abdul Kayum al Nasyri: a Tatar Reformer of the XIX Century, Central Asian Survey*, vol. 1 no. 4, April 1983.
16   Swietochowski, *Russian-Azerbaijan, 1905–1920*, pp. 61–2.
17   Ilber Ortayli, *op. cit.*, p. 45; on the bad feeling among the Kazakh élites, see Lazzirini, in Manz (ed.), *Central Asia in Historical Perspective*, pp. 90–1.
18   Rohrlich, *The Volga Tatars*, p. 69.
19   Swietochowski, *Russian-Azerbaijan, 1905–1920*, p. 92.
20   The basic book on Sultan Galiev is Bennigsen and Lemercier-Quelquejay, *Sultan Galiev.*
21   One should remember that the Islamic Renaissance Party, at the time of its founding conference in Astrakhan in 1990, was also opposed to independence for the Muslim republics on an ethnic basis, preferring at that time the framework of a renewed USSR rather than a framework of nationalism in the modern sense of the term.
22   See the articles in *Central Asian Survey* by Glenda Fraser (vol. 6 nos. 1 and 2, 1987), Héléne Aymen (vol. 6 no. 3, 1987) and Marie Broxup (vol. 2 no. 1, 1983).
23   For a translation of extracts of the biography which Sangak himself gave to the Russian journalist V. Medvedev ('Saga o Bobo Sankake, Voïne', 'the saga of Baba Sangak, warrior', in *Drujba Narodov*, June 1993), see Reinhard Eisener, 'Zum Bürgerkrieg in Tadshikistan', *Osteuropa Zeitschrit für Gegenwartsfragen des Ostens*, Stuttgart, 1994, pp. 777f; also cited in Stéphane Dudoignon, 'Chronique bibliographique', CEMOTI, no. 16, 1993, pp. 393f. We find another version of the story, which has Ishan Sultan dying in 1922, but it is not clear that this is the same person. (Glenda Fraser, 'Basmachi', *Central Asian Survey*, vol. 6 no. 1, 1987, p. 64).

CHAPTER 4

1   The idea is often expressed in various terms, to explain the weakness of Muslim representation in the Soviets: 'It was not that the political leadership ignored the Muslims – it was simply that they were culturally more backward than the rest of the population, and thus the revolutionary groups had no influence over them'. So said Djaparadzide, a (Georgian) cadre of the Baku soviet to a Muslim delegation protesting against the colonial behaviour of the Soviets (Suny, *The Baku Commune*, p. 188). This argument reappears at the other end of Europe's colonial space, where the communist section of Sidi Bel Abbés in French Algeria writes in a resolution that 'the natives of North Africa are composed for

the most part of Arabs resistant to the economic, social, intellectual and moral development that are indispensable for people to form an independent state capable of attaining communist perfection', in Carrére d'Encausse, *Le Marxisme et l'Asie*, p. 270.

2   Rohrlich, *The Volga Tatars*, p. 86.
3   Mirhadi, in *Passé turco-tatar*, collected writings, p. 352.
4   Carrére d'Encausse, in Allworth (ed.), *Central Asia*, p. 223.
5   Kreindler, 'Ibrahim Altynsarin, Nikolaï Ilminskyi and the Kazakh Awakening', *Central Asian Survey*, vol. 2 no. 3, 1983.
6   *Ibid.*, pp. 109–11.
7   *Ibid.*, p. 106.
8   Baldauf, 'The Making of the Uzbek Nation', p. 80.
9   Olcott, *The Kazakhs*, p. 11.
10 Carrére d'Encausse, in Allworth (ed.), *Central Asia*, p. 197.
11 Swietochowski, *Russian-Azerbaijan, 1905–1920*, pp. 26 and 61.
12 *Ibid.*, pp. 14 and 17.
13 Allworth, *The Modern Uzbeks*, p. 191.
14 For the GPU in the 1920s, see Glenda Fraser, 'Basmachi', *Central Asian Survey*, vol. 6 no. 2, 1987, p. 16.
15 Carrére d'Encausse, *Réforme et Révolution*, p. 259.
16 Summarised in the article by Rakowska-Harmstone, *Central Asian Survey*, vol. 2 no. 2, 1983, p. 28.
17 See Skalnik, 'Union soviétique – Afrique du sud', pp. 157–76; and 'Soviet ethnografya and the national(ities) question', pp. 183–92.
18 See Charachidze: 'L'Empire et Babel'.
19 '*Sovremenye etnicheskye protsessy v SSSR*', collective text, Nauka, 1977; translated into French as *Processus ethnique en URSS*, Progress Publishers, Moscow, 1982: p. 10 for a full citation of the definition given by Stalin. For a summary of the German romantic notion of the people, as opposed to the political view, see p. 8: 'Une telle communauté [ethnique] se forme de façon *naturelle* et historique, semble-t-il; et *ne dépend pas de la volonté des hommes isolés* qu'elle comprend, et elle est capable d'une existence stable pendant plusieurs siècles par auto-reproduction' (my emphasis). For a general study of Soviet anthropology, see *Regards sur l'anthropologie soviétique*, *Cahiers du Monde russe et soviétique*. On the practice of Soviet ethnologues, see Marx in Roy (ed.), *Des ethnies aux nations en Asie centrale*.
20 Soviet experts write as if the nationalities existed before the political constructions. 'In Central Asia, the frontiers set up between the territories of Turkestan, Bukhara and Khiva by the hierarchical system of the kháns destroyed the ethnic territories of the Uzbeks, the Tajiks, the Kazakhs, the Turkmens and the Kyrgyz', as if there existed an Uzbek ethnic territory prior to the tribal confederation that founded the khanate (*Processus ethniques en URSS, op. cit.*, p. 49).
21 Oransky, *Les Langues iraniennes*, p. 126.
22 *Processus ethniques en URSS, op. cit.*, p. 26, gives a list of 97 peoples for the 1979 census, excluding 'nationalities of fewer than 10,000 people, and the main body of which is located outside of the USSR (Albanians, Afghans and others)', which did not prevent the census from including 9,400 Slovaks.
23 This is confirmed by the statistics: in 1979 only 212 of the 99,908 Jews living in Uzbekistan admitted to speaking the local language; nevertheless, the thousands of Jews of Samarkand and Bukhara are at least bilingual (Tajik/Uzbek); thus

the 'Jews' in question in the census are immigrant Ashkenazis, considered 'Europeans': Rywkyn, *Moscow's Muslim Challenge* p. 98.

24 Curiously, the taboo word 'Turkestan' was to remain in the Soviet system until 1991, to designate the military region stretching from the Caspian to China.

25 See Wixman, *Applied Soviet nationality policy*.

26 See Georges Agabekov (former OGPU representative in Kabul), *OGPU*, pp. 164–5.

27 For an example of ethnologists having difficulties in explaining how the Uzbeks, Kazakhs and Tajiks were in the process of constituting a nation at the start of the century, see *Processus ethniques, op. cit.*, pp. 41–42:

> Although in overall terms they were still weakly involved in the sphere of capitalist influence, and despite the weight of patriarchal leftovers and the archaicism of their ethnic structure, one saw appear in their midst sizeable strata of bourgeoisie, proletariat and intelligentsia. A movement of national liberation appeared.

As it happened, Soviet Tajikistan had no big city, because of the Soviet determination not to make it a competitor with the Uzbeks, and there was no bourgeoisie, no proletariat and no intelligentsia.

28 On the Koreans, see Songmoo Kho 'Koreans in the Soviet Union', *Korea and World Affairs*, no. 1, Spring 1990, Séoul.

29 Wixman, *The Peoples of the USSR*, p. 120.

30 Wasserman in Ro'i, *Muslim Eurasia*, p. 145.

31 Quoted in Allworth, *The Modern Uzbeks*, p. 204.

32 See Carlisle in Manz (ed.), *Central Asia in Historical Perspective*, p. 115, for a quotation from Akmal Ikramov in 1937, at which time he was first secretary of the Uzbekistan party.

33 Swietochowski, *Russian-Azerbaijan, 1905–1920*, p. 25.

34 On the polemics among the intellectuals at the time of the great division, see Jahangiri in Djallili and Grare, *Tajikistan, The Trials of Independence*.

35 Longuet-Marx, 'L'ethnologue daghestanais'.

36 *Processus ethniques en URSS, op. cit.*, p. 206.

37 For an opposite policy in other countries, see Benedict Anderson, p. 134.

38 On this concept, see Massell, *The Surrogate Proletariat*.

39 However it can be said that the fact of belonging to an old élite made it possible for new notables to emerge after independence, generally at a local level. This was the case with Sangak Safarov (see above, the chapter on the *basmachis*). Another example, from 1991: in the Tajik village of Mazar-i Sharif, Ishan Sayyid Haydar, the son of the last *bey*, who had been deported as a *kulak*, found himself, after having been a simple kolkhozian, with the status of bey, and was the founder of a mosque and of a hotel for pilgrims. The way in which he rebuilt this status is unclear, but it is a fact.

40 Massell, *The Surrogate Proletariat*, p. 206.

41 The figures come from Rakowska-Harmstone, *Russia and Nationalism in Central Asia*, pp. 100, 165.

42 Olcott, *The Kazakhs*, p. 220.

43 See Lubin, *Labour and Nationality in Soviet Central Asia*: in a factory in Andijan in 1979, 81 percent of the unskilled workers were Muslim women, whereas they represented only 25 percent of white-collar staff at a time when Russian women made up almost 50 percent at this level. For other similar figures, see *ibid.*, p. 214.

44 M. Barbieri, A. Blum and E. Dolgikh, 'La Transition démographique en Ouzbékistan', unpublished note, INED, 1992.
45 Blum, 'Systèmes démographiques soviétiques', p. 412.
46 Rywkyn, *Moscow's Muslim Challenge*, p. 54.
47 Fierman (ed.), *Soviet Central Asia*, pp. 38f.
48 Patnaik, 'Agricultural and Rural Out-migration in Central Asia, 1960–1991', in *Europe Asia Studies*, vol. 47 no. 1, pp. 147, 154; M. Rywkin, 'Cadre competition in Central Asia: the ethnic aspect', in *Central Asian Survey*, vol. 5 no. 3/4, 1986, p. 185.
49 Patnaik, *op. cit.*
50 *Ibid.*, p. 157; M. Rywkin 'Cadre competition in Central Asia: the Ethnic Aspect', *Central Asian Survey*, vol. 5 no. 3/4, 1986. Alain Blum ('Systèmes démographiques soviétiques', PhD, EHESS 1992), suggests a negative migration balance of 507,000 for Uzbekistan and 784,000 for Kazakhstan between 1979 and 1989.
51 Rywkyn, *Moscow's Muslim Challenge*, p. 49, for a comparison of wages and savings.
52 Rumer, *Soviet Central Asia*, pp. 138–137.
53 See Blum, 'Systèmes démographiques soviétiques'.

CHAPTER 5

1 Massell, *The Surrogate Proletariat.*
2 See also Bushkov in V. Naumkin, *State, Religion and Society in Central Asia*, pp. 234, 235, and Rakowska-Harmstone, *Russia and Nationalism in Central Asia*.
3 For instance, in Kabadyan in southern Tajikistan one finds, in an Uzbek environment, two *kolkhoz* consisting entirely of inhabitants of Pamir relocated in the 1950s: Lal-i Badakhshan and Nasir Khosrow. The names clearly show the ethnic origins of the *kolkhoz* (the 'Ruby of Badakhshan', the area of derivation of the Pamiris, and Nasir Khosrow, the name of the man who converted the Pamiris to Ismailism); these *kolkhoz* also correspond to a village Soviet (*shura-yé kishlaq*). The neighbouring *kolkhoz* known as Pakhtakâr (cotton worker) is solely Uzbek in ethnic terms.
4 See my section on the war of the *kolkhoz*.
5 Bouchet, *Tribus d'autrefois, kolkhoz d'aujourd'hui.*
6 Olcott, *The Kazakhs*, p. 208.
7 *Ibid.*, pp. 212 and 218.
8 Rakowska-Harmstone, *Russia and Nationalism*, p. 58. Most of the *kolkhoz* that we visited between 1991 and 1992 had been regrouped in this way (for instance the *kolkhoz* of Mazar-i Sharif in Penjikent, around the small town which was known, precisely, as Kolkhoziân); for another example, for instance the transition of 49 *kolkhoz* corresponding to the 49 'villages' of Mastcha, to nine *kolkhoz*, see Naumkin, *State, Religion and Society in Central Asia*, p. 235: here the desire to break traditional solidarities is clear.
9 Figures given by V. Bushkov, *Le Tadjikistan existe-t-il?* p. 20.
10 Bushkov in Naumkin, *State, Religion and Society in Central Asia*, p. 235.
11 See Carlisle in Fierman (ed.), *Soviet Central Asia*, p. 97.
12 Highlighted by Vaisman in Ro'i, *Muslim Eurasia*, p. 109.
13 On Rashidov's family system, see Vaisman in Ro'i, *Muslim Eurasia*, pp. 112–14.
14 Bouchet, 'Tribus d'autrefois, kolkhoz d'aujourd'hui', p. 65.

CHAPTER 6

1 Massell, *The Surrogate Proletariat*, p. 77.
2 See Roy, *Islam and Resistance in Afghanistan*, chapter on agrarian reform.
3 For Kazakhstan, see Olcott, *The Kazakhs*, pp. 200f.
4 On turnover in Tajikistan, see Rakowska-Harmstone, *Russia and Nationalism in Central Asia*, p. 166; see also, for Uzbekistan, Gregory Gleason, 'Fealty and Loyalty: Informal Authority Structures in Soviet Asia', *Soviet Studies*, vol. 43 no. 4, 1991, p. 623.
5 Massel, *The Surrogate Proletariat*.
6 See Kushkin, quoted in Massell, *The Surrogate Proletariat*, p. 68.
7 Rywkin, *Central Asian Survey*, 4/1, 1985, p. 6.
8 Rakowska, pp. 171–2, 174. The author also notes that this turnover masked more of a stability than one might imagine. A 'misdoing' cadre was simply transferred to an equivalent post by his protector in the capital, in general originating from the same region as him. The rotation of cadres is also a way of getting around Soviet rules by a practice of traditional clientelism, while still keeping up appearances.
9 For example, the present head of the Islamic Movement in Tajikistan, Mullah Nuri, told me that after the KGB had arrested students and teachers of a clandestine madrasa when he was in Dushanbe (c.1972), they had all been released when various of their relations who were well placed in the apparatus had negociated directly with the Tajik cadres of the KGB. A general rule of the bureaucracy is 'avoid bother'. Announcing the discovery of a clandestine religious school is tantamount to admitting that a clandestine network has been allowed to develop, and that Islam plays a greater role than the official rhetoric would allow.
10 Rakowska-Harmstone, *Russia and Nationalism in Central Asia*, pp. 147–148.
11 *Ibid.*, p. 149. In the example of Uzbekistan, which we cite below, we shall see that all the higher party cadres in the 1940s and 1950s made their careers in their provinces of origin before going on to climb within the apparatus – for instance Rashidov in Samarkand.
12 Rakowska-Harmstone in Hajda and Beissinger (eds), *The Nationalities Factor in the Soviet Politics and Society*, p. 88.
13 Rakowska-Harmstone, 'Soviet Legacies', *Central Asia Monitor*, no. 3, 1994, p. 28.
14 Lubin, *Labour and Nationality*, pp. 158–9.
15 On the Uzbek élites, see Rywkyn, in Fierman pp. 109–10 and 121; Carlisle in Fierman (ed.), *Soviet Central Asia*, pp. 101f; Carlisle, 'The Uzek Power Elite: Politburo and Secretariat (1938–1983)', in *Central Asian Survey*, vol. 5 no. 3/4, 1986.
16 He is the son of the Stalinist apparatchik Buzrukkhodja Osmankhodjaiev (1896–1977). The repetition of the term '*khoja*' indicates a belonging to the 'caste' of *khwaja*, to which I refer in the first part of this book.
17 On anti-Pamiri repression, see Nazarshayev, *Mubareze-rahi haqiqat*.
18 This function is also noted by Benedict Anderson, p. 164.
19 Thus one finds a Russian writer, Ludmilla Schvyr, wondering naively about the incoherence of Tajik replies on the subject of their identity, because they do not reply in relation to an objective set of definitions of ethnic groups, which exist only in the mind of the author, but in terms of their regional belonging: Naumkin, Vitaly, *State, Religion and Society in Central Asia*, p. 252f.

20 Anderson points to this reality effect in the case of territorial limitation of the promotion of administrative personnel in the Spanish colonies of Latin American: Anderson, *Imagined Communities*, p. 114.
21 Thus the Tajik archaeologist Abdullah Isakov shows that excavations at Sarazm brought to light a Zoroastrian (and thus 'Iranian') site, which was proof of the thousand-year-long existence of that culture in an area that is today peopled by Uzbeks: *Sarazm*, Danesh publishing house, Dushanbe, 1991 (in Russian).
22 See Bennigsen, *L'Islam en URSS*, p. 226.
23 Olcott, *The Kazakhs*, p. 222.
24 Allworth, *The Modern Uzbeks*, p. 287.
25 *Ibid.*, p. 292.
26 The only possibility of fieldwork has to be done in the name of ethnography (*etnografiya*); the word 'sociology' (*jama'shenasi* in Persian) is unknown or, worse, suspect, as is *olum-i syassi*, 'political science'.
27 Including, apparently, not only the Pamiris but also the Koulabis, Darwazis and Karateginis. See Manz (ed.), *Central Asia in Historical Perspective*, pp. 9 and 11.
28 On the crisis of the Tajik intelligentsia, see the pertinent article by Parviz Mullâdjânov: 'Réflexions sur quelques effets du passage des générations dans l'intelligentzia contemporaine du Tadjkistan', in CEMOTI, no. 18.
29 In Nazarshayev, *Mubareze-rahi haqiqat*, p. 43.
30 See the book by the brothers Choukourov, p. 134.
31 'Religion: The Pillar of Society' in Sagdeev and Eisenhower (eds.) *Central Asia: Conflict Resolution and Change*, The Center for Post-Soviet Studies, 1995.

CHAPTER 7

1 There are plentiful examples in Rumer, *Soviet Central Asia*, chapter 8.
2 Schroeder in Hajda and Beissinger (eds.), *The Nationalities Factor,* p. 53.
3 Kamil Ikramov, in *Literaturnayya Gazeta*, quoted by Carlisle, in Fierman (ed.), *Soviet Central Asia*, p. 128.
4 See Allstadt, *The Azerbaijani Turks*, pp. 184–5, for the Azeris.
5 See Gleason, 'Fealty and Loyalty, p. 613, where he quotes both the characterisation of this cultural policy by the Russian press, and the protests by Nishanov, Uzbek first secretary (notes 1 and 2).
6 For a history of the civil war in Tajikistan, see Jawad and Tadjbakhsh, *Tajikistan*.

CHAPTER 8

1 There is recurring mention of the Shiite Tajiks in China in the specialist literature, for example in R. Cagnat and M. Jan, *Le Milieu des Empires*, Robert Laffont, 1981, p. 238.
2 See Bennigsen and Lemercier-Quelquejay, *Le Soufi et le Commissaire*.
3 Roy, *Islam and Resistance*.
4 Metcalf, *Islamic Revival in British India*.
5 We were thus able to compare the personal library of an *âlim* in Panjshir in 1981, Miradj-uddin, and a dozen mullahs in Ferghana and Tajikistan in 1991–3.
6 For a description of these books, see Nazif Shahrani, 'Local knowledge of Islam and Social Discourse in Afghanistan and Turkistan in the Modern Period' in Robert Canfield (ed.), *Turko-Persia in Historical Perspective*, Cambridge

University Press, 1991. Shahrani studies Afghanistan, but everything he says can also be applied to Tajikistan.

7   Bouchet, 'Tribus d'autrefois, kolkhoz d'aujourd'hui', p. 57.

8   J. Anderson, 'Islam in the Soviet Archives: a research note', *Central Asian Survey*, vol. 13 no. 3, 1994.

9   Personal meeting, March 1995.

10   *Tabaddolât-i Tâjikistan*.

11   The change of attitude was announced in an article by Igor Belayev (*Literaturanaya Gazeta*, 13 and 20 May 1987), 'Islam and Politics', in which the vitality of parallel Islam is recognised and legalisation is suggested.

12   Roy, *The Failure of Political Islam*, chapter 3.

13   An Islamic literature printed in Russian in Peshawar also circulated in Central Asia: 'Do we no longer need religion?' by Muhammed Qotb, brother of Sayid, 'Namaz', 'The Greatness of Muhammed', no author's name (personal collection).

14   Interview in the Tajik journal *Sukhan*, no. 18, 12 July 1991.

15   The party's programme appeared in various languages, including Russian. Our source was a journal published by the party in Tajik, *Hedayat*, no. 1, June 1990, no place of publication. All the quotations that follow come from this small journal, which consisted of eight pages.

16   *Al Wahdat*, 9 January 1991, p. 3, in Russian, written by Rashid Khatuev. He described the FIS as a 'fundamentalist organisation', and said that 'It only needed the Algerian authorities to introduce elements of democracy for the FIS, an Islamic organisation, to make its breakthrough, and not liberal, left- or right-wing organisations'. Text translated and cited in Longuet-Marx, 'L'ethnologue daghestanais'.

17   See Kepel (ed.), *Intellectuels et militants de l'Islam contemporain*.

18   Roy, *The Failure of Political Islam*. The victory of the Afghan Taliban against Massoud and Hekmatyar in September 1996 was typical of this sliding from Islamism into neo-fundamentalism.

19   One finds in particular a movement of women preachers, the *otin*, who are in charge of preaching during marriages and educating young girls, within a strictly neo-fundamentalist framework. Habiba Fathi, '*Otines*: The Unknown Women Clerics of Central Asian Islam', *Central Asian Survey*, vol 16, 1 March 1997.

20   Thus the daily paper of the Tajik Communist Party, *Tâjikistân-i shuravi*, in 1991 published an article by A. Istad protesting about a heading in the *Tajik Encyclopaedia* which presented Khwâje Ahrar (1404–90), a Naqshbandi Sufi *pir*, as a 'feudalist'. Interestingly, the author stresses that the *waqf* is not a feudal institution, but an institution that makes it possible for mosques and *madrasas* to prosper.

21   On the neo-brotherhoods, see Roy, 'Groupes de solidarités au Moyen-Orient et en Asie centrale'.

CHAPTER 9

1   One is struck by the attachment to this history among people who were victims of the Soviet system. For instance, the dynamiting of Lenin's statue in Dushanbe in October 1991 was condemned by numbers of Russians who had been exiled to that city in the 1940s for 'counter-revolutionary activities'.

2   For examples of the pamphlets published in Uzbekistan after 1991, see M. Thurman, 'Leaders of the Communist Party of Uzbekistan in Historical Retrospect', *Central Asian Monitor*, no. 1, 1996, p. 23.

3   *Uzbekistan avazi* (8 January 1992, p. 3); see M. Thurman, 'Leaders of the Communist Party of Uzbekistan in Historical Retrospect', p. 24.

4   Nazarshaïev, *Mobâriz-i-yé haghighat*.

5   S. Hegarty, 'The rehabilitation of Temur', *Central Asia Monitor*, 1995, no. 1, p. 30.

6   A Turkmen tourist brochure (personal collection) speaks of the 'ancestors of the Turkmen people (*turkmen khalqinin atababalar*): *massagetes, dahis, parthians, ariis, horasmis, alans, ases, oguses*'; we know that at least the Massagetes, the Parthes and the Alains were Iranian-language.

7   Professor Feridun Jelilov, during the Third International Congress on the Turkish Language, Ankara, 24 September 1996 (in *Turkish Daily News*, 25 September 1996).

8   In a small manual published in Dushanbe (by the Hisar Cultural and Historical Centre) in 1993: *Tajikân, Tâjikistân-i ta'rikhî, Tâjikistân-i mu'âsir*, 'the Tajiks, historic Tajikistan and contemporary Tajikistan'.

9   Akiner Shirin, *The Formation of Kazakh Identity*, Royal Institute for Foreign Affairs, 1995, p. 63.

10   *Le Livre de Babur*, translated by J.L. Bacqué-Grammont, POF, Unesco, 1980, p. 123. For an English version, see *The Baburnama in English (Memoirs of Babur)*, translated by Annette Beveridge, London, Luzac and Company, 1922, reprinted 1969.

11   On the process of nationalizing the poet Ali Sher Nawa'y, see *The Modern Uzbezks*, p. 226

12   See Subtelny in Manz (ed.), *Central Asia in Historical Perspective*, p. 53.

13   The Soviet Russian scholar A.Yakoubovsky, in 1946: Allworth, *The Modern Uzbeks*, pp. 238–43.

14   S. Hegarty, 'The rehabilitation of Temur', *Central Asia Monitor*, 1995, no. 1, p. 28f.

15   It is no accident that one of the republics first scientific publications, prefaced by the president of the republic, is entitled 'La renaissance Timouride' (in the French edition, UNESCO, 1996).

16   The new alphabet was published on 12 October 1993 in the daily *Xalq sözi* (new official transcription) and reprinted in a pamphlet issued by the 'Mehnat' publishing house, under the title *Lotin yozuvidagi özbek Alifbosini örganamiz* ('learning the Uzbek alphabet in Latin script'), and printed in an edition of 100,000 copies in November 1993.

17   On the first four, see Natalie Waterson, *Uzbek-English Dictionary*, Oxford University Press, 1980, pp. xvii, xviii.

18   See *The Modern Uzbeks* for the vocabulary used in Uzbek theatre plays in the 1950s, p. 262; and pp. 262–83 for the maintenance of traditional ethical concepts.

19   Speech to the Communist Party congress, published in *E'teghad* ('conviction') (30 October 1993), the CP journal for the province of *Leninabad*, the address of which is 39 Djerzinski Street.

20   Irina Kostyukova, 'The Towns of Kirghyzstan Change Their Faces', in *Central Asian Survey*, vol. 13 no. 3, 1994.

21 Carol Henderson, 'Grass Roots Aspects of Agricultural Privatization in Kyrgyzstan,' *Central Asia Monitor*, May 1993, p. 33.
22 Mehrdad Haghayeghi, 'Kazakhstan's Declining Agriculture,' *Central Asia Monitor*, no. 1, 1996, p. 16.
23 For Kyrgyzstan, see Irina Kostyukova, *op. cit.*

CHAPTER 10

1 Rywkin, *Moscow's Muslim Challenge*, p. 98.
2 The author of these lines, as head of the OSCE mission to Tajikistan and observer at the negotiations in Tehran and Islamabad in 1994, was in a good position to observe this policy of sabotage, which was discreet but effective.
3 Michael Rywkin notes that the number of villages in the region of Tashkent with a Russian majority population fell by 37.7 percent between 1970 to 1979, and that the number of villages with a mixed population fell by 50 percent, which shows that the decline of the Russian population was indeed linked to departures, and not just to a difference in birth rates. In *Cadre Competition in Central Asia*, p. 185.

Bibliography

USSR Academy of Sciences, *Ethnic Processes in USSR,* (*Sovremenye etnicheskie protsesy ve SSSR*, 1977), (Nauka Publishing House), 1982.

Agabekov, Georges, *OGPU, The Russian Secret Terror,* first edition: 1931 (London: Hyperion Reprint), 1975.

Akiner, Shirin, *The Formation of Kazakh Identity* (London: Royal Institute for Foreign Affairs), 1995.

Allstadt, Audrey, *The Azerbaijani Turks* (Stanford: Hoover Institution Press), 1992.

Allworth, Edward (ed.), *Central Asia: A Century of Russian Rule* (New York: Columbia University Press), 1967.

Allworth, Edward, *The Modern Uzbeks* (Stanford: Hoover Institution Press), 1990.

Anderson, Benedict, *Imagined Communities* (London: Verso), 1992.

Anderson, John, 'Islam in the Soviet Archives: A Research Note', *Central Asian Survey*, vol. 13, no. 3, 1994.

Babur, Zahiruddin, *The Baburnama in English (Memoirs of Babur)*, transl. Annette Beveridge (London, Luzac and Company), 1922, reprinted 1969.

Badie, Bertrand, *L'Etat importé: essai sur l'occidentalisation de l'ordre politique* (Paris: Fayard), 1992.

Baldauf, Ingeborg, 'The making of the Uzbek Nation', *Cahiers du monde russe et soviétique*, vol. 32, January–March 1991.

Barfield, Thomas, *The Central Asian Arabs of Afghanistan* (Austin, Texas: Texas University Press), 1981.

Bayart, Jean François, 'L'Historicité de l'Etat importé', *Cahiers du CERI*, no. 15, 1996.

Bennigsen, Alexandre and Chantal Lemercier-Quelquejay, *L'Islam en Union soviétique* (Payot), 1968.

Bennigsen, Alexandre and Chantal Lemercier-Quelquejay, *Sultan Galiev: le père de la révolution tiers-mondiste* (Paris: Fayard), 1986.

Bennigsen, Alexandre and Chantal Lemercier-Quelquejay, *Le Soufi et le Commissaire: Les confréries musulmanes en URSS* (Paris: Le Seuil), 1986.

Bennigsen, Alexandre and Chantal Lemercier-Quelquejay, *Les Mouvements nationaux chez les musulmans de Russie* (Paris: Mouton), 1960.

Bennigsen, Alexandre and Chantal Lemercier-Quelquejay, *Les Musulmans oubliés* (Paris: Maspéro), 1981.

Blum, Alain, 'Systèmes démographiques soviétiques', PhD thesis, EHESS, 1992.

Bouchet, Bertrand, 'Tribus d'autrefois, kolkhoz d'aujourd'hui', in Olivier Roy (ed.), *Des ethnies aux nations en Asie centrale: Revue du monde musulman et de la Méditerranée* (Aix en Provence), January 1992.

Bremmer, Ian and Ray Taras, *Nations and Politics in the Soviet Successor States* (Cambridge: Cambridge University Press), 1993.

Cahiers du monde russe et soviétique: En Asie centrale soviétique, vol. 32, EHESS, January–March 1991.

Cahiers du monde russe et soviétique: Regards sur l'anthropologie soviétique, editions EHESS, April–September, 1990.

Canfield, Robert (ed.), *Turko-Persia in Historical Perspective*, School of American Research Seminar Series (Cambridge: Cambridge University Press), 1991.

Carlisle, 'The Uzbek Power Elite: Politburo and Secretariat (1938–1983)', *Central Asian Survey*, vol. 5 no. 3–4, 1986.

Carrère d'Encausse, Hélène, *Réforme et révolution chez les musulmans de l'empire russe* (Paris: Presses de la FNSP), 1966.

Carrère d'Encausse, Hélène and Stuart Schram, *Le Marxisme et l'Asie, 1853–1964* (Paris: Armand Colin), 1966.

Centlivres, Pierre and Micheline Centlivres-Demont, *Et si on parlait de l'Afghanistan?* (Paris: Editions de la Maison des Sciences de l'Homme), 1989.

Central Asia Monitor, bi-monthly (Fair Haven, Vermont), pubished since 1993.

Central Asian Survey (CAS), Society for Central Asian Studies (London: Carfax).

Charachidzé, Georges, 'L'Empire et Babel, les minorités face á la pérestroïka', in *Face aux Drapeaux: Le Genre Humain*, no. 20, (Paris: Le Seuil).

Choukourov, Charif and Roustam, *Peuples d'Asie Centrale* (Paris: Syros), 1994.

Digard (ed.), *Le Fait ethnique en Iran et en Afghanistan* (Paris: Editions du CNRS), 1988.

Djallili M. and F. Grare, *Tajikistan, The Trials of Independence* (Curzon), 1998.

Fierman William (ed.), *Soviet Central Asia: The Failed Transformation* (Boulder, Colorado: Westview Press), 1991.

Gleason, Gregory, 'Fealty and Loyalty: Informal Authority Structures in Soviet Asia', *Soviet Studies*, vol. 43, no. 4, 1991.

Hajda L. et M., Beissinger (ed.), *The Nationalities Factor in the Soviet Politics and Society* (Boulder, Colorado: Westview Press), 1990.

Hérodote, nos. 42, 54–55, 64; La Découverte, Paris.

Hopkirk, Peter, *The Great Game* (Oxford: Oxford University Press), 1990.

Jawad, Nassim and Tadjbakhsh Shahrbanou, *Tajikistan: A Forgotten Civil War, Minority Rights Group International Report, 1994/6*, February 1995, UK.

Karmysheva, Bilkis, 'On the History of Population Formation in the Southern Areas of Uzbekistan and Tajikistan', VII International Congress of Anthropological and Ethnological Sciences, Nauka, Moscow 1964.

Keddouri, Elie, *Afghani and Abduh* (London: Frank Cass), 1966.

Kenjayev, Safarali, *Tabaddolât-i Tâjikistan (The Events in Tajikistan)* (Dushanbe), 1993.

Longuet-Marx, Frédérique, 'L'ethnologue daghestanais, agent de l'intégration soviétique ou vecteur de l'identité', in Olivier Roy (ed.), *Des ethnies aux nations en Asie centrale: Revue du Monde Musulman et de la Méditerranée* (Aix en Provence), January 1992.

Lubin, Nancy, *Labour and Nationality in Soviet Central Asia* (Princeton, New Jersey: Princeton University Press), 1984.

Manz, Beatrice (ed.), *Central Asia in Historical Perspective* (Boulder, Colorado: Westview Press), 1994.

Massell, Gregory, *The Surrogate Proletariat: Moslem Women and Revolutionary Strategies in Soviet Central Asia: 1919–1929* (Princeton, New Jersey: Princeton University Press), 1974.

Mendras, Marie, *Un État pour la Russie* (Brussels: Complexe), 1992.

Metcalf, Barbara, *Islamic Revival in British India: Deoband (1860–1900)* (Princeton, New Jersey: Princeton University Press), 1982.

Motyl, Alexandre (ed), *Thinking Theoretically About Soviet Nationalities* (New York: Columbia University Press), 1992.

Naumkin, Vitaly, *State, Religion and Society in Central Asia* (Reading: Ithaca Press), 1995.

Nazarshayev, M., *Mubâriz-i râh-i haqiqat* (Dushanbe: Irfan), 1993.

Olcott, Martha, *The Kazakhs* (Stanford: Hoover Institution Press), 1987.

Oransky, Iosif M., *Les Langues iraniennes* (French translation) (Paris: Klincksieck), 1977.

Orywal, Erwin (ed.), *Die ethnischer Gruppen Afghanistans* (Wiesbaden: L. Reichert), 1986.

Passé turco-tatar: Présent soviétique, (in honour of Alexandre Bennigsen) (Paris: Éditions de l'École des Hautes Études en Sciences Sociales), 1986.

Patnaik, Ajay, 'Agricultural and Rural Out-migration in Central Asia, 1960–1991', *Europe Asia Studies*, vol. 47, no. 1.

Rakowska-Harmstone, Teresa, *Russia and Nationalism in Central Asia: The Case of Tadzhikistan* (Baltimore: The Johns Hopkins Press), 1970

Ro'i, Yakov (ed.), *Muslim Eurasia: Conflicting Legacy* (London: Frank Cass), 1995.

Rohrlich, Azade-Ayse, *The Volga Tatars* (Stanford: Hoover Institution Press), 1986.

Roy, Olivier (ed.), *Des ethnies aux nations en Asie centrale: Revue du monde musulman et de la Méditerranée* (Aix en Provence), January 1992.

Roy, Olivier, 'Groupes de solidarités au Moyen-Orient et en Asie centrale: États, territoires et réseaux', *Les Cahiers du CERI*, no. 16, 1996.

Roy, Olivier, *Islam and Resistance in Afghanistan*, second edition (London: Cambridge University Press), 1990.

Roy, Olivier, *L'Echec de l'Islam politique*, Le Seuil, 1992. Translated as *The Failure of Political Islam* (Cambridge, Massachusetts: Harvard University Press), 1995.

Rumer, Boris, *Soviet Central Asia* (London: Unwin Hyman), 1989.

Rywkin, M., 'Cadre Competition in Central Asia: The Ethnic Aspect', *Central Asian Survey*, vol. 5, no. 3/4, 1986.

Rywkin, Michael, *Moscow's Muslim Challenge*, second edition (New York: M.E. Sharpe), 1990.

Sellier, Jean and André, *Atlas des peuples d'orient: Moyen Orient, Caucase, Asie Centrale* (Paris: La Découverte), 1993.

Skalnik Peter, 'Soviet Ethnografya and the National(ities) Question', Regards sur l'anthropologie soviétique, *Cahiers du monde russe et soviétique*, April–September 1990.

Skalnik, Peter, 'Union soviétique – Afrique du sud: les théories de l'ethnos', *Cahiers d'Études Africaines*, no. 110, 1989.

Suny, Ronald, *The Baku Commune* (Princeton, New Jersey: Princeton University Press), 1972.

Swietochowski, Tadeusz, *Russian-Azerbaijan, 1905–1920* (Cambridge, England: Cambridge University Press), 1985.

Tapper, Richard (ed.), *The Conflict of State and Tribe in Iran and Afghanistan* (London: Croom Helm), 1983.

Vambéry, Arminius, *Voyages d'un faux derviche dans l'Asie centrale* (Paris: You Feng), 1987 (based on the 1873 edition published by Hachette).

Waterson, Nathalie, *Uzbek-English Dictionary* (Oxford: Oxford University Press), 1980.

Wixman, Ronald, 'Applied Soviet nationality policy: a suggested rationale', in *Passé turco-tatar, Présent soviétique* (Paris: Editions de l'École des Hautes Études en Sciences Sociales), 1986.

Wixman, Ronald, *The Peoples of the USSR: An Ethnographic Handbook* (New York: M.E. Sharpe), 1984.

Index